PERPETUATING
PATRIOTIC PERCEPTIONS

PERPETUATING PATRIOTIC PERCEPTIONS

The Cognitive Function of the Cold War

Matthew S. Hirshberg

Westport, Connecticut
London

Library of Congress Cataloging-in-Publication Data

Hirshberg, Matthew S.
    Perpetuating patriotic perceptions : the cognitive function of the
Cold War / Matthew S. Hirshberg.
      p.   cm.
    Includes bibliographical references and index.
    ISBN: 0–275–94165–5 (alk. paper)
    1. United States—Foreign relations—1945-1989—Public opinion.
    2. United States—Foreign relations—1989- —Public opinion.
    3. Cold War—Public opinion.   4. Patriotism—United States.
    5. Public opinion—United States.   I. Title.
    E840.H54   1993
    327.73—dc20   92–16209

British Library Cataloguing in Publication Data is available.

Library of Congress Catalog Card Number: 92–16209
ISBN: 0–275–94165–5

First published in 1993

Praeger Publishers, 88 Post Road West, Westport, CT 06881
An imprint of Greenwood Publishing Group, Inc.

Printed in the United States of America

The paper used in this book complies with the
Permanent Paper Standard issued by the National
Information Standards Organization (Z39.48–1984).

10 9 8 7 6 5 4 3 2 1

Dedicated to
Joan Feynman and Richard I. Hirshberg

Contents

Figures and Tables   ix

Preface   xiii

1   "America Won the Cold War!": An Introduction   1

PART I
The Cold War Schema in America

2   Cognition, Culture, and the Cold War Schema   17

3   Cold War Opinion in America   50

4   Cold War Themes in American Culture   97

5   Central American Elections on Network News:
         Cases of Cold War Framing   107

PART II
Cognitive Effects of the Cold War Schema

6   Common Meanings for Cold War Concepts   127

7   Balance, Stability, and Change
         in the Cold War Schema   144

8   Attributions for Superpower Interventions   163

9   Cold War Goals in American Foreign Policy:
         Nicaragua and the World   181

10 Choosing Sides with the Cold War Schema   188

11 Recalling Information Consistent with the Cold War Schema   197

12 Conclusion   209

References   213

Index   223

Figures and Tables

FIGURES

2.1	Structural Balance in Triads	36
2.2	Structural Imbalance in Triads	36
2.3	The American Patriotic Schema	39
2.4	The American Revolution Schema	40
2.5	The American Civil War Schema	40
2.6	The Nazi Enemy Schema	41
2.7	The Soviet Schema	43
2.8	The Cold War Schema	43
3.1	Favorable Ratings of the Soviet Union, National Samples (1953–1991)	67
3.2	Favorable Ratings of Gorbachev and the Soviet Union, National Samples (January 1987 to January 1991)	90
5.1	Monthly Network News Reports on El Salvador (1980–1982)	114
8.1	Attribution and Cognitive Consistency	167
8.2	Attribution and National Enemies	167
8.3	Expected Attributional Responses to Helpful and Harmful Behaviors by One's Own and Other Nations	169
8.4	Hypothesized Attributional Responses to Helpful and Harmful Behaviors by the United States and the Soviet Union	171
9.1	Highly Significant Correlations in Responses to Goal Statements	186

10.1 Relationships between the Self and Other Elements
of the Cold War Schema   192

10.2 Relationships between Actors in the Text   193

10.3 Hypotheses Concerning the Choosing of Sides   194

11.1 Balanced Relationships among the Superpowers
and Ideological Actors, According to the Cold War Schema   199

11.2 Four Types of Summary Recall Responses   201

TABLES

3.1 Favorability Ratings of the Soviet Union (1953–1991)   66

3.2 Attitudes toward Communism as a Form of Government,
General Social Surveys (1973–1988)   82

3.3 Favorability Ratings of the Soviet Union, Soviet Leaders,
and the Soviet People (September 16–17, 1983)   89

6.1 Words Associated with the United States
by 30% or More of the Subjects   132

6.2 Words Associated with Freedom
by 30% or More of the Subjects   133

6.3 Words Associated with Democracy
by 30% or More of the Subjects   135

6.4 Words Associated with Capitalism
by 30% or More of the Subjects   136

6.5 Words Associated with the Soviet Union
by 30% or More of the Subjects   137

6.6 Words Associated with Communism
by 30% or More of the Subjects   137

6.7 Words Associated with Dictatorship
by 30% or More of the Subjects   139

6.8 Contrasting Association with the United States
and the Soviet Union   139

7.1 Positive and Negative Evaluations of the Relationships
among the United States, Freedom, Democracy, Good,
and You (January 1988)   148

7.2 Positive and Negative Evaluations of the Relationships
among the United States, Freedom, Democracy, Good,
and You (January 1990)   149

7.3 Positive and Negative Evaluations of the Relationships
between Communism and: the United States, Freedom,
Democracy, You, and Good (January 1988 and 1990)   149

7.4 Positive and Negative Evaluations of the Relationships
between the Soviet Union and: the United States, Freedom,
Democracy, You, and Good (January 1988 and 1990)   150

7.5 Mean Differences between 1988 and 1990 Responses
to Word-Pairs Containing the Soviet Union 151

7.6 Effects of Party and Ideology on Responses
to Word-Pairs Containing the United States (January 1990) 152

7.7 Effects of Party and Ideology on Responses
to Word-Pairs Containing the Soviet Union (January 1990) 152

7.8 Balance and Imbalance in the American Patriotic Schema,
by Conceptual Triad (January 1990) 154

7.9 Balance and Imbalance in Conceptual Triads Containing
Communism and Elements of the Patriotic Schema (January 1990) 155

7.10 Balance and Imbalance in Conceptual Triads Containing
the Soviet Union (January 1990) 155

7.11 Mean Differences in Extremity between Balanced
and Unbalanced Responses to the Word-Pairs in Triads
That Contain the Soviet Union (January 1990) 158

8.1 Agreement with the Nature Statement in Response to Acts
by the United States 174

8.2 Agreement with the Forced Statement in Response to Acts
by the United States 174

8.3 Agreement with the Nature Statement in Response to Acts
by the Soviet Union 176

8.4 Agreement with the Nature Statement in Response to Acts
by the Soviet Union, Liberals Excluded 176

8.5 Agreement with the Forced Statement in Response to Acts
by the Soviet Union 177

8.6 Agreement with the Forced Statement in Response to Acts
by the Soviet Union, Liberals Excluded 177

9.1 Percentage of Subjects Agreeing and Disagreeing
with the Eight Goal Statements 185

10.1 The Fifteen Conditions of the Experiment: Superpower Identity
by Government or Rebel Ideology 191

10.2 Percentage of Subjects Supporting Each Side, by Condition 195

11.1 Recall of Superpower–Ideology Relationship by Consistent
and Inconsistent Conditions 204

Preface

This book explores the psychological, cultural, and political causes and effects of international perceptions. It does so with respect to American perceptions in an era dominated by a cold war mentality, but it is not meant merely to be a book about the cold war. Rather, cold war America is used as the setting in which international perceptions are examined. Of particular interest are the relationships among politics, public communication, cognitive structures, and perceptions: each affects the others in profound ways, and their interactions have a major impact on our lives. The theories and methods used in this work are borrowed from social and cognitive psychology, cultural anthropology, and communication studies: it is hoped that this broad-ranging synthesis has produced an approach to the study of political perceptions that others will find interesting and useful.

This work has benefited from the input of a number of people whom I would like to acknowledge. Lance Bennett and Steve Majeski provided ongoing encouragement and critical comments on earlier drafts of this work. Tony Greenwald, Chuck Hirshberg, Ole Holsti, and Jan Thomson also offered valuable comments on drafts of various chapters. Lori Stene helped edit the manuscript, prepared the index, and bolstered morale in the final stages. Kerry Hogan and Andrew Hoy ably assisted with various aspects of the data analysis. The study presented in Chapter 9 was the result of the combined efforts of Bob McChesney and myself. Many of the studies presented in Part II of the book were administered with the aid of graduate students in the Department of Political Science at the University of Washington. Finally, this book would not have taken its present form without the cooperation of hundreds of student subjects. I would like to thank all of the above people for their generous help.

PERPETUATING PATRIOTIC PERCEPTIONS

"America Won the Cold War!": An Introduction

We are predisposed to regard any conflict as a clash between good and evil rather than as simply a clash between conflicting interests. We are inclined to confuse freedom and democracy, which we regard as moral principles, with the way in which they are practiced in America—with capitalism, federalism, and the two-party system, which are not moral principles but simply the preferred and accepted practices of the American people. There is much cant in American moralism and not a little inconsistency.

—J. William Fulbright (1964, pp. 6–7)

I believe we are on an irreversible trend toward more freedom and democracy—but that could change.

—J. Danforth Quayle (Anderson, 1989)

The cold war ended in Garry Trudeau's comic world in mid-June 1988, when the White House decided to interpret change in Eastern Europe and Asia as an American cold war victory. Within hours, "a tumultuous cold war victory parade" erupted in Times Square. Euphoric crowds chanted "We're number one!" and "USA!" and the *Daily News* headline proclaimed, "Cold War Over: We Won!" (*The Seattle Times*, June 13 and 14, 1988, p. F3).

Trudeau's *Doonesbury* strip parodied the readiness among the public and the press to embrace uncritically their government's presumptuous and self-serving interpretations of world affairs.[1] His portrayal of simplistic official interpretations, immediate mass celebration, and enthusiastic press coverage was exaggerated to make a humorous point. Still, America's real cold war victory celebration was not far from Trudeau's comic portrayal. "America won the cold war!" proclaimed President Bush in a January 1991 speech to Congress, and the applause was deafening. As Soviet power dissolved into memory, the press joined the politicians in proclaiming ideological conquest with smug confidence. Fiction and reality merged with alarming ease.

The cold war was, in many ways, a psychological phenomenon. It persisted to the extent that policymakers perceived a "cold war" and discussed policy in those terms, to the extent that supporters and critics joined in accepting a cold war interpretation of policy and using cold war jargon to discuss it. It lasted to the extent that people agreed that the cold war was the proper framework for interpreting foreign affairs. The cold war was not an event: It was a period of history during which a particular paradigm dominated perceptions of international reality. In cold war terms, superpower domination, nuclear proliferation, and support for oppressive regimes were seen as necessary responses to similar actions by the other side.

That period of history is clearly over. The systemic and regime changes that took place in much of the communist world and the ultimate demise of the Soviet Union were a remarkable set of events that have forced us to alter the ways in which we look at international affairs. It has been an exciting time for international relations scholars: new realities appear to be rendering old paradigms dysfunctional, and scholars are happily scrambling to adjust to a changing world. The passing of the Soviet Union indeed marks an end to the era in which U.S.–Soviet relations were central to our understanding of international relations, and this has crucial ramifications across the globe.

Still, like the cold war, its end was largely a psychological phenomenon. Communism rules over a billion people in China and elsewhere in Asia. The poverty and oppression that motivated leftist revolutionary movements in the past have not been eliminated in the Third World. Even if the communist label goes entirely out of fashion (and it hasn't yet), there will be those who will advocate socialist alternatives to liberal capitalism as long as there are vast inequalities in wealth and power. Ideologically guided, materially based, and militarily waged battles will continue in the future, along some of the same lines that defined the cold war. We have decided to call the cold war over, and we will call future conflicts by different names. Yet as significant as the decline and fall of the Soviet Empire was, both the world and the cognitive frameworks we use to understand it remain more similar than they are different.

Perceptions of the cold war were biased on both sides, and it is not surprising that the typical American view pitted American virtue against Soviet depravity. The United States was seen as working to preserve and promote freedom and democracy against the Soviet Union's efforts to inflict communist oppression wherever possible. Through these patriotic lenses, Soviet depravity illuminated American virtue, and apparent efforts by the United States to protect the world from the communist menace reinforced America's benevolent self-image.

The joyous and confident claims of cold war victory stem from the same sorts of beliefs that defined the cold war to begin with. The prevailing American interpretation of the downfall of the Soviet Union and communism in Eastern Europe is that they constitute a victory for freedom, democracy, and the American way. American efforts have succeeded in redirecting the earth's momentum in the direction of freedom and democracy: the Soviet empire has crumbled, communist oppression has been overthrown. Once and for all, American freedom and democracy have overcome communist oppression.

It is not surprising that interpretations of the end of the cold war are based on cold war beliefs. Human belief systems cannot be switched on and off like lamps. Belief change is a gradual process that involves the countervailing influences of numerous political, economic, cultural, and cognitive forces. Demagogues pronounce the cold war over while continuing to use only slightly altered cold war beliefs to interpret and respond to world developments. If the cold war ever existed, then vestiges remain. Rather than quibble about reified beginnings and endings, it makes more sense to examine the nature and effects of the cold war mentality, and to consider how that mentality has changed and continues to change. That is what this book sets out to accomplish.

Cold war beliefs functioned to help perpetuate patriotic perceptions in America (thus the title of this book). Not only did stereotyped notions of the Soviet Union make America seem great and its deficiencies insignificant by comparison, but general conceptions of communist oppression increased the appreciation Americans felt for their own brand of "freedom and democracy." The cold war justified America's massive arms buildup, as well as a succession of large and small interventions around the world. Americans remained proud of their nation's ability to dominate and control other nations "in response" to Soviet and communist threats. Thus the cold war helped perpetuate a proud patriotism by uniting the nation against the common enemy, justifying questionable policies in the name of containment, and drawing attention to a Soviet communist antithesis against which America could be proudly compared.

American interpretations of the end of the cold war perpetuate patriotism in the same way that biased perceptions of the cold war did. Cold war victory bolstered American pride and confidence both at home and abroad. It proved that the United States had the resolve and cunning to win against its great rival superpower. In addition, the miserable failure of communism proved what Americans knew to be true: the American way is the best way. This bolstered support for domestic practices and institutions which, though flawed, appear blessed compared to the proven frailty of "the alternative."

WHAT THIS BOOK IS ABOUT

In general, this book explores the nature and effects of culturally predominant belief systems that structure foreign policy cognition. Specifically, it concentrates on the basic beliefs that form the cognitive foundations of American patriotism, as well as the related beliefs associated with the cold war. It examines how patriotic cold war preconceptions affect perceptions of the "reality" of world affairs, and how these perceptions help to elicit public support for U.S. foreign policy. The book demonstrates the important role of cognitive structures and processes in perpetuating patriotic support in the face of the many twists, turns, tumbles and triumphs of U.S. foreign policy. In the course of showing this crucial relationship between cognition and public support, a constructionist approach to the study of mass foreign policy cognition is developed and applied to post–World War II America. It is hoped that this work will both contribute to a better understanding of American public opinion during the cold war, and stimulate continued thought and discussion on the relationships among culture, cognition, policy, and power.

In the pages that follow, the nature and effects of simple American cold war beliefs are examined. First (in Chapter 2), cultural and cognitive theories are combined to form the conceptual framework upon which the study is based. The concept of a cultural schema is central to this synthesis. Schemata are cognitive frameworks stored in human memory. They organize information about the stimuli that are processed through them, specifying how elements of the stimuli fit together. Schemata determine how information is processed, what aspects of stimuli are attended to and recalled, and what meanings and understandings are attached to them.

A cognitive schema is cultural to the extent that it tends to be stored in the memories of a large number of members of a culture and is repeatedly used by them as they perform particular sorts of tasks. The predominance of a particular set of schemata in a given culture means that members of that culture will tend to process, interpret, remember, and respond to relevant stimuli in predictable ways. The use of a cultural schema by political elites making foreign policy decisions has a clear and direct impact on policy outcomes. But this is only one, albeit crucial, component of the schema-based sociocultural system that has foreign policy as its output.

Schemata that are used to process information about international relations tend to have at least two important attributes. First, just as people tend to favor their own "ingroup" over "outgroups," they tend to favor their own nation. Second, there is a tendency to seek, expect, and assume cognitive balance in international relations. Consequently, individuals use schemata combining own-nation-favoring with cognitive balance when they think about international relations. In the later chapters of this work, hypotheses based on a synthesis of schema, ingroup–outgroup, and balance theories are tested.

The American cultural schema upon which this work concentrates is termed here the "cold war schema." The theoretical and empirical bases of the cold war schema are discussed in the chapters that follow, but a short description here of this central notion will provide a sense for the direction of things to come.

The cold war schema is an expanded articulation of the "American patriotic schema." The patriotic schema is conceptualized as a set of positive relationships (associations) among five key concepts: the United States, freedom, democracy, good, and the self. In the cold war schema, these five elements are negatively related to three others: the Soviet Union, communism, and oppression (which are positively related to one another.) Thus the cold war schema includes an enmity between the United States and the Soviet Union, as well as antitheses between democracy and communism, and freedom and oppression. The schema user (the self) and good are clearly placed on the side of the United States, freedom, and democracy in the cold war schema.

The American patriotic schema is a stable belief system, deeply ingrained in the American psyche. The cultural predominance of the patriotic schema is a crucial component of political stability in America. Significant skepticism concerning any of the schema's components would threaten to replace mass complacency with discontent.

The cold war schema is an internationally oriented articulation of the American patriotic schema which fits it into the post–World War II era of superpower rivalry. The cold war schema was used by Americans to make sense of international affairs, and it structured perceptions along the way. Through cold war lenses Americans saw a world consistent with their biased cold war beliefs, and this helped to elicit support for cold war–oriented policies and to perpetuate the patriotism upon which those beliefs were founded. Thus use of the cold war schema in processing foreign affairs information served to reinforce and reify both schemata.

The cold war schema was resistant, but not impervious, to change. As U.S.–Soviet relations improved, components of the cold war articulation of the patriotic schema became dysfunctional and increasingly discredited. This isolated the American patriotic schema from the potentially adverse effects of policy change, and cleared the way for new international articulations of the patriotic schema.

The cold war schema reigned throughout the postwar period, until the Soviet Union fell apart in the early 1990s. Throughout that period, Americans tended to hold the view that U.S. policy rightfully supported freedom and democracy against the expanding, aggressive threat of Soviet-supported communism and oppression. Forty years of bipartisan use of the cold war schema by political elites forming, explaining, justifying, or criticizing U.S. foreign policy established and stabilized the "cold war" as a major theme in American political culture. The cold war schema structured relevant news reports, fictional stories, and educational materials and served as a cognitive framework through which many Americans processed and responded to information about world affairs. The use of the cold war schema in a variety of information-processing tasks— elite decisionmaking, political rhetoric, news reporting, movie making, teaching, public perception, opinion formation, etc.—was mutually reinforcing and formed a dynamic system that resisted (but did not preclude) schematic change.

Over the years, both in periods of hostility and in periods of reconciliation, a basic conflict between the United States and the Soviet Union, democracy and communism, freedom and oppression was assumed. What varied was the aggressive or conciliatory methods advocated or used for managing the conflict, and the degree of anti-Soviet sentiment (see Chapter 3). When U.S.–Soviet relations were openly hostile, Americans showed strong anti-Soviet sentiments; and when U.S.–Soviet relations improved, so did American attitudes toward the Soviet Union. This allowed for continued public support for the two-track (aggressive and conciliatory) policy of containment.

Within the context of a cold war culture (see Chapters 4 and 5), information relevant to competing interpretations of U.S. foreign policy tended to be ignored or excluded, and support was generally achieved for policies framed in cold war terms. Only recently, in the euphoria of "cold war victory," has it been permissible (and increasingly necessary) to entirely reject the cold war as the backdrop for U.S. foreign policy.

Findings from the cognitive studies presented in Chapters 6 through 11 show the existence of patriotic and cold war–oriented preconceptions among samples of American university students in the late 1980s, as well as some of the effects of these preconceptions on relevant cognition. Consistent with the proposed cold war schema, subjects cognitively linked the United States, freedom, and democracy, in opposition to the Soviet Union, oppression, and communism. As expected, subjects favored the American side. Based on their attitudes concerning the nations in question, subjects made unfounded assumptions about the causes of national behavior and about relations among nations. They perceived opposition to communism and support for democracy to be important U.S. foreign policy goals and had difficulty processing information about American actions inconsistent with these goals.

Flawed perceptions, dogmatic evaluations, and ill-informed responses cannot be discussed simply as the result of an ignorant public, but of a public too well trained in the perspective that dominated the American information environment. Indeed, "public ignorance," such as it was, was the result of mass cognition dominated by socially acquired cultural dispositions. Public perceptions reinforced and reified the culturally predominant predispositions that they were based upon. Thus the cold war schema was perpetuated through its own use, as was the patriotic schema contained within it.

While knowledgeable elites are not subject to exactly the same cognitive effects as the subjects of the studies presented in Chapters 6 through 11, they are not immune from stereotyped conceptions, selectivity biases, or the need to fill information gaps with preconceptions. More important, an understanding of how citizens cognitively structure and process foreign affairs provides insight into the processes by which advantageous interpretations of international relations prevail in American political culture.

The votes and opinions of American citizens may have little direct effect on U.S. foreign policy, but public perceptions are very relevant to policy outcomes. Policymakers have had to justify their actions and politicians have felt the need to support or criticize them in the patriotic, cold war terms the public understands. Journalists, too, have been motivated to present foreign affairs news in a form that is meaningful to an audience of cold war schema users. Because the dominant schema frames public discourse, it is reinforced and reified in the minds of Americans (including policymakers, politicians, and journalists). Some of these Americans are entrusted with the task of formulating U.S. foreign policy; others watch to make sure they do it right. Thus citizen cognition is an integral part of the sociocultural system from which U.S. foreign policy emerges.

SUMMARY OF THINGS TO COME

This book is divided into two sections. In Part I (Chapters 2 through 5), the cold war schema is set in its theoretical context and its manifestations in American culture and opinion are discussed. Part II (Chapters 6 through 11) presents a series of cognitive studies that explore the nature, predominance, and effects of the cold war schema.

Part I: The Cold War Schema in America

The general approach and theoretical framework are articulated in the second chapter. After a general discussion of the relationships between foreign policy and citizen cognition, cultural and cognitive schema theories are combined to yield the notion of a cultural schema. It is argued that schemata concerning international relations tend to favor the "in-nation" and to display structural balance. It is suggested that, throughout American history, the American patriotic schema has served as a stable base for a succession of international relations schemata. It is further argued that the cold war schema has been the predominant American cultural schema concerning international relations since World War II. The elements and relationships that make up the cold war schema are rigorously specified, and the role of the Soviet communist enemy in ensuring patriotic beliefs and national unity is discussed.

Chapter 3 turns to the development and predominance of the cold war schema in America. The chapter begins with a brief discussion of the development of U.S. foreign policy after World War II. It is argued that, over the years, a basic agreement on the Truman Doctrine and containment was accompanied by both militarism and accommodation. Next, a look at public opinion data for the period between World War II and the Vietnam War reveals that while the public was united behind the Truman Doctrine, Americans were willing to support both aggressive and diplomatic means for dealing with the Soviet Union and communism. A critique of claims that a "cold war consensus" was destroyed in the Vietnam era follows. There developed an American inhibition to militarism, but it was due more to a fear of the consequences than to a rejection of cold war beliefs. An inspection of recent public opinion data concludes that, despite significant movement away from anti-Soviet attitudes in the late 1980s, the other components of the cold war schema persist.

In combining cognitive and cultural approaches, this book concentrates more on the cognitive. Chapters 4 and 5 are the exceptions, as they are devoted to cultural manifestations of the cold war schema. Through its use in structuring a variety of forms of communication, the cold war schema was reinforced and reified. Americans lived in a cold war culture, as the schema provided underlying themes for political rhetoric, news, novels, movies, scholarship, and educational materials. Chapter 4 discusses some examples of the cold war schema in television entertainment, the cinema, and academia.

Chapter 5 is a comparative case study of American network television news coverage of the 1982 Salvadoran election and the 1984 Nicaraguan election. It shows how events were interpreted in cold war terms when possible, while information favoring competing interpretations tended to be excluded from public view and discourse. The heavily covered, U.S.-supported election in El Salvador was publicly framed as a victory for freedom and democracy over communist oppression. The Nicaraguan election of 1984 was actively opposed by the U.S. government, and was delegitimized and almost ignored in the news. This reaffirmed the perception that the United States was on the side of freedom and democracy and against communist oppression; but it necessitated the biased exclusion of schema-inconsistent information that threatened to seriously challenge the virtue of American involvement in Central America.

Part II: Cognitive Effects of the Cold War Schema

Studies of the content and effects of the cold war schema can take a variety of forms. On the one hand, they may concentrate on cold war culture, as Chapters 4 and 5 do. Alternatively, they may concentrate on cold war cognition by identifying schematically structured information processing and exploring the schema's effects on perceptions. Chapters 6 through 11 are devoted to this latter approach.

The series of cognitively oriented studies presented in chapters 6 through 11 yield findings that are generally consistent with predictions based on the cold war schema. Although the real world is more complex and varied than the simple theoretical construct designed to capture its essence, the American university students who served as subjects in these studies indeed tended to think in terms of the cold war schema. These studies provide clear evidence that the cold war schema structured cognition and that it was used to process foreign affairs information. They also show how the cold war schema was reified through its use and produced perceptions of world affairs into which a patriotic American self-image could comfortably fit.

The first step was to ascertain whether the hypothesized conceptual links in the cold war schema were, in fact, held in American minds. Free association was used in this initial study to ensure that the sources of the links were the minds of the subjects, not the suggestions of the researcher. In the study described in Chapter 6, subjects were presented with words from the cold war schema (including the United States, freedom, democracy, the Soviet Union, and communism) and asked to write down what they associated with each word. Through these free associations it was possible to identify commonly held meanings for key elements of the schema and to find some of the cognitive links between them.

Results show that cognitive links hypothesized in the cold war schema can be found in American minds. For most subjects, "the United States" freely elicited an association with "freedom," and vice-versa; "democracy" also brought the United States and freedom to mind. These patriotic associations create predispositions to interpret U.S. intervention as prodemocratic and liberating. Most subjects also associated "the Soviet Union" with "communism," and vice-versa. This link made it tempting for Americans to assume that governments or movements labeled as communist were Soviet supported or controlled, and that Soviet allies were communist.

Once conceptual links in the cold war schema are established through free association, suspicions that the schematic relationships are merely creations of the researcher can be put to rest. The next step, in Chapter 7, is to present subjects with pairs of concepts from the cold war schema and measure the extent to which they view the concepts as positively or negatively related. This allows for the detection of negative as well as positive relationships in the schema. It also gives a more accurate impression of how pervasive various relationships in the cold war schema are. Because data are collected in the same form as the cold war schema (positive and negative links between concepts), direct conclusions about the schema's pervasiveness can be made. This also allows for clear detection of balance and imbalance in subjects' cognitions. Finally, the study was conducted in January 1988 and again two years later in order to detect stability or change in the schema's predominance over that period.

The findings presented in Chapter 7 provide additional evidence of the cold war schema in American minds and show the role of structural balance in the process of belief system change. Responses generally support the notion that Americans used a balanced cold war schema to evaluate relevant stimuli. The vast majority of subjects were found to believe in most aspects of the cold war schema and to hold balanced cognitions. However, a tendency for some subjects to have unbalanced perceptions of the Soviet Union was also detected. This tendency was a result of increasingly positive evaluations of the Soviet Union and its relations with the United States, accompanied by continued perceptions of the Soviet Union as unfree, undemocratic, and communist. Still, even among those subjects who held unbalanced cognitions concerning the Soviet Union, cognitive pressure toward balance was evident, serving to moderate unbalanced responses.

In the experiment presented in Chapter 8, hypotheses based on a synthesis of ingroup–outgroup, balance, and attribution theories are tested. Subjects were given fictitious news reports concerning constructive behavior (airlifting relief supplies to a village) or destructive behavior (dropping bombs on the village) by the United States or the Soviet Union (2 × 2 factorial design). Because of the overwhelming perception of the United States as good, subjects tended to perceive constructive American behavior as consistent with America's nature and destructive American behavior as something the nation was forced to do. Constructive American behavior was thus interpreted in a manner that confirmed patriotic perceptions of a benevolent America, while American virtue was protected from destructive American behavior, which was discounted through the attribution process. Since perceptions of the Soviet Union were not uniformly positive or negative, responses to the Soviet behaviors did not exhibit this sort of pattern. More conservative subjects showed anti-Soviet attribution biases, while liberals did not.

Through the study presented in Chapter 9, common conceptions of the goals of U.S. foreign policy were identified, and the relationship between the general cold war schema and its application to a specific case was demonstrated. Attitude questionnaires were administered concerning the goals of the United States, both in world affairs generally and in a specific conflict (Nicaragua). Both opposition to communism and the promotion of democracy were considered by subjects to be important U.S. foreign policy goals. In addition, those who thought the goal of U.S. foreign policy was to promote democracy also tended to think it was to fight communism. This is evidence that the positive U.S.–democracy and negative U.S.–communism relationships were linked through a common belief system (the cold war schema).

Further, those who assumed anticommunist or prodemocratic goals in world affairs generally also tended to do so with respect to Nicaragua, despite frightening ignorance of facts regarding that country. This suggests a general tendency to believe U.S. foreign policy to be driven by anticommunist and prodemocratic motives, as well as a tendency to assume such motives in specific cases about which little is known. This sort of application of the general schema to specific cases reifies and perpetuates the schema while framing reality (in this case U.S. involvement in Nicaragua) in a way that promotes public support for U.S. foreign policy.

Chapters 10 and 11 present different sorts of findings from the same experiment. Subjects were asked to respond to a newspaper article in which a superpower intervened on behalf of a government besieged by rebels. In various conditions of the experiment the superpower was identified as either the United States, the Soviet Union, or "UVW." In addition, the government and rebels were separately described as either democratic or communist in some conditions.

Chapter 10 looks at the effects of those elements of the cold war schema on tendencies to choose sides in international conflicts. When asked which of two sides they would rather see win the conflict, subjects tended to support sides described as "democratic," as supported by the United States, or as opposed by either the Soviet Union or "communists." These findings suggest an automatic tendency for Americans to favor whichever side their government chooses to intervene on behalf of, particularly when it is described as democratic or its opponents are described as Soviet-supported and/or communist.

Chapter 11 explores the effects of the cold war schema on subjects' memories for schema-consistent or schema-inconsistent information. From the perspective of the cold war schema, the United States supported democrats, the Soviet Union supported communists, and the two sides opposed each other. Subjects in the experiment were asked to summarize news reports containing information that was either consistent or inconsistent with these schematic expectations. Responses showed tendencies not to recall inconsistent information, to distort it, and to be confused by it. The schema guided recall in such a way that schema-confirming information was more likely to be recalled than schema-refuting information.

For instance, subjects tended to recall U.S. support for a democratic government and U.S. opposition to communist rebels, but they tended not to recall U.S. opposition to democratic rebels. Antidemocratic U.S. behavior tended to be ignored, forgotten or perceived as prodemocratic. Thus there is a tendency to perceive American intervention as prodemocratic, regardless of the facts of the case. The results suggest that the cold war schema creates tendencies to process information in ways that reinforce its own predominance and resist its own refutation.

Some Methodological Issues

The cold war schema has been pervasive in American culture and has been perpetuated through its own use. Pervasive use of the cold war schema has helped to elicit and maintain public support for and acquiescence to the American government and its foreign policy. The variety of studies that follow support these claims from a number of angles.

The cold war schema was communicated to the American people through a variety of sources. News reports, political speeches, novels, films, advertisements, and scholarly treatises were framed by the cold war schema and served as media through which the schema was communicated to the mass public. All of these are rich sources of data concerning the presence or effects of the cold war schema in American culture. Content analyses can demonstrate the role of the schema in framing communication, and further investigations can yield insights about the processes by which the cold war schema comes to be used in such a role. The analyses in Chapters 4 and 5 demonstrate cold war themes in American culture and examine processes by which the cold war schema was perpetuated.

While additional studies concerning the cold war content of public communication would have been valuable, this work emphasizes the cognitive processes and effects of the cold war schema over its cultural manifestations. The bulk of the book concentrates on how Americans think and what they believe. To this end, two distinct, yet complementary, empirical approaches are used: the public opinion approach and the social cognition approach. Both approaches have advantages and disadvantages, and together they provide well-rounded support for the general claims of this book.

The public opinion approach is taken in Chapter 3. Findings from national surveys are used to assess the extent to which American beliefs and attitudes have been consistent with the cold war schema in post–World War II America.

Poll data have the distinct advantages of valid national samples and an abundance of data collected at various points in time. Since the polls use representative samples of the American public, few would object to using their findings to draw conclusions about the American public at large. Because so many polls have been conducted since World War II, we have at our disposal more than just a snapshot or two of American public opinion. By carefully assembling the many public opinion snapshots taken over time we can create a moving picture that highlights both stability and change.

Poll data also have the distinct disadvantages of being costly to produce and of limited depth. The costliness of polling national samples means that most scholars must use the data produced by those with the resources to do so. The questions pollsters ask are often relevant to the cold war schema, but they are rarely ideal. This imperfect fit is a serious limitation, and the result is that relationships between public opinion findings and the cold war schema are fewer and less direct than desired. While polling is often an effective way to measure beliefs, attitudes, and opinions, more creative and time-consuming methods are necessary to study deeper cognitive processes and effects.

The methods used in studies of social cognition reveal such processes and effects. In the social cognition approach, subjects process information under controlled conditions and theoretically derived hypotheses are tested and refined. The six social cognition chapters in Part II of this book use a variety of methods: Chapter 6 is a word-association study, Chapter 7 is a study of responses to word-pairs, Chapter 8 is an attribution experiment, Chapter 9 uses open- and close-ended survey questions, and Chapters 10 and 11 present an experiment that tests side-taking and memory effects.

The disadvantages of the social cognition approach mirror the advantages of the public opinion approach. First, studies in social cognition tend not to use representative samples. An effort is rarely made by social psychologists to bring cross-sections of Americans into their laboratories; instead, reasonable assumptions are made that the subjects used do not substantially differ from other people in any way that would significantly affect findings.

This limitation may be particularly troublesome for some readers, in that conclusions about Americans in general are made based on studies conducted on university student subjects. Clearly, representative samples would have been preferable, and they would have been used had resources been available.

The sampling problem makes the following question a crucial one: is there any reason to believe that students who enrol in introductory courses in political science at the University of Washington in Seattle (the subject pool for the cognitive studies which follow) are excessive in their belief in or use of the cold war schema? This is a group consisting predominantly of relatively bright and interested young people who grew up in the post-Vietnam era. According to many scholars (Allison, 1970; Levering, 1978; Destler, Gelb, & Lake, 1984; Holsti & Rosenau, 1984) (see also Chapter 3), the "cold war consensus" ended in the Vietnam era; the years since then have shown rocky, yet steady, developments in the direction of U.S.–Soviet accommodation. If anything, bright and interested students who grew up during the "post–cold war" era would be expected to show less of a tendency to use the cold war schema than their parents. Although representative samples were not used in the cognitive studies, then, it is most probable that the subject pool was biased away from confirming the hypotheses. Thus, given the subjects used in the studies, findings concerning the prevalence and effects of the cold war schema are likely to be, if anything, artificially weak.

The second disadvantage of the social cognition approach is a lack of comparable data from earlier periods. Social cognition is a relatively new field, and its application to politics and the issues discussed here is an even newer phenomenon (see Lau & Sears, 1986). There simply is not data on early cold war cognition, and so exclusive reliance on cognitive studies would allow us only to speculate about changes in schema predominance and use since, say, the 1950s. Even if there were data from that time, comparisons would be difficult due to variations in samples and treatments. Thus public opinion data must be relied on for the determination of long-term trends.

The social cognition approach has the great advantage of self-consciously following strict scientific method: attention is paid to establishing a theoretical base, deriving testable hypotheses, empirically testing those hypotheses, and refining theories and hypotheses as a result of findings. The field of social cognition has already established a strong body of well-supported theory concerning cognitive processes and effects. By applying theories and methods of social cognition to American cold war thinking, a great deal can be understood about cold war preconceptions and how they affect public perceptions. Schema, script, ingroup–outgroup, balance, attribution, and memory theories are used to conceptualize the mainstream American cold war mentality in a manner amenable to cognitive research. This research is described in Chapters 6 through 11, which systematically demonstrate the prevalence of the cold war schema in American minds and show some important perceptual effects of the schema's use.

Because of the advantages and disadvantages of the public opinion and social cognition approaches, both are used in this work. This combination of approaches allows each to make up, to some degree, for the deficiencies of the other. For instance, it turns out that the views expressed by subjects in the cognitive studies in Chapters 6 through 11 are generally consistent with the public opinion trends revealed in Chapter 3. In this way the survey data help place the cognitive studies into a historical context and provide some justification for generalizing the findings of those studies to the American public as a whole.

Thus a variety of empirical methods are used in the chapters to come. Chapter 3 traces the development of public opinion, while Chapters 4 and 5 consist of textual content analyses. Chapters 6, 7, and 9 present analyses of the responses of student subjects to selected sets of words, phrases, and statements. Chapters 8,

10, and 11 describe experiments that test subject responses to systematically altered texts. Together, these chapters provide an abundance of evidence that Americans held and used the cold war schema, that the schema's predominance was perpetuated through its use, and that the schema promoted patriotism and public acceptance of U.S. foreign policy.

NOTE

1. In fact, the *Doonesbury* parody was probably prompted by television newsman John Chancellor's declaration following the Moscow Summit of May 29 to June 2, 1988, that "The Cold War is over and we have won. All that remains is to declare victory and have a parade" (Rostow, 1990, p. 133).

PART I

THE COLD WAR SCHEMA
IN AMERICA

Cognition, Culture,
and the Cold War Schema

It is our very commitment to human freedom and dignity that should cause us to view American anti-communism with alarm. Most disturbing to me are the many things the anti-communist does in the name of "freedom." At home we have suffered patriotic hooliganism, collective self-delusion, the propagation of political orthodoxy, the imprisonment of dissenters and the emergence of a gargantuan military establishment that devours the national treasure in the face of worsening domestic ills. Abroad, anti-communism has brought us armaments races, nuclear terror, the strengthening of oppressive autocracies, counter-revolutionary reactionism, the death and maiming of American boys, and the slaughter of far off unoffending peoples.

—Michael Parenti (1969, pp. 8–9)

Communism—they didn't give it a race, they didn't give it a sex, they didn't give it an age. And they never let me believe it was just a philosophy in a man's mind. That was my enemy out there.

—Lieutenant William Calley (Everett et al., 1971, p. 7)

A once-popular T-shirt depicted a dying soldier, arms outstretched, still clutching his weapon, in a slow fall into oblivion. The caption simply said, "Why?" Why do we humans insist on shooting, bombing, and starving each other? On the T-shirt, the question was rhetorical—the wearer was not soliciting a lecture from a social scientist or historian on the causes of war. Yet, for scholars, these sorts of questions are puzzles to be pondered. Endless waves of scholarly papers are produced in quests for partial answers.

Violence and war are not necessary to the nature of man, they are culturally based "solutions" to problems of conflict (Mead, 1940; Montagu, 1978). One of the great ironies of man's powerful cerebral cortex is that it has facilitated the mass killing that has plagued human history. Abelson wrote, "most of the worst inter- and intra-national conflicts of the world are greatly exacerbated by the human penchant for imposing oversimplified symbol systems between themselves and the external world" (Abelson, 1973, p. 288). Conflict is exacerbated, not just because cognitive schemata oversimplify complex realities, but because they tend to simplify in particular ways.

We would not be nearly as effective at destroying each other were it not for our ability to takes sides, to distinguish friend from foe, ingroup from outgroup. We have been further aided in our international conflicts by our ability to assume motives, predict behavior, and process complex conflicts quickly and simply. Culturally predominant belief systems guide us in these tasks, structuring the world in ways that make it easy to support one's own nation or group in conflict.

Citizen cognition plays an important role in the social, cultural, psychological, and political processes that yield a supportive climate for foreign policy decision-making. Studies of public opinion have yielded a good deal of useful scholarship in this regard. The conventional public opinion approach concentrates on how public opinion trends affect foreign policy decisionmakers and how decisionmakers affect public opinion. The focus tends to be on how disagreements among policymakers and the public are played out. In contrast, the constructionist approach proposed and used in this work concentrates on that which is agreed upon and taken for granted by mainstream Americans and policymakers alike. From this perspective, citizen cognition is viewed as an important component of a sociocultural system that has foreign policy as an output.

The concept of a cultural schema is central to this perspective. A nation's citizens and its decisionmakers use the same culturally predominant schemata to understand and respond to international relations. Such schemata are structurally balanced, and they are biased in favor of that nation. From the end of the Second World War until the fall of the Soviet empire, the cold war schema, an extension of the American patriotic schema, predominated in American culture. Widespread use of the cold war schema served to bolster and perpetuate the patriotic schema. This facilitated support for and acquiescence to foreign and domestic policies and contributed to overall political stability. It also perpetuated enemy images which increased international tensions and justified cold war–oriented policy.

This chapter makes these points in detail, thus providing the conceptual and theoretical underpinnings for the remainder of the work. After a general discussion of the value of a cognitive approach, the conventional public opinion approach will be discussed. Constructionism will then be introduced, and a discussion of cognitive and cultural theory will lead to the concept of a cultural schema. It will then be argued that in-nation favoring and structural balance are typical attributes of international relations schemata. Attention will then turn to the American patriotic schema and its various extensions, including the cold war schema. Finally, the cold war schema's role in perpetuating the patriotic schema will be elaborated.

THE COGNITIVE APPROACH TO FOREIGN POLICY

We improve our understanding of human behavior through the study of cognitive predispositions and processes. This is not an uncontroversial claim. Social scientists in the behavioral tradition believe that behavior can be suitably explained as the outcome of observable stimuli. Thus there is no need to study unobservable cognition. One simply looks at what precipitated the behavior (the stimuli) and what behavior resulted (the response) and conclude that the stimuli led to the response. From such a perspective, U.S. cold war foreign policy may be viewed, in the orthodox manner, as a response to Soviet expansionism.

The stimulus–response paradigm is inadequate in explaining complex human behaviors such as foreign policy decisionmaking. The fact that different people would make different foreign policy decisions given the same stimuli can be explained only in terms of different learned predispositions. Jervis (1976) writes, "it is often impossible to explain crucial decisions and policies without reference to the decision-makers' beliefs about the world and their images of others. That is to say, these cognitions are part of the proximate cause of the relevant behavior and other levels of analysis cannot immediately tell us what they will be" (p. 28).

Is the progression of U.S. interventions in Greece, Iran, Guatemala, Cuba, Vietnam, Chile, Nicaragua, and elsewhere to be explained simply by realpolitik, or capitalist imperialism, or the obvious need to respond to communist aggression? Even if these explanations have some validity, they each beg crucial questions concerning the cognitive preconceptions of the leaders of those interventions, and of the publics whose support or quiescence was necessary to sustain them. What do Americans consider to be the "national interest"? Why? Do U.S. policymakers believe it to be their jobs to intervene internationally to promote the interests of American business? Why or why not? Do Americans view progressive movements for change as aggressive communist threats? Why or why not? Are there important differences in these sorts of preconceptions among Americans? Why or why not?

It is important to understand how stimuli are perceived, how they are transferred into behavioral predispositions, what those predispositions are, how they are stored, accessed, and used in determining behavior, and how that use may affect the predispositions of others. A cognitive approach allows us to learn all these things, based on a tradition of rigorous theory and experimentation (on people, not rats).

As Holsti (1976) points out, many scholars view psychological approaches to the study of foreign policy "to be well-intentioned, but often of dubious realism and relevance" (p. 15). It has been the habit of most international relations scholars to accept cognitive predispositions as given, ignoring the social, cultural, psychological, and political processes that resulted in people with particular preconceptions playing particular roles in particular nations. They have treated cognition as a "black box," as an area to be taken as given rather than explored. In the interest of parsimony, scholars have chosen to devote their energies to the study of more observable, behavioral explanations.

There is nothing wrong with building a black box, but there is something wrong with putting a lock on it. Black boxes help us understand by allowing us to simplify complex realities, but they also serve to hide areas of misunderstanding. Opening the black box of international relations cognition threatens the simple explanations that depend on that box remaining shut. Once the box is opened, U.S. foreign policy ceases to appear as a series of rational responses to international exigencies and becomes a series of biased responses based on perhaps reasonable, perhaps unreasonable, preconceptions that predominate among policymakers and supporting publics. Thus cognitive approaches to the study of U.S. foreign policy may present a challenge to the preconceptions held by policymakers, most Americans, and many mainstream international relations scholars.

Holsti argues that the study of individual cognition is important because individual differences sometimes affect outcomes:

In any political system there will be a set of shared beliefs. . . . But especially in a pluralistic polity there may also be variations in beliefs, and these differences may take on considerable importance as they are operative in any given decision-making situation. This is precisely the reason for focusing on the individual policy-maker, rather than assuming homogeneity of beliefs among them. It is thus possible to determine empirically the range of core beliefs that are widely shared, as well as those on which there may be substantial variation. [p. 20]

This work concentrates on cultural similarities rather than individual differences, on "core beliefs that are widely shared" rather than "those on which there may be substantial variation," on the public as a supporting cast for policymakers rather than on the individual policymakers. Because certain ways of thinking and acting tend to dominate a nation's culture, most of the cognitive preconceptions of most of the people are basically the same. The makers of U.S. foreign policy have a particular tendency to be like-minded and in accordance with culturally dominant conceptions, since they were systematically selected through political and organizational processes to be so. While studying differences among the preconceptions of individual policymakers may help explain variations and nuances of policy, studying stable, culturally dominant preconceptions is useful in accomplishing a far more important task: explaining major policy orientations and trends.

It is relatively easy to argue that the preconceptions and thought processes of elite decisionmakers are important subjects for study: elite decisions actually guide national behavior. While studies of elite foreign policy cognition are moving forward, there has been far less concern with foreign policy cognition in the mass public, the focus of this study. It is not obvious that citizen cognition has any affect on foreign policy, since it does not directly determine policy outcomes.

EFFECTS OF PUBLIC OPINION ON FOREIGN POLICY

Is citizen cognition important? Do the thoughts of everyday Americans matter? The sentimental answer is, "yes, they matter, because we are everyday Americans, and our thoughts matter to us!" The ideological answer is "yes" too; according to traditional democratic theory, it is "the people" who "ultimately" determine U.S. foreign policy, or at least ought to.

The scholarly answers are not so clear and simple. The conventional approach has been for scholars to address the role of citizen cognition in the policy process by examining the relationship between public opinion and U.S. foreign policy. Scholars have examined both the ways in which public opinion affects the behaviors of policymakers, and how the behaviors of policymakers affect public opinion.

This conventional approach has its roots in liberal democratic ideology and in concerns about how responsive and "democratic" U.S. foreign policy is or ought to be. Do Americans really determine U.S. foreign policy? What are the mechanisms of citizen input or dissent? Are American citizens capable of the sorts of opinions worth listening to? How do policymakers control or impact public opinion? These are the sorts of questions asked, questions revolving around the fit between democratic theory and American practice.

Scholars have often disagreed on the answers to these questions. Forty years ago American scholars generally accepted and recited the notion of a sovereign citizenry that strongly influences foreign policy. In Bailey's (1948) view, the public's great and important impact on the foreign policy of the most powerful nation in the world created the obligation for every citizen "to inform himself so that he can direct our foreign policy—his foreign policy—along intelligent and far-visioned lines" (p. 319). Markel and his colleagues (Markel, 1949) also took the position that public opinion is crucial to U.S. foreign policy, but they concluded that it must be manipulated through conscious and forceful propaganda in order to ensure that public opinion would influence policymakers in the manner preferred by policymakers.

Subsequent scholars (Almond, 1960; Cohen, 1973) challenged the "democratic myth" of significant public impact on policy. According to Cohen, policymakers take a "public relations perspective" similar to that advocated by Markel and his colleagues, in that they manipulate rather than obey public opinion. While State Department officials do pay some attention to opinions expressed in Congress, in the media, by interest groups, and in opinion polls, they tend to be more concerned with leading public opinion than with following it. Graber (1968) writes that "support, rather than advice, is the major concern of the decision makers and that support is sought more by finding ways to make accomplished decisions acceptable to the public than by adjusting the decisions to public tastes" (p. 363). Policymakers tend to make foreign policy decisions first, and figure out how to sell them to Congress and to the American people second.

Cohen (1973) cites the Truman Doctrine as an example of this:

> To gain the support of the Congress for a program of military and economic aid to Greece and Turkey and to build a broader base of support for any future measures to forestall the encroachment of Soviet power, the Truman Administration enveloped the proposal in a broad doctrine that stressed the ideological menace, the threat of communism to democracy and to "free peoples" everywhere. Once they embarked on this line, foreign policy officials developed it as a central element in their rhetoric on the new U.S. foreign policy of active international involvement. And—again not surprisingly—it immediately came back to them as "public opinion," as the external justification of the government's foreign policy. Anti-communism, which began as the Administration's way of getting domestic allies for its policy of containing the power of the Soviet Union, soon became something of a policy itself, in response to the public response. [p. 180]

In this view public opinion has a role, but not a large one, and not as an independent force. Policymakers are somewhat constrained or encouraged by the public responses that they (and/or their predecessors) have a major hand in eliciting. Spanier and Uslaner (1982) argue that, since the Truman doctrine, public opinion has tended to obediently follow presidential leadership.

> Public opinion . . . has supported hardline anti-Soviet and anti-Chinese policies when they were official policy (as they were from Truman's day right through to Johnson), and it has supported moves toward a relaxation of tensions and negotiating conflicts of interests (as during the Nixon era). Both kinds of moves received widespread popular acclaim. The public looked to the president for its cues. [p. 146]

The democratic myth has given way to a more reasonable position which holds that public opinion has an impact on foreign policy decisions, but only under certain circumstances and to a limited degree. Public opinion matters to the extent that it is perceived by leaders and serves to motivate them to act (or not to act) in certain ways. Since leaders need public support in order to maintain their power, they pay attention to public opinion, which often affects their behavior. An anticipated public reaction may motivate a reelection-conscious or popularity-minded president to pursue or discard, display or hide, a particular policy or action (Spanier & Uslaner, 1982, p. 154). Members of congress may also base relevant legislative action on their interpretations of public opinion.

Public opinion is never monolithic, unanimous, or clearly articulated, so it is difficult to read public preferences. It may be that elections in which foreign policy opinions affect the outcome are rare and politicians and policymakers who respond to perceived public opinion are exaggerating its meaning and potential consequences. Still, as Kegley and Wittkopf (1982) argue, "because policy makers act —evidence to the contrary—as though voters make choices on the basis of their policy preferences, they pay attention to the anticipated responses of voters in shaping their policy choices" (p. 296). In addition, as Wittkopf (1990) argues, "the climate of opinion in which policymakers must forge political support" (p. 220) has an impact on the policies they choose to put forward. The crucial point is that some officials do pay attention to opinion and this affects policy. Public opinion may not make policy, but leaders' perceptions of public opinion do constrain and encourage foreign policy decisions and actions.

Some scholars take the position that the nation is better off excluding the public from foreign policy decisionmaking. "Public opinion tends to be permissive and supportive of presidential decisions in foreign policy. . . . The principal reason is that the vast majority of Americans are poorly informed about and uninterested in foreign policy" (Spanier & Uslaner, 1982, p. 145). Why put the course of U.S. foreign policy in the hands of an amorphous mass of uninformed and uninterested citizens when professional policymakers are available for the task?

According to Almond, "foreign policy attitudes among most Americans lack intellectual structure and factual content" (Almond, 1960, p. 69). Kegley and Wittkopf (1982) describe public opinion as "the simple preferences of an uninformed, uninterested, unstable, acquiescent, and manipulable 'public voice'." As a result, "public opinion provides neither a clear nor meaningful guide to policy" (p. 287). Are such unflattering characterizations of American public opinion accurate?

Shapiro and Page's (1988) answer "is unequivocal: The notion of a capricious public is a myth." They argue "that foreign policy preferences have in fact had considerable stability and, when they have changed, have done so in ways that can be judged as reasonable" (pp. 213, 214). Other recent work (Hurwitz & Peffley, 1987; Wittkopf, 1988) has supported this contention, which views foreign policy opinions as structured and stable, and not easily subject to moods and manipulation.

Wittkopf (1990) provides reasonable evidence to support the claim "that the mass public holds stable foreign policy attitudes and that the American people are capable of relating discreet foreign policy issues to one another in a systematic and coherent fashion" (p. 50). He does not claim, however, that this means that most Americans pay much attention to, or are well informed about, foreign affairs. Rather, Wittkopf points out that opinion stability and constraint need not be accompanied by knowledge or political sophistication:

The mass of the American people are, relatively speaking, uninterested in and ill informed about foreign policy issues. . . . [However,] interest and knowledge are largely irrelevant to whether the American people are able, in the aggregate, to hold politically relevant foreign policy beliefs. These beliefs may not conform to what political scientists and journalists would like to see as they contemplate the theory and practice of contemporary democracy, but foreign policy beliefs may be both coherent and politically relevant even if they are not grounded in political sophistication. [p. 15]

The debate continues concerning just how informed, interested, rigid, and rational Americans are in their foreign policy opinions. The book has also not been closed on the respective impacts of public opinion and foreign policy decisionmakers on each other. Yet while scholars have argued about the answers to these questions, they have agreed that these are the questions to ask. Just like mainstream public discourse, mainstream scholarly discourse tends to exhibit agreement on the general issues and questions, but disagreement on specific approaches and answers. Mainstream scholars, strongly influenced by liberal democratic ideology, have agreed to study how disagreements among policymakers and the public are played out. I propose, in addition, that we examine the role of citizen cognition in U.S. foreign policy by studying that which is agreed upon and taken for granted by mainstream Americans.

THE APPROACH OF THIS WORK

The approach proposed here is not a rejection of the conventional public opinion approach, but it is a different way of thinking about the relationship between citizen cognition and foreign policy. It is a "constructionist" (Gamson, 1988) approach to the study of public opinion, in that the emphasis is on political cognition and culture, and more in-depth empirical methods are used in place of the conventional survey. Gamson views constructionism as a promising new direction being taken in public opinion and mass media research:

There is a shift in focus from attitudes and voting behavior to political cognition . . . the constructionist approach makes interpretive processes central. It draws on concepts rooted in cognitive psychology—schemata, constructs, cognitive maps, frames, scripts, and modes of political thinking. . . . There is a shift away from reliance on the sample survey with pre-coded response categories. To the extent that surveys are used, constructionists are likely to rely more heavily on open-ended questions. . . . Public opinion analysis, in this approach, requires an examination of political culture—the language and symbols of political discourse. . . . The concepts employed in this cultural analysis—frames, scenarios, myths, metaphors, images, condensing symbols—parallel the concepts used by constructionists who focus on political thinking. [pp. 164-165]

As Price (1988) points out, the key to this new approach to public opinion research is the linking of individual cognition with communicative social behavior through unifying concepts ("cultural schemata" in this work). The goal is to explain

the way individuals, through their participation in public debate, collectively construct a common domain of ideas and alternatives and decide upon a course of action. Individuals, not the public, are the ones "doing" the construction; but they do so cooperatively by taking into account what others are doing and saying, by encountering ideas others have proposed, or by formulating ideas in contrast or opposition to the views stated by others. If we are to remain true to a discursive model of public opinion, we want to study individual cognition and opinion formation as forms of social behavior; that is, as means by which members of the public participate in a collective endeavor. [p. 7]

From the constructionist perspective taken in this work, the importance of citizen cognition is not dependent upon the attention paid by policymakers to its manifestations in public opinion. Citizen cognition is important because it is an integral component of a sociocultural system that has foreign policy as its output. The approach will be described briefly here and explicated in detail in the chapters that follow.

The crucial assumption is that foreign policy decisions, public information (news, rhetoric, etc.), and public perceptions are all processed through the same set of culturally predominant cognitive schemata. This differs from the conventional public opinion and foreign policy approach in at least two important ways. First, this approach concentrates on culturally shared thoughts, while the conventional public opinion approach looks at different or competing thoughts. Second, general cognitive predispositions and processes are emphasized here, rather than specific opinions on particular issues and policies.

SCHEMA THEORY

The concept of a cognitive "schema" is central to this work. Schemata are made up of interrelated conceptual categories. Such categories are fundamental to human cognition; it is by dividing stimuli into categories that we simplify our complex world and make it comprehensible. Humans experience stimuli and assign them to categories based on their attributes. These attributes also are categorized (Wyer, 1974). Thus conceptual categories are defined in relation to each other. Once an object has been assigned to a category, it is assumed to have the attributes of that category, whether or not those attributes are actually observed. Categorized stimuli are thus linked to other categories, and they become meaningful in that context. We each have built in our memories complex networks of interlinked conceptual categories and experiences, networks into which we order further experiences and through which we may comprehend and react to them.

Individuals tend to adopt conceptual categories and the interrelationships among them from stocks of conceptual categorizations held commonly in their cultures. By learning and adopting the category networks we hold in common, we gain access to powerful cognitive tools that allow us to order reality effectively and communicate with others. We also learn to fit into our culture this way. "Category learning is one of the principle means by which a growing member of a society is socialized, for the categories that one is taught and comes to use habitually reflects the demands of the culture in which they arise" (Bruner, Goodnow, & Austin, 1956, p. 231).

We give meaning to stimuli and formulate responses to them by applying learned cultural categories to our ongoing experiences. Our cultural categories come to structure our senses of reality. "What is understood to be 'out there'," writes D'Andrade (1984) "is affected by the culturally based associations built into the category system." Not only do cultural categories establish common meanings for physical entities (e.g. cat, mountain, and toothbrush), they also create conceptually based entities (e.g. the United States, freedom, and democracy), which exist only in terms of the systems of meaning through which they are defined (p. 91).

Categories are made meaningful through their linkages with one another and linkages between categories and experienced entities. *"Schemata" are the networks of interlinked conceptual categories that serve as frameworks for meaning.*

Although the notion of a "schema" was first used by Head (1920), Bartlett (1932) is generally credited with introducing the term in his path-breaking research on the effects of culturally based knowledge on memory for culturally specific stories. Schema theories (Neisser, 1976; Hastie, 1981; Bobrow & Norman, 1975; Taylor & Crocker, 1981; Thorndike & Hays-Roth, 1979) posit that humans process information through the use of cognitive frameworks stored in memory. These frameworks, or schemata, organize information about the stimuli that are processed through them and specify how elements of the given stimulus are expected to be interrelated. Once cued for use, schemata determine what aspects of stimuli are attended to, stored within the schematic context, and recalled.

Ashmore and Del Boca (1981) describe a schema as "a cognitive structure that influences all the perceptual–cognitive activities that together are labeled 'information processing' (e.g. perceiving, encoding, storing, retrieving, decision making) with respect to a particular domain" (p. 2). According to Taylor and Crocker (1981), the schema for a particular domain "contains general knowledge about that domain, including specification of the relationships among its attributes as well as specific examples or instances of the stimulus domain. . . . The schema provides hypotheses about incoming stimuli which includes plans for interpreting and gathering schema-related information" (p. 91).

Tesser (1978) describes the effects of schemata on information processing as follows:

When we apply a particular schema for thinking about some stimulus object it does two things. First, it tells us what to attend to . . . it makes some attributes relevant, that is salient, while allowing others to be ignored. Second, a schema contains the network of associations that is believed to hold among the attributes of the stimulus and thereby provides rules for thinking about the stimulus. Thus if information conveying some relevant attribute is unavailable from the stimulus itself or is ambiguous or is unavailable from memory, the schema allows for the "filling" of such information with "default options." [p. 290]

Schemata serve as psychic guides for systematic, selective perceptual omissions and additions. Schemata determine which attributes of stimuli are noticed or ignored, and schematic elements are attributed to stimuli whether they are there or not. The ease with which schemata operate on frequently encountered stimuli frees the mind to think of other things. Such processing empowers while distorting; it delivers quick meaning but results in perceptions and memories that combine experience with schematic elements. The "real" and the schematic become indistinguishable as they are merged into perceptions and memories: schematic elements are thus reified.

For instance, most people have and use schemata for stereotyped country-types (democratic, communist, etc.). The "communist schema" typically held in American culture consists of an authoritarian and repressive government that denies its citizens personal freedom and is bent on expansion beyond its borders. Labeling a country, for instance Nicaragua, as communist brings all these things immediately to mind. If an individual has little information about that country, he or she will fill information gaps with elements of the schema. What is assumed to be true about communist countries is thus assumed to be true about Nicaragua.

Schemata structure behavior as well as perception. First, schemata determine our interpretations of past and present stimuli, structuring and giving meaning to the situations we think we are in. Second, schemata for stereotyped event sequences, or "scripts," instruct us on how to act in those sorts of situations.

According to Abelson (1981), scripts consist of "conceptual representations of stereotyped event sequences . . . activated when the understander can expect events in the sequence to occur . . . a script is a hypothesized cognitive structure that when activated organizes comprehension of event-based situations" (p. 717). Schank (1975) describes scripts as "episodes which occur in memory [and] serve to organize and make sense of new inputs. . . . A script is an elaborate causal chain which provides world knowledge about an often experienced situation" (p. 264). Schank and Abelson (1977) describe a script as "a structure that describes appropriate sequences of events in a particular context. A script is made up of slots and requirements about what can fill those slots" (p. 41).

Abelson and his colleagues (Abelson, 1973; Carbonell, 1978) conceptualized political belief systems in terms of scripts and created artificial intelligence simulations of ideological political cognition. Abelson (1973) proposed a "master script" which structures international conflict scenarios in terms of a struggle between "good guys" and "bad guys."

The bad guys have evil plans which are succeeding, and only the good guys can stop them. Unfortunately, the good guys haven't done it yet, and the reason is that the bad guys have the help of dupes, fools, lackeys and running dogs who wittingly or unwittingly intervene with the efforts of the good guys. The only hope, therefore, is to rouse the wrath of the people against the bad guys and their puppets. [p. 292]

His orthodox cold war script consists of this master script applied specifically to the struggle between "the free world" (the good guys) and "the communists" (the bad guys). The "Goldwater machine" was a script-based computer simulation of such a cold warrior. Carbonell's "POLITICS" was a more elaborate effort to simulate "humans in comprehending and responding to world events from a given political or ideological perspective" (Carbonell, 1978, p. 27).

Scripts are a type of schema; what has been said about schemata goes for scripts as well. Once a script is cued for use, stimuli are plugged into their appropriate places within the framework of the script and understanding occurs with respect to this "content-in-structure" (stimuli in script). What is special about scripts is that they structure event scenarios. They set up causal chains and temporal progressions, and include standardized roles, goals, plans, and appropriate behaviors.

Not only do scripts allow us to interpret event sequences as observers meaningfully, they also allow us to play our proper scripted roles in day-to-day situations. Culturally driven behavior is behavior that is structured by the culturally derived scripts that we each have come to call our own. When we behave correctly in restaurants, when we dress and groom ourselves in the style of our culture, when we become politically active in the traditional manner, and when we judge the behaviors of others as appropriate (fitting scripted expectations) or "out of line," we are behaving according to cultural scripts. For this reason, D'Andrade (1981) characterized "the learning of scripts" as "the guided discovery of cultural knowledge" (p. 186).

Particular schemata tend to become prominent in the minds of members of certain groups (Bower, Black, & Turner, 1979; D'Andrade, 1981). These common schemata constitute the cognitive elements of culture. This is not meant to imply that all schemata are cultural. Casson (1981) distinguishes among "universal schemata," which are "shared by all humans," "idiosyncratic schemata," which are "unique to particular individuals," and cultural schemata:

Cultural schemata are neither unique to particular individuals nor shared by all humans—they are shared by the members of particular societies. Examples of cultural schemata include classification systems of plants, animals, material objects, and kinsmen; rules for assigning residence location and decent group membership; procedures for diagnosing illness and disease; constructs used in mathematical computation and deductive reasoning; strategies for making legal decisions and solving technical problems; and rules for behaving appropriately in specific cultural events. Linguistic schemata, which . . . are a subset of cultural schemata, include the abstract categories of meaning associated with words. [p. 20]

CULTURE

Clearly there is more involved in foreign policy than culture; just as there is more to foreign policy than the necessities of power politics, the lure of the profit motive, and the logic of bureaucratic politics. Still, a nation's foreign policy, like its cuisine, like its literature, like its architecture, is a product of its culture.

"Culture" has its roots as a social scientific concept in the field of anthropology. Tyler (1871) defined culture as "that complex whole which includes knowledge, belief, art, morals, law, custom, and any other capacities and habits acquired by man as a member of society" (p. 1). Like most crucial concepts in the social sciences, scholars have argued for years over the best meaning of "culture," and endless streams of definitions have been produced (see Kroeber & Kluckhohn, 1952).

The most significant disagreement concerns the scope of the concept: is culture conceived of as mental, symbolic, behavioral, or material, or some combination of these four components? Kroeber's (1948) definition included both thought and behavior; culture is "the mass of learned and transmitted motor reactions, habits, techniques, ideas and values—and the behavior they induce" (p. 8). In Rossi's (1980) view, "Culture encompasses all that humans have produced to help adapt themselves to the physical environment and to one another" (p. 16), and that includes both "mental culture" and "material culture."

Other anthropologists have preferred to distinguish between culture and its physical manifestations. For instance, Redfield (1941) viewed culture as "the conventional understandings, manifest in act and artifact, that characterize societies" (p. 132). Culture is viewed as "manifest in," but separate from, behaviors and material products.

While emphasis was placed on observable aspects of culture (act and artifact) during the behavioral age, the computer age and the cognitive paradigm that accompanied it led to renewed emphasis on "the role of internal representations" in culture (D'Andrade, 1984, p. 88).

The conception of culture as knowledge and symbol rather than habit and behavior was rapidly assimilated into anthropology and the human sciences. Culture came to be seen as an information-holding system . . . the instructions needed for coping with the environment and performing specialized roles are provided in learned information, which is symbolically encoded and culturally transmitted. [pp. 88–89]

Among those who view culture as an "information-holding system," there remains disagreement about where that information is held. Goodenough (1957) and the "cognitive anthropologists" who took his lead place culture squarely in the human mind.

A society's culture consists of whatever it is one has to know or believe in order to operate in a manner acceptable to its members. Culture is not a material phenomenon; it does not consist of things, people, behavior, or emotions. It is rather an organization of these things. It is the form of things that people have in mind, their models for perceiving, relating, and otherwise interpreting them. [p. 167]

In contrast, Geertz locates culture, not in people's minds, but in systems of symbols through which members of society interact (Keesing, 1981). According to Geertz (1973), a symbol is "any object, act, event, quality, or relation which serves as a vehicle for a conception—the conception is the symbol's meaning" (p. 91). Thus, for Geertz, culture is both behavioral and material, consisting of the symbols that transmit meaning among social actors. "Cultural patterns . . . give meaning . . . to social and psychological reality both by shaping themselves to it and by shaping it to themselves" (p. 93).

Both approaches are strongly rooted in linguistics, and both emphasize the role of meaning in culture. While Goodenough concentrates on the *conceptual frameworks for interpreting meaning* in the human mind, Geertz emphasizes the *representations of meaning* in the social world.

The question, as D'Andrade (1984) frames it, is "where does one look for meaning—in culturally produced messages of various sorts or in the minds of the people who interpret these messages?" (p. 102). In studying American cold war culture, for instance, does one look for evidence of the cold war schema in political rhetoric, news reports, educational materials, and movies such as *Moscow on the Hudson*, or does one try to look into the minds of Americans?

It is important to look in both places. The acts and products (such as the products of mass media) that have portrayed cold war conceptions to Americans, as well as the cognitive schemata that have allowed Americans to properly interpret and respond to those symbols, are necessary to the transfer of meaning. The schemata are learned from the symbols, and the symbols are created out of, and are meaningful in terms of, the schemata. As D'Andrade (1984) argues, "if meanings are simply internal representations of external forms, then ambiguity about whether the external or internal forms are being referenced makes no great difference" (p. 104). Thus it makes little sense to restrict one's pursuits to either domain; greater understanding is achieved through the study of both.

While culture tends to be viewed from a cognitive perspective in this work, the study of symbolic acts and products is considered to be equally important. Ultimately, many symbolic acts are of tremendous consequence. For example, U.S. involvement in such places as Korea, Cuba, Vietnam, El Salvador, Nicaragua, and Grenada consisted of *symbolic acts that were made by cold war schema users and that communicated cold war themes to other cold war schema users.* They were also events with profound human consequences.

Cultural schemata are learned by individuals and stored in human memory, but they are also stored socially in myths, rituals, and other cultural behaviors and products. Schemata structure human cognition (perception, memory, etc.), behavior (talking, deciding, etc.), and products (stories, statues, etc.); schemata are stored where they serve to structure. We can study a cultural schema by examining those things that it structures, by looking at its cognitive, behavioral, and material results. Still, if culture is to have manageable and useful meaning, it must be distinguished from its results. Culture is neither internal cognition nor external symbols; culture consists of the commonly shared schemata that structure both. *Culture consists of cultural schemata.*

This view is consistent with D'Andrade's (1984) conception of culture:

In summary, the position taken in this chapter treats culture as consisting of learned systems of meaning, communicated by means of natural language and other symbol systems, having representational, directive, and affective functions, and capable of creating cultural entities and particular senses of reality. Through these systems of meaning, groups of people adapt to their environment and structure interpersonal activity. . . . Analytically, cultural meaning systems can be treated as a very large diversified pool of knowledge, or partially shared clusters of norms, or as intersubjectively shared, symbolically created realities. On the individual level, however, the actual meanings and messages that people learn, encounter, and produce are typically not divided into separate classes of items that can be labeled knowledge, norm, or reality, but rather form multifunctional complexes of constructs, organized in the interlocking hierarchical structures, which are simultaneously constructive, representative, evocative, and directive. [p. 116]

In defining and describing culture, anthropologists have used a number of related concepts, including "ideas, or conventional understandings, or cognitive models, or world view, or cultural code" (Rossi, 1980, p. 18). Other concepts used to describe the content of culture include beliefs, values, norms, habits, customs, knowledge, skills, morals, rules, and attitudes. How does "cultural schema" relate to this array of concepts?

"Schema" is a general concept that refers to any cognitive framework. From a cognitive perspective it is useful to think of all of the above concepts as types of schemata. Why use one term to characterize an array of cognitive frameworks that have meaningful and important differences? Without minimizing the differences between, for example, beliefs and norms, their inclusion in the larger category of schema allows us to apply the advances of schema theory and research to all sorts of cultural schemata. It allows us to discuss the interrelationships between culture and cognition in a way that is broadly applicable to a variety of cultural schemata. While this work does concentrate on one particular type of schema (a belief system called the cold war schema), the approach suggested here is applicable to a wide array of cultural schemata.

Culture is a crucial concept because it links individual psychological predispositions with patterns of social behavior. In a sociocultural system, members of society learn through social interaction the schemata that are common in their culture, and their ongoing social behavior is then guided by those schemata. Thus, the structures and processes of the social system and of human cognition are joined: members of a particular society learn a common set of schemata, and the predominance of those schemata among members of that society produces particular patterns of social behavior and interaction. *It is this ongoing interaction between cultural schemata and social behavior which constitutes a sociocultural system.*

According to Montagu (1964), culture is the "non-organic, learned, manmade part of the environment. . . . It is the socially transmitted body of customs, knowledge, and skills which enable the individual to function as a member of his society" (p. 84). Socialization, the process by which members learn and relearn their culture through social interaction, is a vital component of a cultural system. As Goodenough (1971) points out, once one has defined culture as *learned*, only a radical behaviorist can ignore the structure and processes of human cognition, since learning is a cognitive process.

Each child learns and internalizes his or her culture through contact with family, teachers, peers, mass media, and other "agents of socialization." As the individual applies these cultural schemata to his or her social world the schemata are made salient, reinforced, and reified. Socialization continues through adulthood, as the cultural schemata held commonly in a society structure social behavior and must be utilized to process information meaningfully. Socialization creates an overall cultural stability over time, as each generation builds on the last. "The culture of today," Kroeber (1948) wrote,

is always largely received from yesterday; that is what tradition or transmission means; it is a passing or sending along, a "handing-through" from one generation to another. Even in times of the most radical change and innovation there are probably several times as many items of culture being transmitted from the past as there are being newly devised. [p. 256]

Members of the same culture are not identically programmed computers. They do not each learn and adopt all of the schemata of their culture, and there are personal and subcultural variations on common cultural schemata. Cultures are not entirely homogeneous, but variations do not destroy the usefulness of recognizing and understanding the commonality that is culture. "The ways of behaving which compose the culture of any society," wrote Beals and Hoijer (1959), "represent generalizations of the behavior of all or some of the members of that society; they do not precisely describe the personal habit system of any individual" (p. 230). Thus reference to a "cultural" or "culturally predominant" schema does not imply that all members of society have or use it, that it takes precisely the same form in the minds of all individuals, or that they all use it in the same way and under the same circumstances. It simply reflects the fact that most members of society have and use the schema, or one very much like it. It postulates further that the schema had to have been learned through a socialization process and that it continues to contribute to certain observable social behaviors.

SCHEMATA FOR INTERNATIONAL RELATIONS

Schemata for different realms differ in structure and content; different sorts of schemata are adopted to facilitate the processing of different sorts of stimuli. Since the "cognitive revolution" in social psychology (George, 1980; Larson, 1985; Markus & Zajonc, 1985), a number of scholars have advocated and practiced the application of schema theory to the study of politics (Axelrod, 1973; Lodge & Wahlke, 1982; Fiske, Kinder, & Larter, 1983; Conover & Feldman, 1984; Lau & Sears, 1986). Research in the field of social cognition has been fruitful and important. Given the success of social cognition, political cognition promises to be a low-risk, high-yield area of study.

Schemata for international relations tend to take on a particular sort of structure that results in predictable responses to relevant stimuli. There appear to be at least two common tendencies in cognition concerning international relations. First, people tend to favor their own nation over other nations. Second, there is pressure toward structural balance in cognitions concerning international relations. These tendencies, combined with tendencies to perceive, remember, and present information in schematic contexts, yield particular sorts of cognitions and behaviors in response to relevant stimuli. The empirical chapters to come consist of investigations of a number of these response patterns, based on the theoretical foundations explicated here.

Ingroup Favoring

Tajfel and his associates have demonstrated that people tend to favor individuals on the basis of the group to which they belong (Tajfel, Billig, Bundy, & Flament, 1971; Wilder, 1981). Subjects tend to like members of their own "ingroup" more than members of a different "outgroup." They tend to treat ingroup members better and to attribute more desirable characteristics to them. They assume members of the ingroup are more similar to themselves than to members of the outgroup, and that members of the outgroup are more similar to each other than to members of the ingroup. There is also a tendency to prefer information consistent with ingroup biases, and to remember it better. These tendencies exist for ethnic, racial, social, and national groups, as well as for groups based on trivial criteria of the sort Tajfel used in his experiments.

Humans tend to favor the ingroup for a number of reasons. First, group loyalty is important to a viable society, so people are socialized to favor their own groups over others. While the exact nature and extremity of ingroup-favoring norms vary from culture to culture, they are an important way in which group cohesion is maintained. Egoistic individuals are taught to submit to the group and transfer their egoism to the intergroup level. American children learn to favor their families, friendship groups, schools, sports teams, businesses, and political parties. They also learn to favor their nation. This general tendency to favor one's own group over others constitutes a general ingroup–outgroup schema which is used whenever people are confronted with group differentiation.

Second, ingroup favoring has a self-esteem function. An individual may feel worthy or unworthy by association with the group to which he or she belongs. Given a general desire for positive self-image and the associated need for a sense of belonging, one is motivated both to belong to groups and to assume a relatively positive image of the groups to which one belongs.

Third, human groups serve as categories used to differentiate sets of people. They allow for informed (prejudiced) responses to group members, given preconceptions about the group.

The use of social categories narrows the amount of information that a person needs to have about someone in order to act. Paradoxically, . . . it also expands the scope of information about an object. Thus you may need very little information to decide that a person is Jewish, but once you assign him to this category you now (ostensibly) know a great deal about him. [Ehrlich, 1973, p. 38]

An ingroup–outgroup schema has the same sorts of functions and liabilities as any schema; it helps the user quickly and easily process new stimuli, but it often brings with it unfounded assumptions which may, in fact, be wrong (or at least questionable). We expect and assume differences among well-defined, mutually exclusive groups, so we find them even where they may not actually exist. We come to perceive our own groups in characteristically different ways than we perceive the groups of others. This is in part a difference of perspective; a group looks different from the inside than it does on the outside. It is in part a practical matter; it may be reasonable and prudent most of the time not to respond in the same way to one's own group as one does to other people's groups. The result is a schema that structures responses to groups in such a way that ingroups tend to be favored over outgroups.

The tendency to favor the ingroup over outgroups does not imply that all outgroups are treated equally. This is particularly true in international relations; some "out-nations" may be allies, and others enemies. Tajfel (1970) found that small children, who had not yet developed any understanding of international relations, already favored their own nation and those allied to it over enemy nations. These findings show, not only that national attitudes and stereotypes may precede political knowledge and sophistication, but also that they tend to be consistent with actual international relations. Such attitudes about other nations are promoted by elites and reified in international interactions through "behavioral confirmation" (Pettigrew, 1981). They are perpetuated by black-and-white news and become manifested in culturally predominant stereotypes.

Not only do citizens have the tendency to view their own nation as good and to favor it over other nations, they will tend to view allied nations as good and enemy nations as bad. For Americans, the United States is the "in-nation" and is perceived as good. A clear ally, such as Great Britain, is generally thought of positively, while a clear enemy, such as Iraq, is perceived as bad. Many relations among nations, however, are characterized by enough complexity, by enough hostility yet, at the same time, harmony of interest, that it is not easy to characterize each relationship as clear alliance or enmity. Citizen attitudes toward nations in such relations with the United States may vary or be characterized by ambivalence.

U.S.–Soviet relations included periods of frigid hostility as well as periods of optimism and accommodation (this will be explained more fully in Chapter 3). American public opinion reflected the uneven path of U.S.–Soviet relations, varying from intense hostility toward the Soviet Union (in 1983, for instance) to the relatively positive attitudes witnessed as the Soviet Union fell apart in the early 1990s. Attitudes toward the out-nation, in this case the Soviet Union, depended on its perceived relations with the favored in-nation, the United States.

Attitudes toward the United States remain a stable anchor in this process. Attitudes toward other nations, anchored to American patriotism, are responsive to ebbs and flows in relations. American attitudes toward the United States remain overwhelmingly favorable, and attitudes toward other nations are established or shift in response to events, elite rhetoric, and other indications of friendly or hostile relations. Thus attitudes toward the in-nation (the United States) are primary, whereas attitudes toward the out-nation (the Soviet Union) are secondary. For this reason, attitudes toward other nations are able to shift enough to permit public support for complex and changing U.S. policies and relations in an uncertain world.

Balance Schemata

One sort of schema upon which a good deal of research has concentrated has been given the term "balance schema," based on Heider's theory of structural balance (Heider, 1958; DeSoto, Henley, & London, 1968; Press, Crockett, & Rosenkrantz, 1969; Cottrell, Ingraham, & Monfort, 1971; Delia & Crockett, 1973; Picek, Sherman, & Shiffrin, 1975; Sentis & Burnstein, 1979). A structurally balanced system of relationships is one in which the sides are clearly drawn. Given three entities (which may be people, groups, nations, concepts, etc.), structural balance implies that if there is a positive (friendly, compatible, or supporting) relationship between two of them, then they are both expected to have the same sort of relationship (positive or negative) towards the third. If two have a negative (hostile, incompatible, or opposing) relationship, then they are expected to relate to the third in opposite ways. Thus structurally balanced triadic relationships may take one of two general forms: all positive relationships, or one positive and two negative (see Figure 2.1). Unbalanced triads consist of all negative relationships, or one negative and two positive (see Figure 2.2). Balanced situations are assumed to create a good Gestalt in which elements fit together harmoniously. Unbalanced situations are assumed to create pressure for change.

A balance schema is one that operates according to the balance principle. The balance principle creates a tendency to organize stimuli into dichotomous structures that clearly distinguish between good and bad elements and contain rules for the relationships among such elements, as Abelson and Rosenberg (1958) observe:

In common-sense terms, a balanced cognitive structure represents a "black and white" attitude. The individual views some elements as good and the other elements as bad. All relations among "good elements" are positive (or null), and all relationships among "bad elements" are positive (or null), and all relationships between good and bad elements are negative (or null). [p. 5]

FIGURE 2.1
Structural Balance in Triads

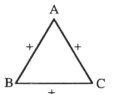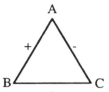

This sort of balance structure is well suited to ingroup–outgroup stereotyping. The stereotyped ingroup consists of the "good guys" who have good motives, do good things, and are related positively with other good guys and with the self (who is part of the ingroup). The stereotyped outgroup is opposed to all this. Such stereotyping occurs with respect to national as well as social groups, and citizen stereotypes concerning their own and other nations exhibit structural balance (Scott, 1965).

Balance theory predicts that perceptions of intergroup relations will tend to be more balanced than the actual relations. Applied generally to international relations, the balance principle takes the following form (Levine & Campbell, 1972, p. 182):

1. An ally of an ally will be an ally.
2. An enemy of an ally will be an enemy.
3. An ally of an enemy will be an enemy.
4. An enemy of an enemy will be an ally.

Harary (1961) suggests that actual relations among nations generally follow this balance principle. In general, a balance schema is a relatively accurate and useful simplification of world politics.

Because many of the structures in the world are balanced, the tendency to perceive balance will often serve people well. It will of course lead people astray when the

FIGURE 2.2
Structural Imbalance in Triads

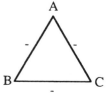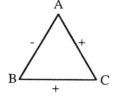

stimuli do not fit this pattern. This is one reason why American decision-makers were slow to recognize that two of their enemies (i.e. Russia and China) were hostile to each other. But errors like this and the associated finding that people perceive their environment as more consistent than it is do not mean that they should perceive it differently. [Jervis, 1976, p. 125]

Although applying a balance schema to international relations may result in occasional errors in the processing of relevant information, this does not mean that it is irrational to use such a structure (Jervis, 1976; George, 1980). Whatever schema is used, it will affect how information is processed, and its relative value as a cognitive tool will vary from situation to situation. In any case, the tendency to perceive balance translates into tendencies to view international actors as good or bad based on their alliances, and to assume international actors to have positive or negative relationships with each other based on whether they are considered to be "good elements" or "bad elements."

THE AMERICAN PATRIOTIC SCHEMA

Hunt (1987) takes a cultural approach in his historical study of the role of ideology in U.S. foreign policy. After Geertz, he views ideologies as "integrated and coherent systems of symbols, values and beliefs" (p. 12). From this perspective,

an American foreign-policy ideology [consists of] a relatively coherent, emotionally charged, and conceptually interlocking set of ideas. These core foreign-policy ideas would have to reflect the self-image of those who espoused them and to define a relationship with the world consonant with that self-image. They would in all likelihood derive from and be sustained by a diversity of domestic values or arrangements. [p. 14]

Hunt argues that U.S. foreign policy cognition has been guided by an ideologically based national self-image, one in which visions of national greatness are tied to the promotion of liberty (p. 17):

By asserting broad propositions about man and society, a nation's self-conception provides the intellectual underpinnings—the guiding assumptions and concerns—for foreign policy and may even in crucial respects dictate its terms. By defining what the nation is about and how it relates to the world, it orients thinking, sets conceptual bounds that make some solutions to problems more obvious and appealing than others, and in general reduces the complexities of the international environment to manageable terms. [p. 191]

Though a different set of concepts are used in this work (i.e. cultural schema rather than ideology), a similar claim is being made about the bases of U.S. foreign policy cognition. Conceptions of international relations are fundamentally based in conceptions of the in-nation. All international relations schemata adopted in American culture are grounded in the American self-image. This self-image, the "American patriotic schema," is the most important, most salient, and most stable political schema in American culture, and it forms the core of international relations schemata such as the cold war schema.

The American patriotic schema, fully articulated and filled out with related scripts and schemata, is broad, deep, and complex. It contains the cultural themes portrayed in a plethora of American myths, rituals, and symbols. Its meaning is found in the flag and the Statue of Liberty, in elections and fireworks, in the bald eagle and baseball, in George Washington and Horatio Alger, in the Declaration of Independence and the Truman Doctrine. It includes countless deeply held notions about the virtues of American freedom, democracy, and capitalism. It also requires a conception of the world and what happens in it into which a virtuous America can fit.

There is not room, in this limited discussion, to attempt to articulate fully the patriotic schema that predominates in American culture. A statement of the fundamental schematic elements that have the most important impact on American orientations toward international relations must suffice.

Fundamental to the patriotic schema is the conception that the United States is the in-nation. Americans perceive a positive relationship between themselves and their nation, and they think of the United States as good.

Basic in-nation favoring is bolstered by other important elements of the schema. The United States is conceived of as the best country in the world, not only because it is the in-nation, but because the United States has achieved greatness through the most clever and moral set of sociopolitical systems—those comprising American liberal democratic capitalism. Levels of sophistication obviously vary, and many Americans have shallow, symbolically based conceptions of their own nation's systems. Still, the notion commonly held among Americans is that the United States is quintessentially "democratic," and that democracy, like the United States, is a very good thing.

Democracy is seen as the best way of doing things, not only because it is seen as the American way, but also because it is viewed as providing the best conditions for human existence. Democratic America is seen to have what many other countries are seen to lack: "freedom." Americans have learned to cherish freedom, to live and die for it. Freedom, as will be demonstrated in Chapter 5, is the concept that is most commonly linked with the United States. Freedom is arguably the great American value. Because freedom is viewed by Americans as undeniably good and important, its strong positive association with the United States serves to bolster positive thoughts and feelings about America. Thus the perceived positive relationships among the United States, freedom, and democracy bolster positive sentiments toward America in general.

The basic American patriotic schema consists of five concepts (the United States, the self, good, democracy, and freedom) and ten positive relationships among those concepts (see Figure 2.3). This basic schema can be expanded upon

FIGURE 2.3
The American Patriotic Schema

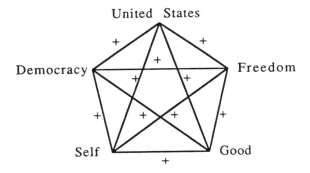

in numerous directions, both domestic and international, and each expanded articulation of the American patriotic schema serves to reinforce and perpetuate it. For instance, a rather detailed script of the American democratic process articulates the America–democracy link. This script contains knowledge of how politicians campaign, citizens vote, and bills become laws in America. The script also helps frame the political process in ways that put American democracy clearly in harmony with freedom, good, and the self. The American democratic process script fills out the patriotic schema and serves to legitimate American policies in the minds of the script-using public. This helps to perpetuate public acquiescence and support for the U.S. government.

Other scripts frame social and economic processes in America in a manner that bolsters the United States–freedom schematic link. Schematic notions about the workings of American capitalism, or "free enterprise" as it is called, define freedom and economic life in America in a harmonious fashion. Upward mobility and free capital accumulation are made salient, while restrictions experienced by those lacking the human or monetary resources to compete are discounted and overshadowed. Schematic idealizations of American social freedoms, such as freedom of speech, further reinforce the United States–freedom link.

The same American patriotic schema structures mainstream American thinking about both domestic and international politics, providing a stable cognitive basis for patriotic perceptions in both arenas. As we move this patriotic schema into the world of international conflict, we see that at various times in history, the United States, freedom, and democracy have had to do battle with opposing forces. According to the conventional American conception, a variety of enemies have opposed this holy trinity throughout American history. Images of these enemies served to bolster and perpetuate the patriotic national self-image by providing the evils against which the nation could favorably compare itself and the threats in terms of which it could justify questionable policies and actions (Finlay, Holsti, & Fagen, 1967).

FIGURE 2.4
The American Revolution Schema

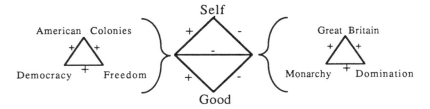

In the late eighteenth century, the British opposed the very establishment of the United States and tried to prohibit free and democratic self-rule. The British monarchy sought to dominate and exploit the American colonies, but their revolution successfully paved the way for a free and democratic United States of America. The American Revolution schema (see Figure 2.4) is an extension of the patriotic schema in which the American colonies oppose Great Britain, democracy opposes monarchy, and freedom opposes domination. The colonies that would become the United States and the freedom and democracy they sought constitute the favored side in the schema, while the dominating British monarchy constitute the enemy. Mainstream American interpretations of the American Revolution fit into this schema.

In the mid-nineteenth century, Southern rebels tried to tear the United States apart while perpetuating slavery, a clear affront to freedom. Although this may not be the interpretation of many Southern whites, most Americans have learned and accepted this characterization of the American Civil War. According to the conventional view, the North preserved the United States by defending the union against the Southern Confederacy. In the process, freedom and democracy were upheld through the eradication of slavery. This typical set of simple beliefs is expressed in the American Civil War schema (see Figure 2.5), another example of an extension of the American patriotic schema. The North is identified with the United States, and thus the self, and is considered to be the good side in the conflict.

FIGURE 2.5
The American Civil War Schema

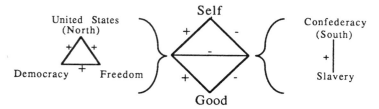

FIGURE 2.6
The Nazi Enemy Schema

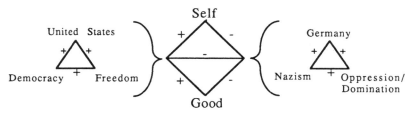

In World War II, the United States faced fascist enemies who threatened to remove freedom and democracy from the face of the earth. Nazi Germany, for example, is viewed as having been the most malevolent of enemies, intent on extending its genocidal domination throughout the world. The United States, in defeating Germany and its allies, was defending democracy from Nazi fascism, freedom from the threat of oppressive domination. What, for the lack of a better term, might be called the Nazi Enemy schema (see Figure 2.6) is another extension of the American patriotic schema into the international realm.

The Revolution, Civil War, and Nazi schemata are examples of balanced schemata that structure past conflicts and wars in terms of the American patriotic schema. They provide enemies and antitheses, set in balanced opposition to the United States, freedom, democracy, the self, and good. While scholars may find more truth in some of these interpretations of history than in others, the point is not the veracity of these interpretations, but their consistency. The acceptable American view has had the United States fighting for freedom and democracy in a world littered with those that would oppose these virtues.

Because these schemata structure interpretations of different historical events in the same patriotic manner, they serve to help perpetuate the patriotic schema upon which they are based. Perceptions of the American Revolution, the Civil War, and World War II all confirm the patriotic schema that structure them. This helps to maintain and promote the predominance of the patriotic schema in American culture, which increases the likelihood that further conflicts will be interpreted in a like manner. Thus the American patriotic schema is self-perpetuating: its use reinforces its cultural dominance, which increases its use. The various extensions of the patriotic schema contribute to this process. Since World War II, the cold war schema has been particularly important in this regard.

THE COLD WAR SCHEMA

In the years since World War II, the cold war schema has been the most salient and important international extension of the American patriotic schema. Following the war, the Soviet Union emerged as America's chief rival for control of

Europe and Asia. The Truman Doctrine framed American policy as the defense of freedom and democracy from Soviet encroachment, and numerous events were interpreted in that light. In this way, the cold war schema set the Soviet Union in opposition to the United States, freedom, and democracy.

Americans' conceptions of the Soviet Union, while not as elaborate as their conceptions of their own nation, were nonetheless embodied with an array of ideas and images. When thinking of the Soviet Union, Americans tended to picture a cold, depressed, sad place crawling with secret police, prisons, and propaganda. However, putting aside such details of American perceptions of the Soviet Union, a simple Soviet schema which fits neatly in with the American patriotic schema can be specified.

When asked, in open-ended interviews in the winter of 1985–1986, to identify current enemies of the United States, 87% of a sample of New York University students spontaneously mentioned the Soviet Union (Holt, 1989). Furthermore, Holt found that "communism, conceived as antithetical to democracy" (p. 47) was a primary reason for identifying nations as enemies of the United States.

Just as American virtue is linked with its ideological and systemic attachment to "democracy," Soviet villainy was tied to its ideological and systemic attachment to "communism." From the perspective of the cold war schema, democracy and communism are negatively related opposites, and each was promoted by one of the two negatively related superpowers. Both democracy and communism are perceived in extremely general terms: democracy is the way we do things in the United States, and communism is the way they did things in the Soviet Union. The democracy–communism dichotomy added substance to the notion that democracy was at stake in the cold war.

The opposite of "freedom" goes under a variety of names: tyranny, oppression, repression, domination, slavery, prison are but a few. Unlike other important elements in the cold war schema, freedom's antithesis lacks a unifying word that is broadly and conventionally used to sum it up. The word "oppression" has been chosen to encompass antifreedom in the cold war schema. The many different words used to describe freedom's antithesis should not blind us to its important role in the cold war schema. What was considered to be the most dangerous thing about the Soviet Union and communism was the oppression they were seen as inflicting.

The Soviet schema consists of positive relationships among three concepts, the Soviet Union, communism, and oppression (see Figure 2.7). The cold war pitted the Soviet Union against the United States, communism against democracy, and oppression against freedom. Thus the cold war schema consists of the American patriotic schema, the Soviet schema, and negative relationships among the elements of those two schemata. As Figure 2.8 shows, the sides are clearly drawn in a cognitively balanced fashion. According to the cold war schema, our good side (the United States, democracy, and freedom) opposes a bad side (the Soviet Union, communism, and oppression).

FIGURE 2.7
The Soviet Schema

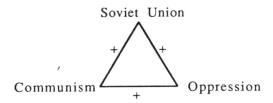

It is important to note that the cold war schema is firmly rooted in long-standing American ideological beliefs. According to Hunt (1987), ideology ties America's virtuous national self-image with the perception that the United States promotes freedom in the world. The new cold war policy that emerged after World War II was based firmly in old ideological preconceptions: "Ideology defined for the advocates of containment the issue at stake: survival of freedom around the world. That ideology also defined the chief threat to freedom: Soviet communism—which the United States had an incontestable obligation to combat" (p. 153).

Hartz (1955) has argued that American anticommunism is based on the same liberal ideology that defines "Americanism" and has guided the nation from its inception (pp. 302–309). In Bailey's (1948) view, antagonism against the Soviet Union and communism stems largely from an ideological attachment to the American way: "We have long cherished a powerful democratic and liberal tradition, and we dislike those nations that represent aristocracy, illiberalness, and repression, whether of Communism or Fascism. . . . We dislike those nations with an ideology which may bring about undesirable changes in our social or economic structure, whether it be French syndicalism or Russian Communism" (pp. 217, 219).

According to Walsh (1947), American anti-Soviet attitudes had their roots in that anticommunism, in anti-Russian attitudes dating back to the tzarist era, and

FIGURE 2.8
The Cold War Schema

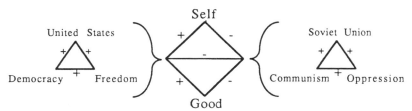

in ignorance concerning the Soviet Union. American images of the Soviet Union, in the absence of factual information, combined images of autocratic, oppressive Russia with dreaded communism. This image, set against an idealized conception of America, completes the cold war schema.

Hurwitz and Peffley (1990) see anti-Soviet and anticommunist attitudes as based in the very patriotism they helped to perpetuate:

Patriotism has recently been linked with anti-Soviet/communist sentiment in the public opinion literature. Whether expressed as an unswerving love of country or a chauvinistic view of superiority of one's nation, patriotism implies an inherent preference for American institutions and customs and, consequently, should translate into a hostile view of a system such as the USSR which, for many, threatens all that is distinctly "American." [p. 8]

The positive thoughts and feelings that most Americans have toward their nation make them "good citizens" who can generally be depended upon to support their nation in times of doubt and danger. The ultimate political function of the cold war schema was to perpetuate its pro-American component, the patriotic schema, thus stabilizing patriotic public support. While some elements of the schema showed flexibility in response to changing realities, the patriotic schema formed the unmovable anchor to which other elements were tied. Thus the Soviet schema had to shift around a bit to accommodate the stability of the patriotic schema. This peripheral flexibility allowed for the cognitive processing of a complex and changing international reality in the continued context of stable pro-Americanism.

SCHEMATIC THINKING IN A COMPLEX WORLD

People do not generally rely on a single schema, particularly when they think about subjects as complicated as international relations. Those who used the cold war schema to think about international relations did so in conjunction with other schemata. The cold war schema cohabited American minds along with intervention scripts, realist conceptions of national interest, theories of deterrence, and an array of other relevant schemata. The cold war schema often, but not always, was the dominant thought structure. While some schemata blended harmoniously with the cold war schema, others created disturbing contradictions. Depending on the international issues or events under consideration, the cold war schema and its various elements were more or less dominant in structuring cognition. Effects of the cold war schema therefore varied in their form and intensity.

As will be argued in the pages to follow, the cold war schema perpetuated itself in a number of ways. In public discourse, news, and popular culture, information was presented in ways that confirmed the schema, and alternative perspectives were undermined. Cold war schema users tended to remember and interpret international issues and events in ways that confirmed the schema and resisted its refutation. Political, cultural, and cognitive forces tended to work against public recognition of conditions and events that were inconsistent with cold war preconceptions. As a result, for most people, most of the time, most of reality seemed to fit the cold war schema.

The patriotic schema creates a tendency to assume, for example, that a nation supported by the United States is more democratic than a nation opposed by the United States. While some information may contradict simple schematic notions, information that is consistent with the schema is more likely to penetrate one's belief system. Although the simple schema does not always dominate and exclude contradictory information, it usually does.

For instance, American politicians and policymakers justified the Vietnam War by framing it in terms of the cold war schema. Mainstream public discourse and news coverage did not tend to stray from this interpretation, even to criticize policy. Most Americans accepted and used the cold war schema, and this made them susceptible to cold war appeals. It also made them resistant both to criticism of U.S. policy in Vietnam and to evidence that the United States was not supporting freedom, democracy, or good. In the end, the war was rejected, but not because it was not generally seen as a noble cause. The major American lesson from the war was that war hurts: more recent interventions (Nicaragua, Grenada) were motivated and justified in terms of the cold war schema, but American leaders have learned to minimize the American pain involved.

Still, people who became aware of schema-inconsistent facts did not completely disregard them in favor of a simple schema. Counter-schematic information sometimes slides through schematic defenses. Some Americans questioned or rejected the application of the cold war schema to Vietnam and, occasionally, some aspects of the schema itself. Many Americans found it difficult to support the United States, or to view it as good, during the Vietnam War. Some experienced great internal conflict as they tried to reconcile national behaviors they considered wrong and could not support with a nation they considered right and could not oppose.

People are not simple-minded automatons who unceasingly force incompatible stimuli into an idealized cognitive structure. The picture is more complex, involving individual differences, psychic conflicts, and the possibility of schematic change over time.

While excessively rigid and uncompromising acceptance or rejection of the cold war schema may occur in extreme cases, the cognitive styles of most mainstream Americans mix rigidity with some flexibility. At one extreme, there existed those true believers who steadfastly disregarded all that might have created doubt and remained religiously faithful to the cold war schema in all its Manichaean glory. At the other extreme were those who, in the face of evidence that elements of the cold war schema were not entirely true, completely rejected either those elements or the entire schema, often replacing them with competing, anti-American schemata.

Most people, however, hovered somewhere in-between the extremes of the orthodox cold warriors and their radical opposition. Although the biases of most Americans guarded against counter-schematic information, it sometimes got through anyway. Occasionally, normal American cold war schema users encountered evidence of U.S. opposition to democracy (in Vietnam, for instance), of positive Soviet behavior, or of improving U.S.–Soviet relations. Under such circumstances, many Americans began to experience some doubt, ambivalence, and limited attitude change. Still, as long as Americans were able to get their "fix" of Soviet or communist oppression, and of U.S. promotion of freedom and democracy, the cold war candle continued to burn in the minds of Americans. Supported by proschema cultural and cognitive biases, the cold war schema remained in American brains so long as schema-consistent cues were intermittently supplied. In fact, a certain amount of flexibility in the cold war schema was necessary to the long-term perpetuation of the American patriotic schema, and to the maintenance of public support for cold war policies. As is argued in Chapter 3, the American cold war policy of containment has consisted of two tracks, one aggressive, the other accommodative. Long-term support for this dual approach to dealing with the Soviet threat depended upon the ability of Americans both to rally behind their leaders against the evil empire, and to celebrate superpower summits and improved U.S.–Soviet relations.

If American images of the Soviet Union were set in stone, then the shifts made necessary by America's two-track Soviet policy would have been met with strong opposition. If the Soviet Union was always viewed as a hated enemy, then accommodation would have appeared as immoral and unwise as making deals with the devil. Had anti-Soviet sentiments entirely dissolved, however, then U.S. leaders would have been unable to justify aggressive acts as necessary responses to the evil empire. The Soviet Union, communism, and the oppression associated with them served again and again to justify questionable American behavior, and to provide an unsavory image against which a flawed America could be favorably compared in times of doubt and discontent. Thus perceptions of communist oppression and the evil empire were vital to the maintenance of the idealized positive conceptions of America contained in the patriotic schema. Although it was necessary at times to ease anti-Soviet attitudes, it was just as necessary at other times to rekindle them.

Given America's dual containment strategy, a somewhat flexible anti-Sovietism was necessary to the stabilizing rigidity of the American patriotic schema. Positive perceptions of the United States were the immobile anchor of the cold war schema. Perceptions of the Soviet Union varied as the tides of aggression and accommodation changed. Through this mix of rigidity and flexibility, the cold war schema functioned to perpetuate patriotism and public support for U.S. foreign policy throughout the cold war era.

NATIONAL UNITY AND THE ENEMY

Sumner (1906) suggested that "the relation of comradeship and peace in the we-group and that of hostility and war towards other-groups are correlative to each other. The exigencies of war with outsiders are what make peace inside" (Stein, 1976, p. 143). Coser (1956) presented and refined the ideas of Simmel (1955) concerning the relationships among ingroups, outgroups, and conflict. In their conception, the ingroup–outgroup distinction emerges from conflict, which establishes both ingroup and outgroup identities and the boundaries between them. The existence of the outgroup fosters cohesion in the ingroup. Based on a review of the relevant literature in sociology, anthropology, psychology, and political science, Stein (1976) concluded "that external conflict does increase internal cohesion under certain conditions" (p. 165).

Freud (1961) wrote, "it is always possible to bind together a considerable number of people in love, so long as there are other people left over to receive the manifestations of their aggressiveness" (p. 61). The disliked or enemy outgroup functions as a target against which hostility can be directed. The existence of the outgroup as an outlet for aggression facilitates cohesion within the ingroup. The ingroup is united against the common enemy, and this allows it to justify otherwise unjustifiable acts as necessary responses to the outside threat (Finlay et al., 1967).

Thus, according to the cold war schema, the favored United States was defined in terms of its contrast and conflict with the Soviet Union, and vice-versa. As Keen (1986) writes,

it becomes more and more difficult to imagine who we are without reference to our enemy. Our negative identity, or orientation *against* becomes primary. The enemy . . . becomes our symbiotic partner. . . . Without him who would we blame for the slings and arrows, the failures, the wounds, the inchoate anger, the gnawing frustration, the injustice? [p. 108]

American virtues are defined by their antitheses. For instance, Americans view their nation as quintessentially free, yet that idealized American freedom has meaning only in relation to its unfree antithesis. The reality of freedom in America is mixed: Americans are free in some ways, restricted in others. There are differences between the freedoms exercised in America and those in other countries, just as there are differences in the freedoms exercised by some Americans compared to others. How can this complex and ambiguous reality be reconciled with a simple, strong, schematic link between America and freedom? In order to maintain the idealized image in the face of a mixed reality, an idealized antithesis is necessary for comparison.

The stereotyped "totalitarian" state, so closely associated with the Soviet Union and communism, provides the relative unfreedom against which American freedom can favorably compare. American freedoms that do not exist in the stereotyped oppressive state are paraded as clear examples of how remarkably free America is. Restrictions, contradictions, limitations, and exceptions to American freedom are discounted as part of life in an imperfect world. Thus America is seen as perfect in an imperfect world, quintessentially free despite obvious restrictions on freedom. American freedom is verified relative to an image of the unfree which is vague, schematic, and unexperienced. Against a black background, grey seems white; against the Soviet–communist stereotype, the United States appears to be the epitome of freedom.

As Dallek (1983) argues, the Soviet communist threat functioned to divert the attention of Americans from their alienation and powerlessness, and to unite them against a common enemy:

The Communist danger . . . justified the need for "togetherness," conformity, or organizational loyalty as a substitute for the traditional individualism to which so many Americans are still drawn. Tied to the material benefits provided by the impersonal machine culture, Americans rationalize its necessity by pointing to Communist threats. Though other influences contribute to this exaggerated fear, its usefulness as a device for encouraging "Americanism" or "belongingness" has been a consistent reason for its centrality in U.S. foreign policy since the Second World War. [p. xix]

In its schematic manifestation, U.S. foreign policy became American freedom and democracy opposing the threat of Soviet communist oppression. As a result, it was easy for Americans to unite within this nobly defined in-nation against the threatening out-nation. Stereotyped, schematic notions of an oppressive, communist dungeon in the Soviet Union formed a stark contrast with idealized schematic images of American freedom and democracy.

The schematic contrast and conflict between the Soviet Union, oppression, and communism on the one side and the United States, freedom, and democracy on the other functioned to help Americans define their in-nation in a way that facilitated in-nation favoring. The cold war schema that emerged from U.S.–Soviet conflict served to foster social cohesion and political acquiescence in the United States. Despite inequalities and social strife at home, most Americans remained grateful that they did not live in an oppressive, Soviet communist hell. Despite U.S. interventions that have caused immeasurable destruction and suffering abroad, most Americans have remained proud that they live in a nation that has been willing to protect the world from the grave threat of communist oppression. This is because Americans have used the cold war schema to interpret the political world.

The recent downfall of the Soviet Union means that America will need some other prominent out-nation against which to compete and be compared. The cold war schema cannot continue, unaltered, in the absence of the Soviet Union. "Terrorists" like Khadafi, "drug dealers" like Noriega, "communists" like Ortega, and other minor villains have provided quick enemy fixes, and it may be that a succession of Irans, Nicaraguas, Lybias, and Iraqs will suffice to fill the enemy role. It may not always be necessary to have a nation of the Soviet Union's stature to provide the ongoing out-nation that will ensure the maintenance of enthusiastic American unity. Although the jury is still out, the recent conflict with Iraq suggests that the powerful, threatening enemy superpower may be adequately replaced by a series of pesky, deranged, and deluded minor conquerors.

3

Cold War Opinion in America

I believe that it must be the policy of the United States to support free peoples who are resisting attempted subjugation by armed minorities or by outside pressures.

—Harry S. Truman (Gati, 1974, pp. 6–7)

What is our battle against communism if it is not a fight between anti-God and a belief in the Almighty.

—Dwight D. Eisenhower (Parenti, 1969, p. 64)

I believe that we can check the Communist advance, that we can turn it back, and that we can, in this century, provide for the ultimate victory of freedom over slavery.

—John F. Kennedy (Destler et al., 1984, p. 51)

It may seem melodramatic to say that the United States and Russia represent Good and Evil. But if we think of it that way, it helps to clarify our perspective on the world struggle.

—Richard M. Nixon (Keen, 1986, p. 31)

The march of freedom and democracy will leave Marxism-Leninism on the ash heap of history.

—Ronald Reagan (Stoesinger, 1985, p. 292)

First there were dinosaurs, then there were cavemen, then there were Russians, and then there were people.

—Casey, age 5

Each past president (and future anthropologist) had a different perspective on the cold war. While in office, each president altered his views. Still, the road from Truman to Bush, with all its dips and turns, was built on a solid foundation of core beliefs. "The more things change, the more they remain the same." This old aphorism, at once profound and trivial, was not initially intoned with U.S. foreign policy in mind. Yet as we look for continuity and change in U.S. foreign policy orientations and opinions, we find an abundance of both; though opposites, continuity and change are inescapable aspects of the development of all things. The challenge is to understand what has and has not changed, in what ways, when, and why.

In the four decades that followed World War II, Americans lived through wars and interventions, arms races and arms agreements. They engaged in debates over the relative merits of containment and rollback, militarism and diplomacy. Throughout those four decades, however, the basic beliefs articulated in the Truman Doctrine provided a relatively stable foundation upon which discourse, policy, and perceptions rested. This foundation was the cold war schema: the basic notion of a Manichaean conflict between the United States, freedom, and democracy, on the one side, and the Soviet Union, oppression, and communism on the other. The schema's nature, its manifestations, its effects, and its resilience constitute the central focus of this book.

The cold war schema justified U.S. foreign policy and provided a cognitive basis for public support, but it also provided grounds for limited dissent. The schema set up the ideal against which Americans were able to judge their foreign policy. Some complained that the United States had not fulfilled its promise to protect the world from communist oppression. Others lamented that the United States had forsaken freedom and democracy in its quest for order. Opposing political camps repeatedly made these sorts of claims, often about the same policy or event. For instance, the war in Vietnam and interventions in Central America elicited these sorts of opposing arguments. The contrasting critiques may have emphasized different aspects of the cold war schema, but both sides appealed to that same culturally legitimated belief system. The cold war schema was the organizing framework that provided the criteria for judging post–World War II U.S. foreign policy.

Did the cold war schema maintain its position of cultural prominence, even in the era of detente? At least two opposing arguments can be (and are) made, each with some legitimacy. The conventional wisdom, to be discussed in greater detail later in this chapter, is that the cold war consensus died during the late 1960s and that the 1970s were the beginning of a post–cold war period. According to this argument, the events of the 1960s and 1970s—the Vietnam War, detente with the Soviet Union, and normalization of relations with China—were accompanied by a large-scale rejection of the old cold war orthodoxy. Vietnam bankrupted the Truman Doctrine both morally and monetarily. The old claim that the United States was fighting for freedom and democracy against Soviet-supported communist oppression lost much of its credibility. At the same time, improved relations with the Soviet Union and China made the Manichaean image incongruent with U.S. diplomacy. This led to greater tolerance for, and milder stereotypes of, the communist superpowers. Later liberalizations in the Soviet Union and Eastern Europe improved the image of the Soviet Union, and this led to a further erosion of the cold war schema.

The alternative argument developed in this chapter is that, through all these developments, mainstream Americans remained united in their general use of the cold war schema. American rhetoric, opinion, and behavior in the cold war period were both aggressive and accommodating, and often shifted from one to the other. This duality derived from the realities of power politics in a dangerous world; peace and cold war victory were both goals. As America's nuclear advantage declined, however, the costs and dangers of militarism increased and diplomacy became more attractive as the primary tool for cold war conflict management. This development was not, as some interpreted it, a rejection of the cold war schema, but a prudent choice of tactics. While it was accompanied by some lessening of negative perceptions of the Soviet Union, it was never clear that these developments were stable or lasting. Not until the recent decline and fall of the Soviet empire did the cold war schema become obsolete, and even then, not completely so.

It cannot be argued that there was no attitude change; negative attitudes toward the Soviet Union were clearly less pervasive during periods of U.S.–Soviet accommodation. Still, periodic U.S.–Soviet conflicts repeatedly revitalized latent anti-Soviet sentiments and maintained the cold war schema in the minds of most Americans. Like racist and sexist attitudes and ethnocentric prejudices, anti-Soviet attitudes and stereotypes were suppressed when the political and social atmosphere encouraged intergroup tolerance, but lay in waiting for the times and places where their expression would be acceptable. As an examination of public opinion data from the 1970s and 1980s will show, anti-Soviet attitudes re-emerged almost instantly, and with a vengeance, when political conditions were right.

Over time, improved intergroup relations and nonexpression of anti-outgroup attitudes and stereotypes *can* change the culturally predominant perceptions of the outgroup. Thus, had friendly U.S.–Soviet relations continued uninterrupted for an extended period of time, anti-Soviet perceptions would have gradually faded away. The fall of the Soviet Union preempted this eventuality and made the Soviet stigma irrelevant. Although many stereotyped conceptions of the Soviet Union will be transferred to the new states that have emerged from its ashes, automatic associations with communism and oppression are not likely to persist.

This chapter considers the ways in which the cold war schema weathered the ebbs and flows of post–World War II U.S.–Soviet relations. It looks at the development of American cold war orientations and considers whether developments during the 1960s and thereafter removed aspects of the cold war schema from cultural predominance. It argues that while administrations swung back and forth between aggressive and accommodative policy stances, they continued to think in terms of the cold war schema. A look at public opinion during the era of the "cold war consensus" reveals that while there was consensual antipathy toward the Soviet Union and communism and a universal desire to contain them both, the American public remained open to both military and diplomatic initiatives by their government. Claims that consensus was destroyed in the Vietnam era are critiqued, and it is suggested instead that diplomacy increased in desirability relative to militarism while consensus remained intact around the cold war schema. The cold war schema has recently lost its relevance due to the dissolution of the Soviet Union. Still, it is not clear that the positive perceptions of the Soviet Union that many Americans held in the early 1990s would have otherwise persisted.

The central argument made in this chapter is that although there were fluctuations in attitudes toward the Soviet Union and an increasing desire to use accommodation as the main method for dealing with the Soviet threat, the cold war schema generally prevailed into the Gorbachev era. America's leaders sometimes vilified the Soviet Union and took harsh stances, and they sometimes treated the Soviets with friendly respect. The American public showed a willingness to accept both tacks, and aggregate changes in their attitudes toward the Soviet Union reflected the official position of the moment. Until the demise of the Soviet Union, there was no clear indication in U.S. policy or public opinion that the cold war schema had left the American scene for good.

THE DEVELOPMENT OF COLD WAR POLICY

This brief discussion is not meant as a summary of the cold war: it is intended simply to demonstrate that America's Soviet policy was at times aggressive and at times accommodative throughout the post–World War II period. Thus later developments were not a miraculous transition from an all-out, frigid, cold war to a sudden peace. Rather, U.S.–Soviet relations had their ups and downs, and aggression and accommodation were alternative means for managing relations within a cold war context. American leaders and the American public were united in their belief in the cold war schema, but fluctuating realities led to changes in the schema's manifestations in policy and opinion. The point is that accommodative policy preferences were not a rejection of the cold war schema, but a prudent choice of cold war tactics.

Based on the American patriotic schema, the cold war schema had deep roots in the American diplomatic tradition. Woodrow Wilson personified the American crusade for freedom and democracy with vision and moral fervor that few have matched. From the Wilsonian perspective, the United States was a divinely enlightened missionary saddled with the heroic, if unsavory, task of doing battle with the forces of oppression so that other peoples of the world could enjoy America's unique gifts (Stoesinger, 1985). Intervention by the United States was morally right by definition, as America, freedom, democracy, goodness, God, and Wilson were inextricably bonded in holy harmony. Self-determination meant the adoption of American ways, and, paradoxically, it sometimes had to be imposed through American domination (Nathan & Oliver, 1985, p. 16).

It was under Wilson that the United States first confronted the Soviets, intervening against the Bolsheviks in a half-hearted attempt to keep what was viewed as an oppressive minority from subjugating a great nation. Since that time, interventions in Greece, Korea, Cuba, Vietnam, Grenada, Nicaragua, and elsewhere have been officially interpreted as struggles with that same enemy. According to the schematic interpretations of these American interventions, they have involved the United States, freedom, and democracy, engaged in a Manichaean struggle for the future of mankind against the Soviet Union, oppression, and communism.

After World War II the Soviet Union acquired the status of premier enemy of the United States. The war had been a time of strained alliance against common enemies. In the postwar period, the United States and the Soviet Union repeatedly found themselves at odds over the futures of other nations. As both sought to form others in their own very different images, each found the other to be both constraining and threatening. Disputes arose over Eastern Europe, Germany, Iran, and Japan. Economic issues and the new presence of nuclear weapons caused further tension (Levering, 1988, pp. 16–23). U.S. and Soviet policy goals clearly conflicted, and U.S. policy, in rhetoric and behavior, began to concentrate on a perceived Soviet communist threat. The Soviet Union and communism replaced Nazi Germany and fascism as the great national and ideological enemies of the United States and democratic capitalism.

The cold war was inaugurated by President Truman in 1947 with the establishment of the Truman Doctrine and the policy of containment. A believer in the Wilsonian ideal, President Truman was also strongly anti-Soviet. Faced with a Congress that was not about to spend tremendous amounts of money to finance foreign aid and adventures without good justification, Truman provided that justification in his famous speech of March 12, 1947. The issue of $400 million in aid to Greece and Turkey provided the impetus and opportunity for the statement of America's self-defined role in the postwar world. According to the Truman Doctrine, the United States would use its power to defend freedom and democracy from the tyranny of aggressive, oppressive regimes and rebels.

Totalitarian regimes imposed upon free peoples, by direct or indirect aggression, undermine the foundations of international peace and hence the security of the United States.

The peoples of a number of countries of the world have recently had totalitarian regimes forced upon them against their will. The Government of the United States has made frequent protests against coercion and intimidation, in violation of the Yalta agreement, in Poland, Rumania, and Bulgaria. I must also state that in a number of other countries there have been similar developments.

At the present moment in world history nearly every nation must choose between alternative ways of life. The choice is too often not a free one.

One way of life is based upon the will of the majority, and is distinguished by free institutions, representative government, free elections, guarantees of individual liberty, freedom of speech and religion, and freedom from political oppression.

The second way of life is based upon the will of a minority forcibly imposed upon the majority. It relies upon terror and oppression, a controlled press and radio, fixed elections, and the suppression of political freedoms.

I believe that it must be the policy of the United States to support free peoples who are resisting attempted subjugation by armed minorities or by outside pressures. [Truman, in Gati, 1974, pp. 6–7]

The Truman doctrine clearly divided the world between good (the American side) and evil. The implied enemy was the Soviet Union and, inseparable from it, the communists of the world. Vigilant American involvement in the world was seen as necessary to maintaining the American way of life at home and abroad.

This was to be achieved through, as Kennan (1947) phrased it, "a long-term, patient but firm and vigilant containment of Russian expansive tendencies . . . a policy of firm containment, designed to confront the Russians with unalterable counter-force at every point where they show signs of encroaching upon the interests of a peaceful and stable world." (pp. 575, 581). The policy of containment grew to combine economic, military, and diplomatic means for the purpose of checking what was seen as Soviet communist expansion around the world. Under Truman, such efforts included the Marshall Plan, the formation of NATO, and the Korean War. The year 1950 marked not only the outbreak of the Korean War, but also Truman's approval of National Security Council Paper Number 68, which advocated the militarization of containment and suggested substantial U.S. military buildup to meet the challenge.

The Truman Doctrine and the policy of containment made it clear who the enemy was and framed U.S. policy as a series of responses to enemy activities and threats. This cold war conception with the sides well drawn would later serve to structure official U.S. interpretations of various involvements around the world: in Korea, in Vietnam, in Nicaragua.

According to Trout (1975), "both the United States and the Soviet Union defined and then sustained the cold war through an ideological division of the world" (p. 251). On both the American and Soviet sides ideologically grounded conceptions of international relations defined and structured cold war antagonisms and made them relevant to domestic politics. The symbolic antithesis between communism and democracy, which was consciously promoted in the Truman Doctrine and served to structure American conceptions of foreign policy, "helped to establish an identity between societal goals and policy goals" (p. 259). The result, Trout argued, was that cold war policy and rhetoric served a political legitimation function. In fact, the "normative frameworks" (p. 279) that served to define the cold war emerged from legitimation processes in both superpowers.

Despite the Truman Doctrine and the policy of containment, the Truman administration was attacked by critics from the right for being insufficiently vigorous in its anticommunism. The "loss" of China was portrayed as an avoidable catastrophe, and containment was viewed as almost treasonous constraint when liberation was possible.

Anticommunism swept the nation in the Red Scare years of the early 1950s, as the nation purged itself of suspected communist subversion. For the American people, the Soviet Union took the role of Nazi Germany, the role of feared, evil enemy. Communist ideology became the antithesis of American loyalty, the hidden membership card of the enemy.

The issue was not whether opposing communism was of utmost importance, but what sorts of actions, investments, and risks were to be undertaken in doing so. The disagreements between Truman and MacArthur over the running of the Korean War was symbolic of the debate over anticommunist tactics, and the strong support MacArthur found in both the public and the political elites tells of the strong disagreements on these matters.

The Eisenhower administration operated under similar strains, which they managed through a mix of tough rhetoric and controlled action. While a presidential candidate, Eisenhower had expressed a desire to liberate Eastern Europe, and he spoke in stark, Manichaean terms as he entered office: "Forces of good and evil are massed and armed and opposed as rarely before in history. Freedom is pitted against slavery, lightness against dark" (Dallek, 1983, p. 187).

Once he settled into office, however, Eisenhower pursued a prudent policy of containment. The religiously anti-Soviet, anticommunist John Foster Dulles spoke of rollback and massive retaliation, while the pragmatic President Eisenhower held the line against potentially dangerous policies and action. Low-risk covert interventions were undertaken in Iran and Guatemala, but the United States did not intervene when the Soviet Union invaded Hungary. Clear efforts were made to improve U.S.–Soviet relations and reduce tensions through diplomatic meetings and visits. While mistrust and animosity toward the Soviet Union remained strong, Soviet power forced pragmatic American leaders to deal with the Soviets in a constrained, diplomatic fashion.

Claiming that the Eisenhower administration had not been vigorous enough in its anticommunism, Kennedy made aggressive cold war rhetoric a mainstay of the 1960 presidential campaign: "I believe that we can check the Communist advance, that we can turn it back, and that we can, in this century, provide for the ultimate victory of freedom over slavery" (Destler et al, 1984, p. 51). Vigorous or overzealous, the Kennedy administration was soon to find itself in embarrassing (Bay of Pigs) and dangerous (Cuban Missile Crisis) cold war confrontations over Cuba. Yet despite the rhetoric, Kennedy, too, displayed constraint as a cold warrior. Bay of Pigs was a limited operation, and he resisted more bellicose action in the Cuban Missile Crisis.

Having gone to the brink in the Cuban Missile Crisis, and realizing the rapid Soviet progress toward parity, Kennedy, in the last year of his life, sought accommodation with the Soviet Union. In June 1963, Kennedy suggested a reexamination of "our attitude toward the cold war" and stated that "both the

United States and its allies, and the Soviet Union and its allies, have a mutually deep interest in a just and genuine peace and in halting the arms race." The "pause in the Cold War," as Kennedy described it, resulted in important agreements such as the 1963 Test Ban Treaty and the sale of American wheat to the Soviet Union. Subsequent American presidents followed Kennedy's lead and continued to make arms control agreements with the Soviet Union (Levering, 1988, pp. 99–101, 185).

Ten years before Kennedy's death was to make him president, Senator Lyndon Johnson proclaimed his belief in the cold war schema and the doctrine of massive retaliation:

We should announce, I believe, that any act of aggression anywhere, by any Communist forces, will be regarded as an act of aggression by the Soviet Union. . . . If anywhere in the world—by any means, open or concealed—Communism trespasses upon the soil of the free world, we should unleash all the power at our command upon the vitals of the Soviet Union. That is the policy we should build toward. [Parenti, 1969, p. 152]

As president, Johnson vastly increased American involvement in Vietnam in an effort to hold the line against communism. The heated national debate over Vietnam not only ended the Johnson presidency, it also led many to question the cold war as a justification for U.S. intervention.

By the early 1960s, the undeniable Sino–Soviet split had made the accepted American conception of a powerful and monolithic world communist movement implausible to many (Levering, 1988, p. 98). Separately the Soviet Union and China seemed less threatening, and their disagreements provided an opportunity for playing one off against the other. Seeking both to improve the U.S. position and achieve stability in the world system, Nixon and Kissinger opened dialogue with China and pursued detente with the Soviet Union.

Nixon had cut his political teeth as a staunch anticommunist cold warrior, and the fact that he continued anticommunist interventions in Indochina and Latin America provided living (and dying) proof that the cold war had not been abandoned. On the one hand, Nixon and Kissinger were covertly working to depose the president of a small South American democracy (Chile) because of his Marxist views, progressive economic policies, and international communist connections. On the other hand, they were seeking dialogue and stable relations with two far more powerful and "dangerous" communist enemies. Nixon and Kissinger, of course, could not treat the Soviet Union or China like Chile or Vietnam (ultimately, they couldn't even treat Vietnam like Vietnam). The emergence of the Soviet Union and China as formidable communist powers motivated the prudent use of diplomacy in managing relations. Through diplomacy, they reasoned, both strategic stability and containment could be achieved.

The Carter administration wavered with the conflicting influences of an anti-Soviet national security advisor (Brezinski), a secretary of state (Vance) who favored a more accommodating stance, and a president who considered human rights to be relevant to U.S. foreign policy. After a rough start, the Carter administration did manage to negotiate a SALT II Treaty, but it was never ratified. The Soviet invasion of Afghanistan and the American response brought U.S.–Soviet relations to a low point, halting any progress toward detente. By the end, as Levering puts it, "the president who had criticized Americans' 'inordinate fear of communism' in 1977 had been virtually transformed into a Cold Warrior" (1988, p. 168). When Reagan came along to declare detente dead and the cold war alive, the Carter experience had lent some credibility to such a view.

Reagan went through a development not unlike that of Kennedy; ferociously anti-Soviet early in his presidency, he then developed an eagerness to negotiate later on.

At the outset, Reagan told the world that the Soviet Union was the "evil empire," the "focus of evil in the modern world." In his first news conference as president, he asserted that the goal of the Soviet Union was to impose "a one-world Socialist or Communist state." "The only morality they recognize," he proclaimed, "is what will further their cause: meaning they commit any crime, tell any lie, to cheat, in order to obtain that."

As Hunt argues, Reagan's new cold war reaffirmed national pride and simplistic ideological truths that were deeply rooted in American political culture (Hunt, 1987, pp. 188–189). The vehement cold war rhetoric was employed in efforts to promote interventionist policies and increased arms expenditures. "Peace through strength" was the goal, and an arms buildup was the means. The Reagan administration quickly stepped up efforts to prohibit or overturn revolutionary change in Latin America. Revolution was to be denied, not simply because it was considered communist, but because of assumed direction and sponsorship, through Cuba, by the Soviet Union. "Let's not delude ourselves," Reagan suggested in December 1980, "the Soviet Union underlies all the unrest that is going on." He continued, "If they weren't engaged in this game of dominoes, there wouldn't be any hot spots in the world" (Kegley & Wittkopf, 1982, p. 560).

While the Reagan orientation toward Latin America did not change, the administration's approach to dealing with the Soviet Union did. After vilifying and refusing to negotiate with the Soviets, Reagan met and concluded agreements with them and even visited the "evil empire." Once again, a crusading cold warrior, faced with the responsibilities of maintaining relative peace in the nuclear age, was motivated to seek a relief of tensions between the United States and the Soviet Union.

The Bush administration continued a cautious but friendly policy of accommodation. At his December 1989 meeting in Malta with President Gorbachev, President Bush spoke of a "vastly improved" relationship between the two superpowers, with reduced, but "not eliminated," tensions. "With reforms under way in the Soviet Union," he proclaimed, "we stand at the threshold of a brand-new era of U.S.–Soviet relations. It is within our grasp to contribute each in our own way to overcoming the division of Europe and ending the military confrontation there" (*The New York Times*, Dec. 4, 1989, pp. A1, A11). While endorsing the notion of progress toward an end to the cold war, Bush steadfastly refused to prematurely declare the war over. Although he agreed that "things have moved dramatically since the days when the two sides often confronted each other," Bush pointed out to reporters that "if I signal to you there's no Cold War, then you'll say, 'Well, what are you doing with troops in Europe?'" (*Seattle Post-Intelligencer,* December 5, 1989, p. A9). Although Bush was later to declare, "we won the cold war" (TVNZ News, January 13, 1992), he, like many Americans, did not jump at the first opportunities to do so.

The 1991 coup that temporarily deposed Gorbachev and hastened the dissolution of the Soviet Union also showed how fragile the improved relations with, and perceptions of, the Soviet Union were. Americans were cognitively prepared for a new cold war, but events intervened to the contrary: after a short return to the helm, Gorbachev resigned and the Soviet Union was dissolved. American perceptions of the republics that have emerged from the Soviet ashes no doubt are strongly influenced by schematic images of the Soviet Union. Still, the association with communism has clearly been broken, and the cold war schema has ceased to be a relevant framework for thinking about international relations.

The end of the Soviet Union clearly ended, not only the cold war, but also the relevance of the Soviet component of the cold war schema. Until that point, however, the cold war had remained the principle guiding theme of U.S. postwar foreign policy. As Nathan and Oliver (1985) state it:

The constancy of U.S. foreign policy is striking. . . . Debates have persisted concerning the most appropriate means for constraining Soviet power. But with the exception of a brief period at the onset of the Carter administration, the Soviet Union has remained the singular focus of U.S. foreign policy since the end of World War II. [p. 424]

All administrations felt the sometimes conflicting, sometimes complementary desires to contain the Soviet Union and communism, on the one hand, and to maintain American peace and security, on the other. All administrations employed a mix of resolve and constraint, aggression and diplomacy, in dealing with the perceived Soviet–communist challenge.

Why the many shifts of U.S. policy postures toward the Soviet Union, from pugnacious to tolerant and back again? One explanation may be the tendency for American presidents to exaggerate Soviet threats or positive changes in order to obtain public and congressional support (Nye, 1984). In this context, what appear to be significant changes in U.S. or Soviet policy or opinion may be more accurately characterized as yet another wave in the ongoing fluctuations between two complementary, though symbolically opposed, sides of the same policy: hanging tough and easing tension.

Ernest May points out that the need for the executive branch to recruit public support and overcome the institutional separation of powers presses presidents to feel that the issues must be oversimplified or exaggerated. One of the ironies of the historical record is that, while public opinion has appeared to support a two-track policy of peace and strength, presidents have found it difficult to formulate and implement strategies that appeared to the public to be effectively pursuing both goals at the same time. [Nye, 1984, p. 207]

Over time, the Soviet Union became both the rival superpower and the major negotiating partner of the United States. Had the Soviet Union been viewed exclusively as the "evil empire," then U.S.–Soviet negotiations would have amounted to "making deals with the devil." Detente and its offspring required that American leaders adopt dual rhetoric toward the Soviet Union. The sometimes hated enemy was depicted at other times as a respected opponent.

Nincic (1988) suggests that the two-track Soviet policy may have been encouraged by the American public's responses to presidential behavior. He argues that the public has preferred a safe balance between an aggressive and cooperative Soviet policy. When a president who was perceived as relatively hawkish (e.g. Reagan) made relatively friendly moves toward negotiations with the Soviet Union, or when a president with a "soft" reputation (e.g. Carter) took a hard-line stance toward the Soviets, public approval increased. Behavior counter to the president's reputation provided a reassuring sense that a balanced and reasonable policy was being pursued, while tough behavior by a hawk or soft behavior by a dove fueled fears of war or weakness. Presidents who were sensitive to such public opinion shifts may have become conditioned to moderate their behavior and pursue a two-track Soviet policy.

Though opposites, continuity and change are inescapable aspects of the development of all things, and post–World War II U.S. foreign policy is no exception. The central continuing theme was the notion that the United States was competing with the Soviet Union and a worldwide communist movement. It was not only a struggle for control, it was a struggle to determine the present and future character of human existence, both in specific countries and the world at large. From this perspective, two important cold war goals emerged. First, it was important to promote American systems and ideals, as well as American influence and control in the world. Second, the United States had to limit the dominance of communist systems and ideals, and Soviet influence and control worldwide.

In pursuing these first two, generally (but not always) complementary, goals, policymakers were constrained by a third goal, that of keeping the cold war "cold." In the cold war, that which one side controlled, reformed, and/or maintained in its own image was lost to the other, but efforts to maximize gain and minimize loss were constrained by the threat of mutual loss in a hot war. Thus there were tradeoffs, and no goal could be achieved completely. Cold war policymakers differed in the emphases they placed on each goal, and in the means they preferred to achieve the goals. Whether it was containment or rollback, through economic aid or covert operations, detente or "peace through strength," these three goals were part of the equation. While cleavages developed over U.S.

policy in Korea, Vietnam, Nicaragua, and other important issues, such cleavages generally did not go deep enough to influence a substantial portion of policymakers or the American public to challenge the most basic of American cold war preconceptions.

While there was continuity in the basic preconceptions, however, there was also a rocky, but continuing development in the direction of improved relations between the United States and the Soviet Union. Parity in the nuclear age created a common interest in stability that moderated U.S. and Soviet pursuits of their conflicting ambitions. The real and potential costs of U.S.–Soviet confrontation motivated the two sides to seek accommodation.

Recent findings from the Foreign Policy Leadership Project (Holsti, 1987, 1989; Holsti & Rosenau, 1990a) provide a taste of change and continuity in the attitudes of samples of American leaders. Between 1976 and 1984 there were dramatic declines in the percentage of leaders who accepted the domino theory and who agreed that "detente permits the USSR to pursue policies that promote rather than restrain conflict." In their latest survey, in 1988, Holsti and Rosenau (1990a) found an increasing tendency among American leaders to favor improved relations with the Soviet Union. While in 1980, 26% felt that better superpower relations were not in America's interests, only 7% felt this way in 1988. There was also a clear decline in the salience of the Soviet threat. In 1980, when asked to choose the two greatest future threats to American national security, 50% chose a decline in U.S. military strength relative to the Soviet Union, and 35% picked Soviet expansion into the third world. In 1988, only 21% opted for the relative increase in Soviet military might, and 25% chose Soviet expansionism.

Thus it is fair to say that, by 1988, "opinion leaders as a group [were] moving toward a more benign interpretation of the Soviet Union and its external relations" (Holsti & Rosenau, 1990a, p. 580). Two caveats must be added, however. First, many leaders remained cautious in their optimism, and evidence of continued cold war animosity and suspicion tempered evidence of more friendly attitudes. The cold war conception of an expansionist Soviet Union in need of containment was very much alive in 1988. In 1988, 73% of the sample agreed that "the Soviet Union is generally expansionist rather than defensive in its foreign policy goals." It is true that the percentage of leaders with this view has steadily declined from 1980, when 85% expressed agreement, but it is also clear that this unflattering conception of Soviet goals continued to predominate among American leaders in 1988 (Holsti, 1989). Continuity is also found in attitudes toward containment; in 1976, 1980, and 1984, over 80% of the leaders viewed containing communism as an important foreign policy goal (Holsti, 1987). In 1988, there was little appreciable decline in the importance placed on containing communism, or in the tendency for some leaders to automatically equate communist victory with American defeat. On the other hand, 89% agreed that "the Soviet Union and the U.S. share a number of foreign policy interests such as prevention of war, arms control, and stabilizing relations between them." American leaders remained suspicious of the Soviet Union, but showed a strong realization of common superpower interests and the desirability of positive relations.

The second caveat is that the softening attitudes and opinions concerning the Soviet Union and containment were not equally held across party and ideological lines. In 1988, Republicans and conservatives continued to show great concern about the Soviet threat, while Democrats and liberals did not rank Soviet military might or expansionism high on their lists of future security threats. About two-thirds of both the Republican and conservative subsamples felt that "the U.S. should take all steps including the use of force to prevent the spread of communism." Only 16% of the Democrats and 12% of the liberals agreed with this statement (Holsti & Rosenau, 1990a).

Holsti and Rosenau's data show that by 1988 there was a near unanimous desire for positive U.S.–Soviet relations, and generally warming attitudes toward the Soviet Union. Among Democrats and liberals, there was also a decreased emphasis on the Soviet threat and an overwhelming unwillingness to use force to contain communism. Republicans and conservatives tended to put greater emphasis on cold war threats and military solutions. Thus dissensus existed along party and ideological lines regarding the relative importance of the superpower rivalry and the role of force in containment. This change notwithstanding, basic concerns with Soviet expansion and the containment of communism continued.

PUBLIC OPINION AFTER WORLD WAR II

Mass public opinion was consistent with elite trends: Americans tended to be anticommunist and anti-Soviet and to support containment, but within this cold war context they showed, over time, an increasing desire for accommodation. For the prime cold war years between World War II and the Vietnam War, the poll data[1] show what most scholars agree upon: Americans were clearly anticommunist and feared and distrusted the Soviet Union. Americans generally believed in the Manichaean conflict between Soviet promotion of communist oppression and American defense of freedom and democracy. Like today, however, Americans were willing to explore a variety of means to achieve their noble ends safely; they were willing both to use military force to deter or repel Soviet advances, and to use diplomacy to ease cold war tensions. In regard to means, but not ends, the American people were reasonably flexible and open to policy fluctuations during the heart of the cold war.

As one might expect, the survey questions themselves very often displayed cold war biases based on anticommunist, anti-Soviet and pro-American premises. Americans were not asked *if* the United States should pursue anticommunist or anti-Soviet policies, they were asked *where and how* such policies should be pursued. Such questions tell us that the pollsters themselves were cold war schema users, but they do not reveal much about the basic preconceptions of respondents. For example, in January 1951, Gallup asked whether the United States should use its troops only to defend North and South America from communism, or whether the U.S. should help fight communism in Europe as well. In December 1952, respondents were asked which was "more important for the United States to do—try to keep the rest of Asia from falling under Russian control, or try to stop Russia from taking over Western Europe." In June 1954, respondents were asked who they would rather see investigate communists, Committees of Congress or the FBI and the Department of Justice. Five months after the Truman Doctrine speech of March 12, 1947, Gallup asked the following:

As you know the United States is now sending military supplies and other aid to Greece to keep her and neighbor countries from coming under Russia's control. If we find within the next few weeks that this help is not enough, which one of these steps (on card) do you think we should take? [*Gallup Poll*, 1972, p. 675]

Given the Soviet Union's lack of effort to control Greece, this question seems ludicrous to us now. In the immediate post–World War II period, however, pollsters and respondents alike believed Truman and others when they explained that the Soviet Union and communism were a threat in Greece and elsewhere, and that American vigilance was necessary to preserve freedom and democracy at home and abroad. In this context, and given the above question, it is not surprising that 68% of the respondents chose firm U.S. action, in cooperation with the United Nations, to stop the Soviet Union's (imaginary) move into Greece.

Anticommunism

The Red Scare of the 1950s reflected public attitudes that had been strongly anticommunist well before the cold war. American communists had long been viewed as un-American, loyal to and directed by the Soviet Union. In fact, America's first red scare, which occurred in the 1920s, was based in the same ideological preconceptions that later fed cold war chauvinisms (Hartz, 1955, pp. 293–302).

Communists were viewed as threats to the American way of life, and many saw this as necessitating and justifying repressive measures against them. In November 1939, 25% of respondents thought that American communists took orders directly from Russia, 27% thought they formulated their policies in consultation with Russia, and only 9% thought that they made independent policy decisions. In December of that year, 70% of those who expressed opinions thought that it was more important for the Dies Committee on Un-American Activities to investigate Communists, rather than Nazis. In April 1941, 78% blamed strikes in the defense industries on communists (8% disagreed), and 69% suggested repressive measures or imprisonment to deal with American communists (23% did not offer suggestions). In May of that year, 71% thought that the Communist Party should be outlawed in America (22% did not).

Anticommunism and concern about the pro-Soviet loyalties of American communists subsided somewhat during World War II, when the United States and the Soviet Union were fighting on the same side. In 1946, slightly less than half felt that the Communist Party should be forbidden by law (Niemi, Mueller, & Smith, 1989, p. 127). In the post–World War II period, however, anticommunism quickly returned to prewar levels. Two-thirds of Americans supported outlawing the Communist Party in the late 1940s, and by December 1950 that figure had risen to 80%. In 1948, the political party of former Vice President Henry Wallace, who had expressed strong support for a cooperative stance toward the Soviet Union, was considered to be "run by communists" by 51% of Americans polled (21% disagreed). The notion that American communists were loyal to the Soviet Union was also accepted during this period. In October 1947, 62% thought that American communists "actually take orders from Moscow" (13% did not). In August 1948, 73% thought that American communists would work against the United States in the event of a war with the Soviet Union, while 8% thought they would help the United States. In July 1949, only 10% thought it possible to be a good Christian and a communist at the same time (77% thought it impossible).

Given these perceptions of communists, it is not surprising that in 1946 and 1947 two-thirds of Americans thought communist Americans should not be allowed to hold civil service jobs (under 20% thought they should). In July 1950, 90% thought that all communists should "be removed now from jobs in United States industries that would be important in wartime." When asked, "What do you think should be done about members of the Communist Party in the United States in the event we get into a war with Russia?", 40% felt they ought to be put in internment camps or prisons, about a quarter thought they should be exiled or sent to the Soviet Union, and one in eight suggested execution. One American in a hundred suggested that they be left alone.

In July 1949, only 15% agreed that communists should be allowed to teach at the university level (73% disagreed), and 72% approved of a University of California requirement that its teachers swear that they were not communists (22% disapproved). In March 1953, 63% felt that even former members of the Communist Party should not be allowed to teach college (23% thought they should). In November 1953, two-thirds of Americans felt that "a person known to favor communism" should not be allowed to make a speech in their city (29% thought that they should).

A June 1954 survey conducted for Stouffer found that about 90% of Americans felt that admitted communists who worked at defense plants or taught at the high-school or university level ought to be fired. Approximately two-thirds thought that communist store clerks or radio singers should be fired, that communists should not be allowed to give speeches, and that books written by communists should be removed from public libraries. Three-quarters thought that American communists should lose their citizenship, and half favored putting communists in jail (Niemi et al., 1989, pp. 115–118, 127).

The Taft–Hartley Law required that labor leaders swear that they were not communists before being permitted to take a case to the National Labor Relations Board. There was strong popular opposition in 1947 to changing this provision (18% wanted it changed and 64% did not). In 1949, 80% approved of this law (10% disapproved). During 1948 and 1950, two-thirds of all Americans supported the Mundt–Nixon bill requiring that communists register with the Justice Department (20% opposed it). When, in 1965, this law was declared unconstitutional by the Supreme Court, 58% disapproved of the decision (27% approved).

In October 1961, Gallup presented respondents with an unpleasant choice: "Suppose you had to make the decision between fighting an all-out nuclear war or living under communist rule—how would you decide?" Eighty-one percent of American respondents preferred all-out nuclear war to living under communism (6% chose the opposite). In contrast, only 21% of British respondents preferred nuclear war to living under communism. While this difference is due in part to a view among some Americans that the United States would win such a war, it also reflects the prevailing American attitude that living under communism is worse than violent death.

Attitudes toward the Soviet Union

Attitudes toward the Soviet Union also became increasingly negative as World War II ended. Public distrust of the Soviet Union had been muted during the war, while the Soviets were an ally against Nazi Germany. From 1943 through 1945, 44% to 54% thought that the Soviets could be trusted to cooperate with the United States in world affairs when the war was over (29% to 38% did not think so). The war's end, however, brought with it conflict and suspicion; in August 1946, 62% reported feeling less friendly toward the Soviet Union than they had in the previous year (only 2% felt more friendly). By May 1949, only 20% still expected Soviet cooperation (62% did not).

In July 1946, only 7% approved of Soviet foreign policy (71% disapproved), and 60% believed the Soviet Union was trying to build up "to be the ruling power of the world" (26% thought they were "just building up protection against being attacked"). By October of the following year (1947), 76% believed the Soviets were building up to rule the world, and this belief pervaded for years (79% thought so in July 1953). In January 1949, only 16% of Americans believed that the Soviets sincerely desired peace (72% thought they did not). Americans perceived the Soviet Union as aggressive and threatening, and their own nation as defensive. In January 1948, 73% thought that the Soviet Union "would start a war to get something she wanted (such as more territory or more resources)," while only 5% thought the United States would do such a thing. Instead, an overwhelming 92% of the sample of Americans thought that their nation would "fight only if attacked."

Table 3.1 and Figure 3.1 present the percentages of Americans who held positive attitudes toward the Soviet Union from October 1953 through January

TABLE 3.1
Favorability Ratings of the Soviet Union (1953–1991)

Month/year	Pollster	Favorable Response (1 to 5)	Most Unfavorable Response (-5)
October 1953	Gallup	1%	72%
August 1954	Gallup	5	7 2
December 1956	Gallup	5	6 8
December 1966	Gallup	1 7	3 9
December 1967	Gallup	1 9	
May 1972	Gallup	4 0	2 5
April 1973	Gallup	3 4	2 3
July 1973	Gallup	4 6	1 6
March 1974	NORC	4 5	2 2
March 1975	NORC	4 4	2 1
June 1976	Gallup	2 1	3 6
March 1977	NORC	3 1	3 0
April 1978	Gallup	2 6	
February 1979	Gallup	3 4	3 2
January 1980	Gallup	1 3	5 3
January 1981	Gallup	2 2	3 8
March 1982	Gallup	2 0	4 3
September 1982	Gallup	2 1	4 0
March 1983	NORC	2 3	3 4
September 1983	Gallup	9	
March 1985	NORC	2 1	3 6
March 1986	NORC	3 2	2 6
1987	Gallup	2 5	
March 1988	NORC	4 4	2 2
December 1988	Gallup	4 4	
Feb/March 1989	Gallup	6 2	
August 1989	Gallup	5 1	
May 1990	Gallup	5 5	
September 1990	Gallup	5 8	
January 1991	Gallup	5 7	

Sources: Niemi, Mueler, & Smith, 1989; *Gallup Poll*, 1984, 1990, 1991; Kohut, 1988.

FIGURE 3.1
Favorable Ratings of the Soviet Union, National Samples (1953–1991)
Sources: Niemi, Mueler, & Smith, 1989; *Gallup Poll*, 1984, 1990, 1991; Kohut, 1988.

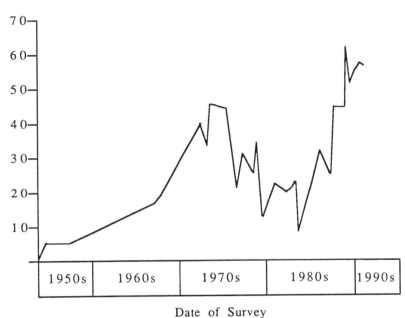

Percent
Favorable

Date of Survey

1991. Table 3.1 also shows the percentages who gave the most unfavorable possible response (–5) to the Soviet Union on the 10-point Stapel Scalometer. Findings clearly show that during the 1950s American attitudes toward the Soviet Union were overwhelmingly negative. At best, one American in twenty was favorably disposed toward the Soviet Union, while over two-thirds viewed the other superpower in the most negative terms available.

Strategies for Containment

Public opinion in the postwar period, like the public rhetoric and official policy orientation of the day, was clearly anticommunist and viewed the Soviet Union with fear and distrust. On the other hand, also consistent with public rhetoric and policy, opinion was not clear, united, stable, or consistent concerning how the Soviet threat ought to be dealt with. Both aggressive and cooperative approaches to containment received public support.

In the early 1950s, containment was a more important goal than peace for most Americans. For example, in a July 1950, Gallup survey, 68% thought that stopping Soviet expansion in Asia and Europe was more important than keeping the United States out of a major war (25% felt the other way). Given these priorities, military means to achieving containment made sense. Thus, for instance, Americans overwhelmingly (79% to 11%) thought that the United States should go to war with the Soviet Union "if Communist troops attack the American Zone in Germany."

Surveys conducted in the early 1950s by the National Opinion Research Center yielded similar findings. Given the choice between containing communism and staying out of another war, respondents chose containment by large margins in July 1951 (63% to 29%) and February 1952 (67% to 27%). In September 1950, and again in May 1952, 59% favored threatening Russia with massive retaliation in the event that "any communist army attacks any other country." In the 1952 survey, 70% favored first use of atomic weapons in the event of a war between the superpowers, and in April 1954, 51% favored dropping hydrogen bombs on Russian cities if the Soviet Union attacked one of America's European allies (Wittkopf, 1990, pp. 305, 326).

However, at the same time as Americans expressed a willingness to use massive destructive force to contain communism, there is ample evidence that diplomatic efforts were also favored. Soviet nuclear capabilities posed a great threat to the American people, and they showed a willingness to try even unpromising ways to lessen that threat. In February 1950, 80% of those who knew of the hydrogen bomb thought that the Soviet Union would use one on the United States. While only 17% thought that an attempt at an arms control agreement with the Soviet Union would be successful, 68% thought it was worth a try. During a period of intense cold war fervor, and long before nuclear parity and the predominance of the notion of mutually assured destruction, the American people overwhelmingly favored trying to negotiate an arms agreement with the Soviet Union.

Despite U.S.–Soviet animosities, 65% thought it would be "a poor idea for the United States to break off diplomatic relations with Russia" in December 1954 (21% thought it would be a good idea). After the Geneva Conference of 1955, 58% felt the conference had been worthwhile (18% did not), and 52% felt that relations with the Soviets would get better (only 11% thought they would worsen). In March 1958, 52% favored (and 23% opposed) an Eisenhower–Khruschev summit meeting. In August 1959, Americans overwhelmingly approved of Eisenhower's visit to the Soviet Union (70% to 18%) and Khruschev's visit to the United States (64% to 23%). In April 1959, 71% felt it would be good for U.S., British, and French leaders to meet with the Soviets regularly.

American approval of diplomatic initiatives during the cold war did not stem from an acceptance of the Soviet Union and communism, but from a willingness to try peaceful methods for managing an ongoing conflict. In August 1959, only

7% held the opinion that "the United States agreement to exchange visits . . . mean(s) that there has been a softening in basic United States attitudes toward communism." Instead, an overwhelming 73% interpreted it "as mainly a new effort to reduce tensions."

The cold war 1950s were also a time when ideas of increased cultural and commercial exchanges between the United States and the Soviet Union received general, but not overwhelming, approval in the American public. In March 1955, most Americans approved both of having American athletes take part in events in the Soviet Union (by a 59% to 31% margin), and of having Soviet athletes compete in the United States (63% to 29%). In June 1957, 52% approved and 39% disapproved of the Soviet suggestion that educators be exchanged in order "to learn more about each other's culture." In November 1957, most Americans approved (60% to 31%) of a student exchange between the two countries. From the mid-1950s and into the 1960s, about half thought that the two superpowers should work out business arrangements to increase commerce, while about a third disagreed.

This sort of public support for U.S.–Soviet cooperation increased in the 1970s and 1980s. For instance, support for business agreements between the superpowers stood between two-thirds and three-quarters in the post-Vietnam era (Wittkopf & McCormick, 1990). Still, the increased public desire for superpower cooperation that later accompanied detente did not negate the clear evidence of cooperative tendencies in American public opinion during the heart of cold war hostilities in the 1950s.

In the 1950s, then, both military and diplomatic means were accepted as worth pursuing in dealings with the dangerous Soviet enemy. According to Almond, almost all Americans in the early postwar period "experience(d) Russian and Communist pressure as a grave threat to fundamental values" (1960, p. 17). By 1950 he detected a foreign policy "consensus" that included "resistance to Communist expansion by economic, diplomatic, propaganda, and, if necessary, military means" (p. 159). The Gallup data support Almond's summary of 1950 American attitudes:

American sentiment, while not fixed on a war course toward Russia, is permissive of actions which involve the risk of war. The prospect of war with Russia is not a sufficient deterrent to dispel popular support of American policy in those areas in which we have assumed commitments. American sentiment does not preclude negotiations with the Russians in principle; but it has little confidence in their usefulness. [p. 99]

Given vast American strategic superiority and deep suspicions of the Soviet Union, hot war seemed more plausible than negotiations. Still, Americans never closed the door on either conflictual or cooperative relations with the Soviet Union. The risks brought by increased Soviet nuclear capabilities helped keep the war cold and motivate negotiations.

The public's willingness to try a variety of means for managing the cold war was in part an understandable response to uncertainty about the future prospects for war and peace. A mixed set of responses to related questions asked around 1960 will demonstrate this uncertainty. In May 1960, half of the sample thought that there was "bound to be a major war sooner or later" with the Soviet Union, while 37% thought that Western countries could "continue to live peacefully" with the Soviets. Six months earlier, in December 1959, 58% did not think there was much danger of war between the Soviet Union and the West (31% thought there was). At that time, only 23% of the sample believed that "a peaceful settlement of differences between Russia and the West" was impossible (66% thought peaceful settlement was possible). In December 1960, 27% of the sample thought peaceful settlement impossible, and 34% thought so in 1962. Findings from the mid-1950s were similar (*Gallup Poll*, 1990, p. 53).

These findings show a mix of hope and fear rather than an overwhelming mood of collective expectation or dread. Some Americans expected war with the Soviets eventually, while others expected it soon. Some anticipated peace, while relatively few viewed a peaceful settlement to be impossible. Disagreements and uncertainties were reasonable; the combination of mutual hostility and restraint that characterized the cold war produced both the danger of an eventual hot war and hope for peaceful coexistence between the Soviet Union and the West. Given uncertainty about the future and a desire for both containment and peace, the American people tended to be willing to try a variety of military and diplomatic methods for holding off the Soviet–communist threat.

In summary, then, the period between World War II and the Vietnam war is considered to be a time of "cold war consensus," and it is true that Americans overwhelmingly supported their government's anticommunist and anti-Soviet goals and policies. Within the confines of that consensus, however, disagreement thrived; debates raged on how assertive or militaristic American anticommunist policy should be. The public was, in those days of American superiority, more willing to risk military confrontation than Americans today, but they also showed a willingness to negotiate and a desire for peace and understanding.

WAS CONSENSUS DESTROYED IN THE VIETNAM ERA?

The notion that the cold war consensus was destroyed in the Vietnam era has become more or less accepted among scholars (Allison, 1970; Levering, 1978; Destler et al., 1984). A number of studies (Mandelbaum & Schneider, 1979; Maggiotto & Wittkopf, 1981; Holsti & Rosenau, 1984; Wittkopf, 1990) attempt to articulate the post-Vietnam dissensus by distinguishing among separate, coexisting belief systems. The studies have made valuable contributions by examining elite and public opinion trends and cleavages in the post-Vietnam period. They show the emergence of important divisions in U.S. foreign policy beliefs and preferences.

These studies have not, however, presented evidence of a rejection of the cold war schema (they did not, of course, set out to do so). What these sorts of studies have shown is variations on a common theme. Some Americans emphasize certain elements of the schema over others (i.e. U.S. opposition to communism over support for democracy), or emphasize other things (i.e. world peace, economic interest, or domestic concerns) over the cold war schema. But this does not refute the claim that the cold war schema remained in the minds of most Americans and continued to affect information processing, cultural content, behavior, and policy.

Because it is tempting to assume that findings on competing belief systems in the post-Vietnam era prove that the cold war schema ceased to be prominent in American culture, these works will be addressed in some detail. The research findings of Holsti and Rosenau (1984) and Mandelbaum and Schneider (1979) appear to suggest that a cold war belief system was but one of three relatively equal, competing belief systems that Americans may have chosen from. A careful look at these studies leads to a different conclusion. Although they show that individual differences existed at the level of policy emphasis, they do not show that these differences reached the deeper level of the cold war schema. The fact that many Americans did not express obsessive, orthodox cold war attitudes does not mean that they did not believe in the basic cold war schema.

Maggiotto and Wittkopf (1981) built their belief systems around basic policy orientations; they divided Americans into categories based on whether they approved of cooperative and/or militaristic U.S. foreign policy. Their distinctions are important and their categories are useful, but none of their belief systems preclude the cold war schema. While these works do identify important cleavages in foreign policy attitudes, then, they do not refute the claim that the cold war schema survived Vietnam.

The Scholarly Consensus

Allison (1970) proposed ten "axioms of the postwar era" which guided American thinking about world affairs after World War II. According to Allison, "these propositions, in more or less sophisticated versions, formed the foundation of the American world view during the cold war. For twenty-five years after World War II U.S. foreign policy was roughly consistent with them" (p. 151). The first five axioms are:

1. The pre-eminent feature of international politics is the conflict between Communism and the Free World. . . .
2. The surest simple guide to U.S. interests in foreign policy is opposition to Communism.
3. Communism is on the march. . . .
4. Communism is monolithic. . . .

5. The United States has the power, responsibility, and right to defend the Free World and maintain international order. [p. 150]

Allison saw, in 1970, a general modification of these axioms, as well as what he interpreted to be a wholesale rejection of them by the "Vietnam generation." The 25- to 35-year-old elite Americans he interviewed had witnessed the use of cold war axioms in defense of an ill-advised, if not immoral, war, and they were not buying them. Earlier generations, with memories of Munich, Hitler, and Stalin, were far more prone to accepting the conventional cold war axioms. Allison correctly predicted that "No More Vietnams!" would be the "No More Munichs!" of the 1970s and 1980s (p. 160).

In a test of Allison's generation effect, Holsti and Rosenau (1984) found that leaders from the Vietnam generation did not show a greater tendency to reject hard-line cold war attitudes than did members of other generations. Still, the scholarly consensus concurs with Allison's view that the cold war consensus was shattered by the Vietnam experience. Holsti and Rosenau argued that "the post–World War II consensus on foreign policy has been shattered; the Vietnam experience has been a critical causal factor; and the resulting views on foreign policy can appropriately be designated as competing belief systems" (1984, p. 74). Destler et al. (1984) proposed that the cold war anticommunist consensus held within it the seeds of its own destruction:

The anti-Communist-policy consensus was at the heart of centrism and majorityship, and gave it steadiness and direction. But it led to rigidity as well, and in this rigidity lay the seeds of the center's destruction. The doctrines at the heart of the consensus, and their political force, called for American intervention in Vietnam. . . .

The endless and seemingly hopeless agony of the Vietnam War destroyed the consensus, sprayed power out from the center toward the political extremes, and made the forging of majorities a trying affair. Moderates and liberals joined with the inheritors of the Henry Wallace tradition in a coalition of the left that, for the first time, enjoyed real political power. This coalition began to question the basic principles of postwar U.S. foreign policy as rigidly ill-suited to the new and far more pluralistic world and ill-equipped to understand the limits of American power in such a world. [p. 19]

Levering (1978) viewed Vietnam as one of a number of important developments that contributed to a breakdown in the consensus:

For many Americans the Vietnam War was the major catalyst for a general re-evaluation of the assumptions upon which the Cold War consensus had been built, but it definitely was not the only factor contributing to changing attitudes toward U.S. foreign policy. Improved relations with Russia in the aftermath of the Cuban missile crisis, the open split between Russia and mainland China, changes in the Western alliance, the emergence of a new generation of Americans who remembered neither Munich nor the Czechoslovakian coup—these and other developments of the 1960s contributed to the drift away from the dominant Cold War approach. [pp. 120–121]

Vietnam and Dissensus

The Vietnam War and other developments of the 1960s did have a divisive effect, as many came to see fallacies in the orthodox cold war perspective. The Vietnam experience contributed to the growing tendency for some Americans to shy away from the use of force (Wittkopf & McCormick, 1990). While Americans continued to be concerned with containing communism, Vietnam made the severe costs of military intervention salient. This, accompanied by increasing concerns about the disastrous costs of nuclear confrontation with the Soviet Union, shifted public preferences away from hard-line, militaristic approaches to containment.

Still, the image of a dramatic shift from consensus to discord, while perhaps descriptive of political cleavages, does not describe the cognitive dynamics involved. How is it that some Americans were able to maintain their support for the Vietnam War throughout, others opposed it early, while still others gradually came to oppose it? Why did some break away from the cold war "consensus," while others did not? Different Americans saw Vietnam from different perspectives; their roles and predispositions differed, and so did their responses. Hard-line cold warriors tended neither to lose faith nor to oppose the Vietnam War; for them the lessons of Vietnam involved the need for true commitment, clear goals, and a muzzled press. Their predispositions helped them stay cold warriors throughout the Vietnam period. For those who grew to reject the war and, along with it, aspects of the conventional cold war perspective, their experiences and predispositions were of a different sort, a sort that left them open to challenge and change.

Vietnam formed the battle lines for an intensified public debate over U.S. foreign policy. Prior to Vietnam, public critiques of U.S. foreign policy tended to consist of complaints that the administration was not fighting communism vigorously enough. Direct challenge to an aggressive cold war stance was considered by many to be un-American and treasonous, and thus a sense of "consensus" was perpetuated in an environment of relatively closed debate. Aggressive cold war doctrines had the function of a loyalty oath, recited and even believed in order to fit in and remain safe. Given the Red Scare atmosphere of the time, the Korean War could not have spurred quite the debate that Vietnam did.

International realities, the American domestic climate, and views toward the cold war had all developed by the mid-1960s to the point that public discourse could be significantly expanded. Still, it took an issue as serious and tragic as Vietnam, along with an active and persistent antiwar movement, to force onto the agenda challenges to some of the accepted notions that had guided American perceptions in the cold war era.

Vietnam did not function as a proverbial bolt of lightening, randomly striking certain individuals and stripping them of their cold war orthodoxy. Instead, Vietnam drove a wedge into preexisting differences, magnifying them, in the context of a salient issue, into a perceptible "dissensus." Yes, the Vietnam War precipitated change, but it was neither as sudden, nor as complete, as it might first appear.

Holsti and Rosenau

Holsti and Rosenau (1984) based their conclusion that the consensus had been shattered on their study conducted in 1976 and again in 1980 of the foreign policy opinions of over 2,000 American leaders. The lessons of Vietnam, they argued, tended to go against Allison's axioms; although the leaders strongly agreed with the domino theory and the conception of the Soviet Union as an expansionist power, they tended to be mixed in their endorsements of the axioms (pp. 75–77).

Holsti and Rosenau suggested that three competing belief systems emerged in the post-Vietnam era, which they christened "Cold War Internationalism," "Post–Cold War Internationalism," and "Semi-Isolationism." Holsti and Rosenau (1986) provided concise descriptions of the three perspectives:

Cold War Internationalists are inclined to view the international system as bipolar in structure. A relentless Soviet drive against the United States and its allies, buttressed by a rapid military buildup in the USSR, is thus the primary threat. Although seemingly muted during periods of détente, Moscow's determination to expand its influence by whatever means is the unvarying driving force behind Kremlin policies. In order to forestall the threat, it is vital for the United States and the West to maintain a high level of military capabilities, a determination to match or exceed increases in Soviet force levels and a willingness to use military power if necessary to discourage adventures by the USSR. . . .

Post–Cold War Internationalists tend to view the international system and primary threats to its stability in terms of North–South issues, including but not limited to the growing gap between rich and poor nations, threats to the environment, population, resources, racial conflict, trade, Third World debts and other international economic issues. Although not unmindful of East–West tensions, they are inclined to view problems between Moscow and Washington as tractable. Détente, arms control, and other such measures can . . . stabilize relations between the superpowers. . . .

Semi-Isolationists believe that excessively internationalist American policies, whether to cope with East–West or North–South issues, are of themselves the major threat to the United States. By taking on the role of the world's policeman, the world's do-gooder, or the world's conscience—with only selective success at best—the United States has squandered vast material and non-material resources that are vitally needed to deal with a long agenda of neglected domestic problems. [p. 379]

Cold War Internationalists maintain the conventional cold war perspective, the "consensus" of old. Post–Cold War Internationalists and Semi-Isolationists have rejected the cold war orthodoxy, but in different ways. Post–Cold War Internationalists emphasize the complexities of world affairs that create the need to approach the world in terms other than ideological superpower confrontation (i.e. diplomacy), while Semi-Isolationists challenge the need to be so involved in the world at all.

To test whether these belief categories are descriptive of divisions among leaders, Holsti and Rosenau gave their respondents a series of statements. Each statement corresponded to a belief type; if their categories were good ones, then correlations among responses to statements for the same belief type (i.e.. Cold War Internationalism) would be high, while correlations with responses to statements for the other two types would be low or negative.

In both 1976 and 1980, the mean correlation among Cold War Internationalist items was .40, and they tended to correlate negatively with the other items. Orthodox cold war beliefs do seem to form a distinctive, coherent belief system. Evidence is weaker for the other two belief systems, however. The mean correlation among Semi-Isolationist items (.22 and .21) is negligibly different from the mean correlation among all non–Cold War Internationalist items (.19 and .20), and not much greater than the mean between-group correlation (.13) for the two non–Cold War Internationalist belief systems (Holsti & Rosenau, 1984, p. 211). In short, the evidence is not strong enough to support the assertion that Post–Cold War Internationalism and Semi-Isolationism are separate, distinct, and well-constrained belief systems. They lack both the internal consistency and exclusive nature of Cold War Internationalism.

Holsti and Rosenau also found that individuals they classified as Post–Cold War Internationalists and Semi-Isolationists had strong tendencies to be liberals, Democrats, and critics of U.S. policy in Vietnam, while Cold War Internationalists tended to be conservatives, Republicans, and supporters of U.S. policy in Vietnam. Cold War Internationalism was popular among military officers and business executives, while educators and journalists tended to be Post–Cold War Internationalists and Semi-Isolationists. These cleavages are all the more reason to conclude that the distinctions between those who have maintained the cold war orthodoxy with its emphasis on force and those who have not are the meaningful ones, and that cleavages among non–Cold War Internationalists are not strong, clear, or important enough to warrant separate categories with equal status.

Like Allison, Holsti and Rosenau attribute the breakdown of consensus to the divisive influence of the Vietnam War. To back up these claims they show that support of the Vietnam War strongly correlates with the items they use to test general foreign policy orientations. The assertion is that the Vietnam War caused the splitting up of the consensus among leaders, as only the Cold War Internationalists maintained the old line. However, given that Holsti and Rosenau lack comparable pre-1976 data, their results can only be speculative and suggestive; it is unclear whether Vietnam caused the breakdown in consensus, whether the dissensus on Vietnam was a salient symptom of a previous breakdown, or whether the consensus never was all that consensual to begin with. All three are possibilities, and each captures an important piece of what happened.[2]

In any case, it is important to delimit where cleavages formed and where they did not. Within any culture or subculture, competing variations on agreed upon themes form the bases for discord. A rejection of extreme cold war orthodoxy is not the same as a rejection of the cold war schema, which is a far more general and encompassing belief system.

In a survey conducted in the summer of 1981, Cottam (1986) asked U.S. foreign policy officials to list what they considered to be perfect modern or historical examples of enemies of the United States. Two-thirds (66%) of the sample volunteered the Soviet Union (by comparison, 14% mentioned Nazi Germany). Respondents were also asked to evaluate the Soviet Union on a 7-point scale ranging from "perfect example" to "terrible example" of an enemy. Almost all (98%) of the officials placed the Soviet Union on the "perfect example" side of the scale, and 69% chose the most extreme response (7 on the scale). Cottam's findings show a clear consensus, at least among U.S. foreign policy officials, on the enemy image of the Soviet Union.

Holsti and Rosenau's 1988 data (Holsti & Rosenau, 1990a, discussed earlier) showed warming attitudes toward the Soviet Union and an overwhelming desire for good relations. Still, while leaders were divided in their views of the role of force in containment, they generally remained united in their concern about Soviet expansion and containment. While the old cold war orthodoxy became less fashionable as time went on, basic cold war concerns continued to structure much of the thinking of American leaders.

Mandelbaum and Schneider

Mandelbaum and Schneider (1979), in a study very similar to that of Holsti and Rosenau, explored varying beliefs in the mass public. Data from a December 1974 and January 1975 Harris survey were used to examine differences among respondents they categorized (according to their ratings of the importance of certain foreign policy goals) as "conservative internationalists," "liberal internationalists," and "non-internationalists." According to Schneider (1984):

Conservative internationalists were found to picture the world primarily in East-West terms: democracy versus totalitarianism, capitalism versus communism, freedom versus repression. . . . Liberal internationalists emphasized economic and humanitarian problems over security issues and rejected a hegemonic role for the United States. . . . Noninternationalists . . . are suspicious of international involvements of any kind. [pp. 16–17]

Mandelbaum and Schneider looked for opinion differences among the three groups, and they found them. What they *observed* were *relative* differences in opinion among the three belief groups, but they used this data to make *absolute* conclusions about group members and their belief systems. Thus their conclusions must be subjected to question. For instance, 54% of "noninternationalists" (the ones who are suspicious of international involvement) thought that it would be best for the United States to take an active role in world affairs. Mandelbaum and Schneider tolerated this self-contradictory conclusion because 54% is *rela-*

tively low, compared to the percentage of internationalists (75%) who felt that way.

Conservative internationalists did show a greater tendency to view other countries becoming communist as a threat to United States. They also were far more likely to agree that the United States should "have the same kind of dedication to the spread of political freedom and private enterprise of business in the world as the Russians and Chinese have for the spread of communism in the world" (Mandelbaum & Schneider, 1979, p. 76). So conservative internationalists did exhibit greater concern about communist expansion and more desire for U.S. expansionism. But this does not mean that conservative internationalists opposed peaceful dealings with communists, or that liberal internationalists supported the spread of communism or opposed U.S. efforts to promote freedom, democracy, and capitalism.

Mandelbaum and Schneider's data show, not just differences in the response patterns among the three belief systems, but also important similarities, some of which indicate broad acceptance of the cold war schema. Members of all three groups tended to view the United States as "a force for good" in the post–World War II world, but conservative internationalists (82%) were closer to unanimous than were liberal internationalists (60%) or noninternationalists (57%). In no group did more than 10% view the United States as "a force for evil."

Only 12% in each group thought that the United States should "back authoritarian governments that have overthrown democratic governments," even given that there is some advantage in doing so (ibid., p. 84). This consistent unwillingness to sacrifice democracy for "national interest" indicates a clear and pervasive concern for democracy across categories.

Regardless of category, respondents tended to view long-term peace agreements with the Soviet Union or China as possible, but liberal internationalists had greater tendencies to think this way. Both conservative (55%) and liberal (66%) internationalists agreed that "In a nuclear age, when the whole world can be blown up, we have to overcome old animosities and ideological differences and learn to live with countries such as the Soviet Union and China" (p. 76) (only 36% of noninternationalists felt this way). Slightly over half of both internationalist groups felt that "the big breakthroughs in peacemaking in the future will come less from agreements with traditional allies and more from agreements in learning to live together with traditional enemies" (p. 77). Majorities in all three groups felt that a long-term peace agreement between the United States and the Soviet Union was possible, although liberal internationalists had the greatest (70%) tendency to think this way. Given that "keeping peace in the world" was viewed as very important by 87% of the sample, there was a clear motivation, among internationalists of both types, to pursue detente.

On the other hand, there was an almost unanimous rejection, in all three groups, of the notion that improved relations with the Soviet Union and China mean that there is "little chance" of world war. The view, among conservative and liberal internationalists alike, was that grounds for conflict still existed, but cooperation was a viable and acceptable means for managing it. Mandelbaum and Schneider (1979) presented this sort of position, but they limited it (without clear justification) to conservative internationalists:

For conservatives, what appears to have changed is not conservative attitudes toward communism, but conservative attitudes toward U.S. foreign policy. Conservatives still see world politics as a fundamental conflict of values between East and West, but they no longer feel that the United States can lead a crusade against communism by force of arms. The conservative view of detente is that we must learn to live with the communists, trusting them only as far as is necessary for the sake of peace, playing one communist power off against the others, dealing with them to our mutual advantage, but never losing sight of the essentially competitive nature of our relationship and never conceding the legitimacy of their values or intentions. The internationalist consensus in support of detente really goes no farther than this. [pp. 62–63]

In a very different interpretation of the same data, Schneider (1984) concludes that "Conservative internationalists are anti-detente and promilitary. . . . Liberal internationalists are pro-detente and anti-military" (pp. 16–17). Although liberals were more likely than conservatives to advocate diplomatic efforts, and conservatives had a greater tendency to advocate military involvement to protect allies under attack, this does not justify Schneider's reinterpretation of the data or his conclusion that conservative internationalists were anti-detente. In fact, the evidence suggests that they tended to be pro-detente. The differences between liberal and conservative internationalists appear to have been ones of policy emphasis, which occasionally became magnified when applied to specific salient issues in combination with polarizing, partisan public debates. The differences were not as stark and extreme as the authors' portrayals suggest.

Wittkopf and Maggiotto

Yet another, more successful attempt to describe the competing belief systems in the post-Vietnam dissensus is found in the work of Wittkopf and Maggiotto (Maggiotto & Wittkopf, 1981; Wittkopf & Maggiotto, 1983; Wittkopf, 1990). They organize their four belief systems around two main alternative policy orientations toward U.S. involvement in the world: cooperative internationalism (emphasis on cooperative ties and realpolitik) and militant internationalism (emphasis on the military). Militant internationalism correlates positively with perceptions of the Soviet Union and communism as threats and negatively with support for detente, while the opposite is true of cooperative internationalism.

Maggiotto and Wittkopf (1981) demonstrate the validity of these two dimensions through a factor analysis on data from the 1974 Chicago Council of Foreign Relations survey. Wittkopf's (1990) factor analyses of CCFR data from 1974, 1978, 1982, and 1986 add strong support to the notion that militant and cooperative internationalism are two distinct and important dimensions along which U.S. foreign policy beliefs and attitudes are organized.

It was argued above, in different words, that America's policy toward the Soviet Union has felt the dual pulls of cooperative and militant internationalism since World War II. Opinions have reflected this duality, and the dangers of mutual destruction in the nuclear age have increasingly motivated cooperative internationalism. Wittkopf and Maggiotto's two dimensions of mass foreign policy attitudes clearly organize four belief systems around the basic points of contention in post–World War II foreign policy.

Their four belief systems consist of "hardliners" (23% in 1974), who support militant internationalism only; "accommodationists" (27%), who support only cooperative internationalism; "internationalists" (30%), who support both militant and cooperative internationalism; and "isolationists"(20%), who do not support internationalism of any sort (Maggiotto & Wittkopf, 1981, p. 612). Wittkopf (1990) found little change in these ratios from 1974 to 1986. In 1986, 24% were classified as hardliners, 24% accommodationists, 28% internationalists, and 24% isolationists (p. 26).

It is important to recognize, as Wittkopf and Maggiotto do, that many Americans can and do support both militarism and cooperation; this group is instrumental in providing continued public support as American policy shifts from cooperative to militant internationalism and back again. But Wittkopf and Maggiotto's "internationalists" were ignored in the other formulations—neither Holsti and Rosenau nor Mandelbaum and Schneider provided a category for them. These scholars may have been paying a bit too much attention to polarizing public debates between "liberals" and "conservatives," "hawks" and "doves," and this may have temporarily diverted their attention from those who support both militarism and cooperation.

I use the word "temporarily" because Holsti and Rosenau, in response to Wittkopf's (1986) critique of their work, have since endorsed the Wittkopf and Maggiotto scheme. In a study that will surely serve to promote the use of the Wittkopf and Maggiotto dimensions, Holsti and Rosenau (1990b) argue that the dimensions are logical, relevant, and useful, and they show the four-group typology to be applicable to their own data.

The MI/CI [militant internationalism/cooperative internationalism] classification scheme recognizes that the traditional internationalist–isolationist dimension is not sufficient to describe the range of contemporary views, and it is built around two central elements of U.S. foreign policy attitudes . . . the conclusion that clearly emerges from analyses of the three FPLP data sets is that the MI/CI classification scheme has survived a demanding series of tests. When combined with the results of other studies, these findings suggest that it provides an excellent starting point for further inquiries into public opinion on international affairs. [pp. 120, 122]

In the absence of analyses on pre-Vietnam data, we can only speculate about the relative prevalence of cooperative and militant internationalism in the 1950s and 1960s, and about the distribution of hardliners, accommodationists, internationalists, and isolationists. Thus we must remain skeptical of Wittkopf's (1990) assumption that hardliners and accommodationists only emerged in the 1970s (p. 26). Maggiotto and Wittkopf's formulation probably was just as applicable to the pre-Vietnam era as it is today. It is likely that there were more militant internationalists and fewer cooperative internationalists in the early cold war years. Still, as the Gallup data show, Americans were open to both cooperation and militarism well before the Vietnam War.

Wittkopf (1990) does identify two very important and relevant public opinion trends. First, the Vietnam experience contributed to at least a temporary aversion to containment through military means:

Throughout the postwar period, the American people have regarded containing communism as an important goal of U.S. foreign policy, and they continued to see communism as a threat in the 1980s, just as they did in the 1940s, 1950s, and 1960s . . . communism remains a threat, but greater disagreement now exists about the question of how to deal with it. . . . to many people Vietnam symbolized the bankruptcy of military solutions to political problems, and in this sense it doubtless contributed to growing divisiveness about how best to deal with the Communist threat. [p. 191]

In addition, a greater desire for accommodation with the Soviet Union emerged from the Vietnam era:

By the 1970s and thereafter the general climate of opinion was arguably more favorable to accommodations with the Soviets than to confrontations with them. This is not to say that the Soviets may have become either more trusted or less feared than earlier—the contrary may in fact be the case—but only that "compromise" with the Soviets seems to have replaced "firmer" as the preferred approach to them. [p. 192]

While the Vietnam era shifted the emphasis of American policy preferences away from militarism, then, the cold war goal of containing communism persisted in the post-Vietnam era, as did American anticommunist and anti-Soviet sentiments. The next section supports these claims with public opinion data.

PUBLIC OPINION AFTER VIETNAM

The implausibility of any suggestion that Vietnam and detente removed the cold war schema from American minds is demonstrated by the general upsurge in cold war attitudes and fears that occurred during the 1970s and early 1980s. According to a Gallup poll, in 1972 only 24% worried a great deal about "the problem of the Soviet Union"; four years later, that figure had doubled to 50%, and 75% worried at least a fair amount. In July 1973, 46% had favorable attitudes toward the Soviet Union; by September 1983, only 9% did (see Table 3.1). Although the Soviet Union became increasingly popular among Americans in its last few years of existence, anti-Soviet attitudes in the 1980s rivaled those of the legendary 1950s. In short, public opinion trends through the 1970s and early 1980s simply do not support the notion of a stable rejection or significant lessening of cold war attitudes coming out of the Vietnam era. Over that period, Americans retained their concern with containing communism, and although attitudes toward the Soviet Union fluctuated, they tended in the negative direction.

Communism and Containment

The Red Scare ended long before the Vietnam War, and the number of Americans who favored repressive action against fellow citizens who were communists dropped about twenty-five percentage points from the 1950s to the 1970s. An April 1973 Response Analysis replication of the 1954 Stouffer survey found two-thirds favoring the firing of communists who worked in defense plants or taught at the high school or university level. Half thought that communists should lose their American citizenship, and a quarter thought they should be imprisoned. Slightly under 40% favored the firing of communist store clerks and television entertainers. Around 40% also favored removing books written by communists from American libraries and prohibiting communists from giving speeches. NORC surveys found impressive stability in these last two findings that extended through 1988. These findings show a decreasing willingness to sacrifice the Bill of Rights in order to exorcise American communism. In 1973, 70% saw the protection of the rights of the innocent to be more important than finding every communist in America; in 1954, only 32% felt this way (Niemi et al., 1989, pp. 115–118, 127, 130).

This increasing tolerance for American communists should not be confused with an increasing tolerance for communism. All indications are that American anticommunism has outlived Vietnam, detente, and even the cold war.

NORC's General Social Survey asked Americans to evaluate communism as a "form of government." Table 3.2 shows their findings for 1973 through 1988 (Niemi et al., 1989, p. 69). Throughout that period, between 70 and 85% thought of communism as a bad form of government, and no more than 3% viewed communism as good. It also shows an increase during the 1970s and early 1980s in the already staunch anticommunism sentiments of the American people. Americans who viewed communism as the worst form of government rose from 43% in 1973 to 60% in 1984. This figure came back down to 48% in 1988, as the Reagan administration eased its anticommunist rhetoric and improved relations with the Soviet Union. Even so, American anticommunism was alive and well in the late 1980s.

Throughout the 1970s, most Americans saw communism as a dangerous threat. A Yankelovich poll in January 1976, for instance, found that 68% of the public felt that American communists presented at least some danger, while 9%

TABLE 3.2
Attitudes toward Communism as a Form of Government, General Social Surveys (1973–1988)

Month/year	A Good Kind of Govt.	Bad or Worst Kind of Govt.	The Worst Kind of Govt.
March 1973	3%	70%	43%
March 1974	3	75	49
March 1976	1	77	51
March 1977	1	77	53
March 1980	1	83	57
March 1982	1	84	59
March 1984	2	85	60
March 1985	1	85	57
March 1987	1	83	55
March 1988	2	77	48

Source: Niemi, Mueler, & Smith, 1989, p. 69.

thought they presented no danger. A Response Analysis poll of March–April 1973 found that 63% viewed communists in the United States as a threat (26% disagreed). Gallup found in 1976 that three-quarters of their respondents worried at least a fair amount about the threat of communism, and half of the sample worried a great deal. In May 1978, the National Opinion Research Center found communists to be the number one most despised group of people for 29% of Americans; the only other group to even come close (24%) was the Ku Klux Klan (Smith, 1983, pp. 280, 289, 291).

There does not appear to have been any change in the 1970s and early 1980s in American attitudes concerning the importance of containing communism. In Chicago Council on Foreign Relations polls of 1974, 1978, and 1982, 81% to 86% viewed containing communism to be at least somewhat important, while 8% to 13% thought it was unimportant. Containing communism was very important to 54% to 60% of the public (Holsti, 1987, p. 34). These attitudes persisted in 1986 (Rielly, 1987, p. 12), when 57% thought containing communism was very important. When presented with the prospects of communist parties coming to power through peaceful elections in a variety of countries, only 4% to 9% (depending on the country in question) of the 1986 sample did not view such a democratic transfer of power as threatening to the United States. The impressive persistence and stability of these attitudes indicates that American anticommunism and the perceived need to fight communism abroad are deeply rooted in American minds and resistant to fluctuation and change.

Attitudes toward the Soviet Union

American attitudes toward the Soviet Union were unstable and relatively unfavorable until the late 1980s. Figure 3.1 and Table 3.1 both show the development of American attitudes toward the Soviet Union between 1953 and 1991. They demonstrate a clear decline in anti-Soviet attitudes from the Red Scare years of the 1950s (when around 90% of all Americans held unfavorable attitudes toward the Soviet Union) to the Detente years of the early 1970s. In December 1956, 68% of Gallup's respondents gave the Soviet Union "–5" on the 10-point Staple Scalometer. Ten years later, in December 1966, 39% gave the most extremely negative response, and only 16% did so in July 1973. By June 1973, when Soviet Premier Brezhnev visited the United States, only half of Gallup's respondents expressed negative attitudes toward the Soviet Union, and 45% expressed positive ones.

The last two decades, however, showed no clear trend in American attitudes toward the Soviet Union. Attitudes fluctuated as various events and developments affected the Soviet image. Unfavorable attitudes toward the Soviet Union increased to 72% in 1976 and dropped back down to 60% in 1979.

By 1980, the December 1979 Soviet invasion of Afghanistan had pushed unfavorable attitudes toward the Soviet Union over 80%; 53% of respondents gave the Soviet Union the most negative rating on the 10-point scale, and only 13% expressed favorable attitudes. In February 1980, 68% agreed that peace with the Soviet Union was not possible and that a major war would eventually occur. At the same time, a Roper poll found that only 16% of the public advocated negotiation and the careful avoidance of military confrontation between the superpowers. When the November 1980 elections rolled around, the *Los Angeles Times* found 70% desiring "a tougher stand toward the Russians." This they got from the new Reagan administration, and 73% agreed, in a March 1981 Harris poll, that, "by sending military aid to countries threatened by communism and being tough with the Russians, Reagan will rebuild respect for the U.S. in the Kremlin" (Yankelovich & Smoke, 1988, p. 4).

Soviet popularity improved slightly over the next couple of years, but the downing of KAL 007 over Soviet airspace, accompanied by strong cold war rhetoric by the Reagan administration, brought anti-Soviet attitudes back up to the level of the mid-1950s. As late as September 1983, only 9% of all Americans held favorable attitudes toward the Soviet Union.

In 1978 and again in 1982, the Chicago Council of Foreign Relations found "thermometer ratings" of the Soviet Union to be lower than any other country tested. In 1986, ratings of the Soviet Union were still frigid—out of 23 countries, only Iran was judged more coldly than the Soviet Union (Rielly, 1987, p. 18). At 31 degrees, the Soviet Union was viewed with far less warmth than such dubious favorites as South Africa (47 degrees) and Nicaragua (46 degrees). In the same survey, conflict and competition with the Soviet Union was mentioned as America's "biggest" foreign policy problem twice as often (31% of the time) as the next popular problem.

In 1983, 90% agreed that "during the 1970s, when we were trying to improve relations, the Soviets secretly built up their military strength," and 82% believed that "the Soviets are constantly testing us, probing for weaknesses, and they're quick to take advantage whenever they find any." In 1984, by a margin of 61% to 28%, Americans accepted the old Reagan declaration that "The Soviets lie, cheat and steal—do anything to further the cause of communism" (Yankelovich & Doble, 1984, p. 41). In a July 1988 ATS survey, 64% agreed with that statement, and 56% expected that a weak America would elicit a Soviet attack on the United States or its allies (Yankelovich & Smoke, 1988, p. 6).

In May 1984, the Public Agenda Foundation received 56% agreement to the statement, "the Soviet Union is like Hitler's Germany—an evil empire trying to rule the world" (Yankelovich & Smoke, 1988, p. 4). In that same survey (Belsky & Doble, 1984), Americans were asked about important reasons for considering the Soviet Union to be an enemy: "They continually try to spread communist revolution to other countries," was seen as a very important reason by 69% of the sample. In addition, when asked whether they worried more about the Soviet "military threat to the United States," or the "threat to all our beliefs and values—freedom, democracy, religion, and free enterprise," 69% expressed worry about beliefs and values, and 26% worried more about the military threat (Yatani & Bramel, 1989, p. 21). Americans saw the Soviet Union as their enemy, not only because it was the rival superpower, but because they saw the Soviet Union as a promoter of communism and a threat to freedom and democracy.

In this context of anti-Soviet sentiment, Gallup asked Americans, in December 1983, how much freedom they thought there was in various countries; 86% thought there was little or no freedom in the Soviet Union, 5% thought there was some freedom, and 1% thought there was a great deal. At least at that point in time, the perceived negative relationship between the Soviet Union and freedom was strong.

Attitudes toward the United States

At the same time, 80% thought there was a great deal of freedom in the United States, 11% thought there was some, and 1% thought there was little or none. As one would expect, Americans showed strong beliefs in the positive relationship between the United States and freedom.

Overall, Americans' attitudes toward their own country remained overwhelmingly favorable. In June 1986, Gallup found that 99% were proud to be Americans (89% "very proud" and 10% "quite proud"), while only 1% were "not very proud" and even less were "not at all proud." Findings were similar in 1981; the unanimity and degree of national pride in America is truly impressive. A recent Gallup poll (February 28 to March 2, 1989) found 95% expressing favorable attitudes toward the United States, and similar results were obtained in earlier surveys. American patriotism has proved to be strong and stable.

Thus public opinion data do not indicate that the cold war schema died in the era of detente. Survey data from the 1970s and 1980s testify to the survival of anticommunism, anti-Sovietism, pro-Americanism, and the belief that freedom is on the American side in the cold war. The weight of the evidence strongly suggests that in the mid-1980s, the cold war schema remained clearly manifest in American public opinion.

PEACE, NOT LOVE, MOTIVATES DIPLOMACY

Although Vietnam made Americans hesitant about the use of troops to contain communism, they became less gun-shy as the war faded into memory. In a July 1978 Roper poll, Americans were equally divided (43% to 43%) over whether U.S. troops should be used if Soviet troops invaded Western Europe. Support for the use of troops rose steadily through the early 1980s, and, in November 1986, Gallup found that the public favored the use of troops against a hypothetical Soviet invasion of Europe by a 68% to 24% margin. In a December 1981 Harris poll, about half of the respondents favored the use of nuclear weapons "if Western Europe were threatened with a Russian takeover" (Wittkopf, 1990, pp. 313, 326). In the post-Vietnam era, then, there was substantial public support for the use of militaristic means if necessary to contain Soviet expansion.

While most Americans favored dangerous levels of resolve in the face of hypothetical Soviet aggression, they also favored diplomatic attempts to lessen the chances of catastrophic U.S.–Soviet conflict. In seven surveys conducted from April 1977 through April 1979, Harris consistently found that about three-quarters of the public supported a "new SALT" agreement. From 1977 through 1981, NBC News found that between two-thirds and three-quarters favored agreements "between the United States and Russia which would limit nuclear weapons" (Wittkopf, 1990, p. 324).

Although the invasion of Afghanistan temporarily dampened American enthusiasm for U.S.–Soviet accommodation, the desire to reduce superpower tension built steadily over the 1980s. For instance, in January 1980 a CBS News/ New York Times poll found only 20% agreement with the statement, "the U.S. should try harder to reduce tension with the Russians versus getting tougher in its dealings with them." By September 1982, that figure had risen to 38%, in 1986 it was at 44%, and, in October 1987, America Talks Security found 64% agreement (Yankelovich & Smoke, 1988). In 1986, the Chicago Council on Foreign Relations found that 82% of the public favored U.S.–Soviet arms agreements, and 76% favored resumed cultural and educational exchanges (Rielly, 1987).

In a 1984 survey by the Public Agenda Foundation, 96% of all Americans felt that "picking a fight with the Soviet Union is too dangerous in a nuclear world," and 89% agreed that "there can be no winner in an all-out nuclear war; both the United States and the Soviet Union would be completely destroyed"

(Yankelovich & Doble, 1984, pp. 33–34). This is a clear and rational basis for a "live-and-let-live" attitude, but it is also one that assumes U.S.–Soviet conflict at some level.

Data already presented on American attitudes toward the Soviet Union refute any suggestion that this desire to negotiate and reduce tensions was the result of a disappearance of suspicion or hostility toward the Soviet Union. Gallup polls conducted from 1976 through 1987 showed favorable ratings of the Soviet Union varying from 9% to 34%. In the October 1987 ATS survey, 68% expressed distrust toward Soviet leaders, and the perception that the Soviet Union was behind all the trouble in the world was endorsed by 58% of the sample (37% disagreed). As mentioned above, American attitudes toward the Soviet Union on the CCFR "feeling thermometer" were still frigid in 1986, surpassed only by still-hated Iran. It is clear that many Americans desired warmer relations with the Soviet Union before they experienced warmer feelings toward the rival super-power.

According to an NBC/AP poll of September 1979, 71% believed the Soviet Union could not be trusted to live up to agreements that relaxed tensions between the two superpowers (21% thought they could be trusted). At the same time, 62% favored (and 30% opposed) a new agreement between the superpowers to limit nuclear weapons (Smith, 1983, pp. 285, 287). Apparently, a significant propor-tion of Americans felt that accommodation with an untrustworthy opponent was worthwhile, perhaps to reduce tension. Gallup found a similar phenomenon in October 1985: respondents tended to favor a Soviet arms limitation proposal (by a 47% to 32% margin), even though only a fifth of the sample thought the Soviet Union was "really serious about a major arms reduction agreement," and two-thirds saw it as an attempt to influence world opinion.

Roper polls from the early 1980s clearly show the coexistence of anti-Soviet stereotypes and a desire for good relations. In polls of February and November 1980 and September 1981, around 70% consistently saw Russia's primary objec-tive in world affairs as global domination, an additional 20% or so thought Russia sought to compete with the United States, and only around 5% saw the Soviet objective as self-protection. In June of 1980 and 1981, 85% thought that an effort should be made to improve U.S.–Soviet relations, and slightly over 45% thought that it should be a major effort (Smith, 1983, pp. 281–282). Given Soviet power and these perceptions of Soviet intentions, improving relations seems safer than the alternatives.

The danger of nuclear war, not trust in the Soviet Union or the disappearance of anticommunism or anti-Sovietism, explains why many Americans came to prefer diplomacy to militarism. As Kohut (1988) points out, Americans have desired both a strong defense and arms control throughout the post–World War II period. The main change has been a decrease in the public's willingness to risk nuclear war to contain communism, and this change has been due to its in-creased awareness of the potential destructiveness of nuclear war.

Yankelovich and Doble (1984) reported on the research of Lauer, who used a cluster analysis to divide the American public among four opinion groups. The largest group (31%) was opposed to the Soviet Union and communism, but advocated peaceful, "live-and-let-live" relations. The second group (25%) believed in the "evil empire" and were religiously anticommunist. While they would have liked to destroy communism if they could, the threat of nuclear holocaust motivated them to support negotiation over militarism. A third group (23%) felt that a nuclear war was highly unlikely, and so were willing to take greater risks and favored military buildup over negotiations to deal with the Soviet Union and communism. The last and smallest group (21%) consisted of those who were not ideologically anti-Soviet (Yankelovich & Doble, 1984, pp. 39–41).

Lauer's categories reveal crucial opinion dynamics. Most Americans remained anticommunist and suspicious of the Soviet Union, but at the same time most favored negotiations with the Soviets. Fear of nuclear holocaust, not love for the Soviet Union, motivated (clustered with) a desire for peaceful coexistence. Anti-Soviet attitudes were not enough to elicit militaristic policy preferences; regardless of their opinions of the Soviets, those who feared annihilation tended to opt for diplomacy over militarism. While one of Lauer's groups (21%) may have rejected the cold war schema, the other three continued to employ it in their own ways.

Thus the significant development over the last thirty years was not a rejection of the cold war schema, but a realization of the dangers of war and the limits of American power. Regardless of what Americans would have liked their government to achieve in foreign affairs, there was an increasing perception of prohibitive costs, unacceptable risks, and serious danger. In Vietnam for instance, the anticommunist goals of the war were not challenged by most Americans. At issue instead were the high human, economic, social, and political costs incurred in an effort that ultimately failed. More recently, many liberals have accepted anticommunism as desirable in Latin America, but they have not been willing to pay as large a price for it as conservatives have been. Similarly, detente did not indicate an acceptance of communism or the Soviet Union as an ally; it showed a realization of the importance of managing superpower conflict in an age of nuclear parity.

In 1988, Yankelovich and Smoke described the position of the American public in terms of a willingness to negotiate brought on by fears of the nuclear consequences of not doing so:

A global nuclear holocaust remains so colossal a threat that even a small possibility of it, even in the distant future, creates continuing anxiety. Any measure that can credibly reduce the chances of nuclear war without raising other insecurities will receive overwhelming public support. The public appears firmly convinced that Gorbachev means it when he says he too wants to reduce the nuclear threat. ... Americans believe that reducing the global nuclear threat is in the Soviet interest and that the Soviets know it.

They feel that the Soviets may also seek nuclear security from the additional, selfish motive that it could make their conventional superiority more important. . . . But that does not deny Soviet pragmatism in wanting to avoid global destruction. Because of this perception and their own anxiety, Americans are firm that this is a time for negotiation, not confrontation. [p. 13]

Thus the cold war orientation continued, if in muted form. Support for anticommunist military intervention was limited by an unwillingness to pay such high costs, while support for negotiations with the Soviets was bolstered by the benefits of peace between two nuclear powers. In the meantime, the United States went on with its lower-cost, often covert interventions, and U.S.–Soviet competition continued. Ongoing foreign policy developments and changing priorities altered the impact and role of the cold war schema but did not remove it from the minds of American citizens or policymakers.

ATTITUDES TOWARD THE SOVIET UNION DURING THE GORBACHEV ERA

There is no denying that American attitudes toward the Soviet Union improved in the late 1980s, and the Soviet Union enjoyed its greatest popularity among Americans during its final years. American favorability ratings of the Soviet Union improved substantially in the Gorbachev era. In 1983, one in every eleven Americans held positive attitudes toward the Soviet Union. By 1987, one in four were favorably disposed toward the other superpower (Kohut, 1988). Favorability ratings quickly rose to 44% in late 1988 and to 62% by early 1989. After a drop to 51% in August of that year, favorability toward the Soviet Union remained in the 50% to 60% range in 1990.[3] In January 1991, favorable ratings outnumbered unfavorable ones by a 57% to 35% margin.

A similar, though less impressive, picture is drawn by findings of CBS News/ New York Times polls. In September 1987, 15% had favorable opinions of the Soviet Union, 40% had neutral feelings, and 41% were unfavorable. By May 1989, 30% looked upon the Soviet Union favorably, while 43% were neutral and 24% had unfavorable attitudes. In November 1989, 30% still had favorable attitudes, 54% said they were neutral, and only 13% had unfavorable attitudes.

The Gorbachev era also saw an increasing perception among Americans that the Soviet Union was working for peace. In 1985, 10% thought the Soviet Union was doing all it could to keep peace in the world. By 1987, 21% felt this way, and by May 1990, 31% held that opinion. While this is a far cry from the 50% who consistently saw America as doing all it could for peace in that period, it does indicate a clear and substantial improvement in the Soviet image.

Not only were American attitudes about the Soviet Union turning increasingly positive in the late 1980s and early 1990s, many Americans were no longer viewing the Soviet Union as an enemy. When asked in May 1990 if the Soviet Union was an ally or an enemy, 39% chose ally, 31% picked enemy, 21% said

TABLE 3.3
Favorability Ratings of the Soviet Union, Soviet Leaders, and the Soviet People
(September 16–17, 1983)

	Soviet Union	Leaders	People
Very favorable (+5, 4)	2%	1%	9%
Mildly favorable (+3, 2, 1)	7	6	40
Mildly unfavorable (-1, 2, 3)	22	21	30
Very unfavorable (-4, 5)	66	68	15
No opinion	3	4	6
	100	100	100

Source: Gallup Poll, 1984, pp. 225–228.

it was neither, and 9% did not answer. It is clear that by 1990 few Americans were using the cold war schema in formulating their attitudes toward the Soviet Union.

There are a number of explanations for this impressive improvement in the Soviet image among Americans. Table 3.3 shows the September 16–17, 1983 Gallup favorability ratings of the Soviet Union, Soviet leaders, and the Soviet people. The ratings of the Soviet Union and the leaders were essentially the same, while the Soviet people were given much more favorable ratings. It appears that, at least in 1983, attitudes toward the Soviet Union were tied much more closely to the unpopular behavior of leaders than to the relatively well-liked Soviet people. This indicates two avenues through which American attitudes toward the Soviet Union might have improved since 1983.

First, a Soviet leadership that was increasingly popular among Americans improved the image of the Soviet Union in American eyes and created more favorable American attitudes toward the other superpower. As Figure 3.2 shows, the Soviet Union's impressive increase in popularity paralleled an even more impressive rise by Mikhail Gorbachev. Gorbachev's favorability rating rose at a steady rate of 16% per year from 40% at the start of 1987 to 72% at the end of 1988. In that year, Ronald Reagan was the only man more admired by Americans (*Gallup Poll*, 1990, p. 233). In 1989, Gorbachev's favorability rating reached a peak of 77%, and in early 1991 it remained at the 70% level. As the Soviet premier, Gorbachev personified the Soviet Union, and his strong popularity must have contributed to the increasingly positive attitudes toward the Soviet Union. No doubt there was a mutual halo effect—both the Soviet Union and its leader benefited by association from the improved image of the other.

Second, greater attention to the Soviet people in the American media increased their salience to Americans, and increased the extent to which attitudes

FIGURE 3.2
Favorable Ratings of Gorbachev and the Soviet Union, National Samples (January 1987 to January 1991)
Sources: Niemi, Mueler, & Smith, 1989; *Gallup Poll*, 1984, 1990, 1991; Kohut, 1988.

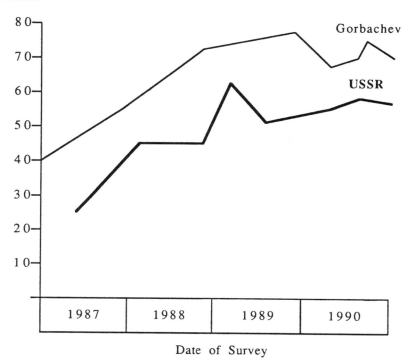

toward the Soviet people had an impact on attitudes toward the country as a whole. The combination of Gorbachev's popularity among Americans and increased attention to the Soviet people explains some of the upsurge in favorable attitudes toward the Soviet Union that occurred in the middle and late 1980s. This is demonstrated nicely in the views of a 67-year-old conservative Republican interviewed in the May 1989 CBS News/New York Times poll: "The Soviets are turning around quite a bit under Gorbachev, with more democracy, more freedom of speech. . . . We carry on against the citizens of China and Russia like they were some kind of 'evil empire.' They're just human beings like us, with a different philosophy" (*The New York Times*, May 16, 1989, p. A10).

This suggests yet a third basis for improved attitudes about the Soviet Union: the perception of positive domestic change there. According to Gallup, in November 1988, 65% thought the Soviet Union was undergoing major changes, while 28% saw the same basic system being run by a different leader. In December 1989, about half (46%) saw events in the Soviet Union and Eastern Europe as "the beginning of the end of communism in the world" (47% disagreed). In June 1989, 66% thought "the Soviet Union's new openness and democracy" would continue, while 25% predicted "return to a more closed society." It is likely that many Americans viewed change in the Soviet Union as a lessening of that which made it worthy of contempt.

This rising optimism about reforms in the Soviet Union gave way to some renewed pessimism as the 1980s gave way to the 1990s. According to a somewhat later Washington Post/ABC News poll, 42% viewed reforms in the Soviet Union as little more than public relations gestures, "and half of those interviewed said it was at least fairly likely that the Soviet Union would revert to the 'hardline communism it practiced before'" (*The Washington Post*, November 23, 1989, p. A22). In January 1991, about as many Americans thought that Gorbachev's economic reforms would fail (42%) as thought they would succeed (46%) (*Gallup Poll Monthly*, 1991). As the events of 1991 clearly demonstrated, even the experts had difficulty accurately predicting the future of the Soviet Union. In 1989, American public opinion about change and the future in the Soviet Union showed some enthusiasm about the lasting and positive nature of that change and some cynicism and skepticism.

The political and economic reforms that the Soviet Union went through provided the perfect opportunity for an image shift; the Soviet Union was increasingly viewed as going through the process of transition from communist oppression toward increased freedom and democracy. Near the end of 1989, for example, 32% predicted that Soviet communism would vanish within the next decade. To the extent that the Soviet Union became dissociated from communist oppression and associated with the United States, freedom, and democracy, Americans felt comfortable with positive feelings toward the Soviet Union.

Apparent progress away from communist oppression and toward freedom and democracy did not have to be completed to allow for pro-Soviet sentiments; the perceived direction of change was enough to allow for the correct symbolic associations. Had souring of U.S.–Soviet relations created renewed pressure to dislike the Soviet Union, it would have been a simple matter to refocus upon what was left of Soviet communism and oppression in order to regain balance. Reform in the Soviet Union *allowed for* comfortable pro-Soviet attitudes, but it did not *cause* them. What went on in the Soviet Union was not as important as how it was interpreted, and interpretations were made in a manner consistent with perceptions of U.S.–Soviet relations.

This brings us to the fourth and probably the most important explanation: improved American public opinion concerning the Soviet Union was to a large degree a response to events and developments in U.S.–Soviet relations. Simply stated, the forty-year record suggests that disagreement and conflict elicited unfavorable attitudes, agreement and cooperation elicited favorable ones. When the Soviet Union invaded its neighbors it was not popular with the American people. Visits, summits, and arms-limitation agreements improved American attitudes toward the Soviet Union. In the late 1980s and early 1990, as U.S.–Soviet relations improved, rhetoric by American politicians and coverage by American journalists lost much of their cold war edges and became increasingly sympathetic to the Soviet perspective. To a large extent, the positive public opinion trends were a response to these sorts of developments.

As impressive as the change in the Soviet image was, as long as the Soviet Union existed there was the possibility of a reverse trend. Given the fluctuations in attitudes toward the Soviet Union during the 1970s and 1980s, it was always possible that unforeseen events accompanied by renewed cold war rhetoric would have rejuvenated latent anti-Soviet sentiments. The wavelike, seesawing pattern of attitudes toward the Soviet Union during its last two decades suggests that when relations between the two superpowers were friendly, attitudes toward the Soviet Union improved, but when relations got strained, anti-Soviet sentiments re-emerged. Thus, intermittent superpower hostility kept the anti-Soviet fire burning in American minds.

Increasing grounds for U.S.–Soviet cooperation meant that Americans became less anti-Soviet over time. Continued and increased pressures toward U.S.–Soviet cooperation in the age of nuclear parity led to changes in official policy and rhetoric, in the structure and content of public information, and in public perceptions; the long-standing tendency to view the Soviet Union in enemy terms was tempered at all levels. Such a process permitted the maintenance of public support through a period of policy change.

However, we just do not know if relations would have continued to improve had the Soviet Union survived, and it is quite possible that a crisis of renewed cold war conflict would have emerged to rekindle America's latent anti-Sovietism. Had the short-lived coup against President Gorbachev succeeded in reinstating a hard-line communist government in Moscow, a renewed cold war fervor in America, accompanied by strongly anti-Soviet attitudes, would have been likely. There certainly was precedence for this. Anti-Soviet attitudes and suspicions were tempered by the World War II alliance, but reemerged with a vengeance after the war. Detente again tamed American anti-Sovietism, only to have it reemerge with a roar in the early Reagan years. Periodic fluctuations in relations and attitudes were the rule in the 1970s and 1980s.

Nincic (1985) suggests another reason why U.S.–Soviet relations may have soured had the Soviet Union survived. He makes the provocative suggestion that fluctuations in American attitudes toward the Soviet Union were a function of domestic economic conditions in the United States: When economic conditions were good, attitudes toward the rival superpower were relatively positive, but when things got bad, the evil enemy reemerged. In fact, Nincic found the expected relationship between changes in per-capita income and anti-Soviet attitudes from the 1950s onward. His findings make it difficult to discount what at first may seem a far-fetched idea.

Nincic relies on two complementary explanations for the phenomenon. The first is based on the frustration–aggression–displacement hypothesis: when income goes down, life gets tough, people get frustrated and hostile, and letting that hostility out against an outgroup, the Soviet enemy, serves as a satisfying catharsis that does not disrupt domestic order. Nincic's second explanation involves official promotion of this sort of displacement: government officials protect themselves by emphasizing superpower animosity, which directs citizen hostility outward against the Soviet Union. If Nincic is right, then the serious economic problems that have recently plagued the United States held the potential for rekindling strong American animosities toward the Soviet Union, had the Soviet Union not fallen apart itself.

Even in those last few years, American attitudes toward the Soviet Union were not unambiguously positive. Although cold war mistrust, suspicion, and fear were clearly on the decline, they were far from eliminated. According to a May 1989 CBS News/New York Times poll, half of the American people thought that the Soviet Union was bent on dominating the world. Twice as many Americans (57%) thought the Soviet Union was an aggressive country that would start a war to get something it wanted, as saw it as a peace-loving nation (27%). By November 1989, that gap had narrowed to 42% to 36%, and Americans tended (by a slim 46% to 41% margin) to think the Soviets would cheat on an arms control agreement.

In interviews, respondents expressed the sorts of cold war suspicions that are hard to shake off. A 65-year-old Illinois man said, "I don't trust the Soviet Union as an open and honest negotiating country." A 32-year-old Virginian offered, "I never trusted them and it's hard to change my view" (*The New York Times*, May 16, 1989, pp. A1, A10, December 3, 1989, p. Y15).

Even as Gorbachev's favorability rating hovered around 70%, Americans were about evenly divided as to whether he could be trusted. In May 1990, 43% trusted him and 49% did not, whereas four months later those figures were approximately reversed. Although Gorbachev was well-liked, forty years of mistrust were not easily dismissed. There was a lag between favorability and trust.

While attitudes toward the Soviet Union were more favorable than they had ever been, underlying suspicions and stereotypes persisted. Yankelovich and Smoke's (1988) characterization of the American mood as "wary readiness" was an apt one. Despite positive developments and ever-improving attitudes toward the Soviet Union and its leader, "the on-again, off-again pattern (cold war–detente–cold war–detente) leaves a residue of skepticism in the public mind" (p. 17). While Americans were ready for an end to the cold war, they were only beginning to have the confidence to declare it over.

In a July 1988 America Talks Security survey, respondents almost unanimously (94%) agreed that U.S.–Soviet relations were stable or improving (Yankelovich & Smoke, 1988, p. 3). Yet despite the enthusiastic pronouncements and joyful celebrations witnessed in the *Doonesbury* comic strip in June of that year, it took a good deal longer for most Americans to believe that the cold war was truly over. A Los Angeles Times poll of November 17–19, 1989 found only 22% claiming that the cold war was over; 61% said that it was not (*Los Angeles Times*, November 21, 1989, p. A12). A CBS News/New York Times poll (November 26–28, 1989) yielded somewhat more optimistic results: 37% thought the cold war was over, while 54% said it was not (*International Herald Tribune*, December 4, 1989, p. 5).

According to a Washington Post/ABC News poll, also conducted in late 1989, 58% believed the cold war was coming to an end (*The Washington Post*, November 23, 1989, p. A22). At the same time, Gallup elicited predictions for the year 2000 which also indicated expectations of an end to the cold war. In November 1989, 68% expected the Soviet Union and the West to be living peacefully by the year 2000, and, in December, 65% thought it likely that the United States and the Soviet Union would be allies within the next ten years. Only 8% predicted nuclear war between the two superpowers. Obviously, there is a difference between the cold war being in the process of winding down and it actually being over. Although most Americans perceived progress toward an end to the cold war at the close of 1989, most did not believe that that end had been achieved. Americans showed optimism that the positive trends in U.S.–Soviet relations would continue, but the prevailing perception was that those positive trends would continue over the next few years in the context of the cold war. This perception was consistent with the Bush administration's position of cautious optimism; cold war tensions had been reduced, the official line had it, not eliminated.

Further Gallup findings indicate that this general orientation continued into 1990. In May, 63% felt that the West could live in peace with the Soviet Union, while 31% saw war as inevitable (responses were the reverse in 1954, during the heart of the cold war). Eighty-four percent saw the peaceful settlement of differences between Russia and the West as possible. At this point, 40% thought the cold war was over, while 52% expressed the belief that there was still a cold war. Four months later, however, those figures were reversed: 40% believed that there was still a cold war while 50% thought it was over. In January 1991, 56% thought the cold war was over, and 62% saw almost no chance of an all-out nuclear war between the United States and the Soviet Union.

THE END OF THE COLD WAR SCHEMA

U.S.–Soviet relations during the cold war were strained and conflictual, but they were not entirely so; in the nuclear age, they became a mixture of competition and cooperation. The Soviet Union became both the rival superpower and the major negotiating partner to the United States. It was possible to cooperate with an enemy, to make agreements and remain suspicious, to meet and remain hostile. Still, cooperation fostered trust, contact led to understanding, and common interests led to favorable feelings. In addition, public rhetoric became less anti-Soviet when diplomacy-minded U.S. leaders were careful not to increase tensions, or to fuel sentiments that would quash their diplomatic policy initiatives.

The mixed nature of U.S.–Soviet relations and the dual policy of aggression and accommodation became reflected in wavering but increasingly positive public attitudes toward the Soviet Union. Substantial fluctuations in attitudes accompanied changes in the mood of U.S.–Soviet relations, and as the mood gradually got friendlier, so did American attitudes. While some Americans maintained strong anti-Soviet sentiments, others came to view the Soviet Union in a more positive light.

Although the cold war schema predominated in the United States after World War II, its anti-Soviet component was waning by the late 1980s. Attitudes toward the Soviet Union and its leader were relatively positive (residual mistrust notwithstanding), U.S.–Soviet relations were perceived as relatively friendly, and there was substantial support for the notion that the cold war was ending.

Had events been different a revival of the cold war schema would have been possible. As it was, the dissolution of the Soviet Union made the anti-Soviet component of the schema irrelevant. The ever-present American patriotic schema remains, as does its schematic opposition to communism and oppression.

As was argued in Chapter 2, the anti-Soviet component of the cold war schema was not as deeply rooted, pervasive, or stable as the pro-American part (the patriotic schema). Pro-Americanism is primary, based firmly in the patriotic and ideological biases that have helped maintain the legitimacy and stability of the U.S. government over two centuries. Anti-Sovietism was secondary, based in traditional anti-Russian and anticommunist sentiments and fueled by cold war conflict and antagonism. Anti-Sovietism served pro-Americanism, but pro-Americanism can survive without anti-Sovietism.

We can only speculate about what future internationally oriented schema or schemata will elaborate the patriotic schema and gain prominence in American culture. Rebellious nations or movements in the third world may be the great enemies of the future. Alternatively, new and powerful competitors for world hegemony may replace the Soviet Union. In fact, the Soviets' shoes may be too big to fill with a unified enemy—a few smaller enemies may yield several schemata to take the place of the cold war schema. Because of the important role such international schemata play in bolstering and perpetuating the patriotic schema, the United States should feel fortunate that it has so many enemies in the world to choose from.

NOTES

1. Most of the public opinion data cited in this chapter are from Gallup surveys (*Gallup Polls*, 1972, 1978, 1981, 1984, 1985, 1986, 1987, 1988, 1989, 1990, 1991). Findings from polls not conducted by Gallup are identified as such in the text; unattributed findings can be assumed to be from Gallup.

2. For more "friendly critiques" of Holsti and Rosenau's assertions regarding Vietnam and dissensus, see Ferguson (1986) and Kegley (1986). Kegley's article also points out a number of important methodological issues pertaining to the Holsti and Rosenau study.

3. There is some discrepancy in the Gallup publications concerning May 1990 findings. According to the compilation of 1990 survey findings (*Gallup Polls*, 1991, p. 53), 55% of the public held favorable attitudes toward the Soviet Union. The February 1991 edition of *The Gallup Poll Monthly*, however, sets this figure at 64%. The 55% figure is used here, as it is more in line with the August 1989 and September 1990 findings.

4

Cold War Themes
in American Culture

No one wants a conflict with the Soviet Union, but it sure makes for thrilling fiction.

> —Television advertisement for B. Dalton Booksellers

1997, after ten years of Soviet occupation, ten years without freedom in a land called Amerika. . . . *Amerika,* next.

> —Television advertisement for the *Amerika* mini-series

The cultural predominance of the cold war schema was perpetuated through the interactions of schema-using individuals and schema-structured products of culture. Cold war schema users wrote novels, screenplays, textbooks, scholarly articles, news reports, and speeches, and they often framed them in cold war terms. In a culture of cold war schema users, these products were in demand; people found the scenarios meaningful and the themes gratifying, and they were willing and eager to spend substantial amounts of time and/or money on the consumption of cold war culture.

In the United States, an Orwellian "Ministry of Truth" is not needed to control entertainment, news, and education; the invisible hand of the market is both effective and insidious. Propaganda is a consumer item—people buy it because they find it gratifying and useful (Ellul, 1965). In the American free market for entertainment, some themes sell, and the cold war schema was one of them. East–West conflict provided the black-and-white backdrop for countless espionage and adventure thrillers. The contrast between stereotyped Soviet oppression and idealized American freedom was a theme of many meaningful and emotionally moving scenes. Cold war themes interested, entranced, excited, angered, and soothed Americans.

The cold war sold in America, not just in the entertainment market, but in the market of ideas as well. The predominance of the cold war schema led some American rhetoricians, educators, and scholars to take it for granted in their work, and their work was positively received by others who shared their preconceptions. Thus the cold war schema was reinforced in a variety of settings and media; schema-use in a variety of tasks merged into a self-perpetuating cultural milieu.

Chapter 5 examines how and why the cold war schema structured television network news reporting of foreign affairs through a comparative case study of Central American election coverage. The current chapter presents a few examples of products of cold war culture on television and in the cinema. It also looks at an example of scholarship that is anchored in the American patriotic schema. Since the primary focus of this book is on the cognitive effects of the cold war schema rather than its cultural manifestations, no complete or systematic analysis of cold war culture will be attempted here. Examples are presented in an anecdotal fashion in order to provide a feel for some of the ways in which cold war messages were portrayed in American culture in the 1980s.

TELEVISION

Imagine that it's 1987, you are an American, it's late, and you can't sleep. You turn on the television and are greeted by the absurd and sadistic spectacle of scantily clad young women writhing in staged combat in a boxing ring. An announcer adds meaning to the scene.

As you watch, "Debutante Debbie" and "Suzy Spirit," appropriately clad as "The Cheerleaders," prevail in their tag-team match against the "Terrorist" team of the hooded "Woman of Darkness" and the dark haired "Palestina." But the forces of light do not achieve total victory on this night; other more dangerous evils are about to appear on "GLOW Gorgeous Women's Wrestling."

"Colonel Nanushka" is a hefty, stern-looking woman from Kiev. A proud Soviet, she sports short blond hair, a hammer and sickle tattooed over her right breast, a red singlet, and red tights. Her partner, "Spanish Red," is seductively beautiful, with fine American Indian features and long black hair. Her bright red leotards clearly declare her true colors, and the tattoos on her arm hint danger.

Their opponents were to be, in a long awaited showdown, "Americana" and her partner. Unfortunately, explains the announcer, Americana could not make it this evening. The communists go bezerk, grab his microphone and demand Americana. "We're here to take on Americana," they snarl, "not some cheap replacement."

The replacements, "The Southern Bells," come out in bloomers, carrying parasols. Frustrated and incensed over their inability to destroy Americana, Nanushka and Red proceed to sadistically and unmercifully punish the Bells. Children in the audience frantically wave small American flags, but it does not help. In a heroic show of American solidarity, "Ebony" (a black woman dressed in red, white, and blue) comes to the aid of the Bells. She is soon beaten back, and the team of Colonel Nanushka and Spanish Red completes its easy conquest. "That was too easy," they sneer, "bring on Americana." The crowd is on its feet, fists are in the air, and a chant drowns out the Communist conquerors: "Russia sucks, Russia sucks, Russia sucks. . . ."

To create clear and satisfying contests between good and evil, the writers of "GLOW Gorgeous Women's Wrestling" presented symbolic portrayals of American stereotypes of the struggle between good and evil in the international arena. Good was symbolized by "Americana," along with "The Cheerleaders," "The Southern Bells," and "Ebony"—in short, by the United States. Evil was symbolized by the Terrorists, consisting of the "Woman of Darkness" (representing Islamic fundamentalists) and "Palestina" (the PLO), and by the communist team of Colonel Nanushka (the Soviet Union) and Spanish Red (Cuba/Nicaragua). These stereotypes were not invented on sadistic American late-night television shows; they developed in American culture in conjunction with post–World War II U.S. foreign policy. But their simplicity and pervasive appeal made them ideal for framing fictitious television conflict. Thus anti-Soviet and anticommunist (as well as anti-Arabic and anti-Islamic) attitudes and stereotypes were reinforced in television fiction.

Probably the most famous, and certainly the most hotly debated, cold war television production in the 1980s was ABC's $40 million, 14½ hour "miniseries" called *Amerika* (which, ironically, was partially filmed on location in Canada). In "Amerika," the United States, freedom, and democracy are crushed under Soviet–communist oppressive rule. The idea for this piece of free enterprise propaganda was expressed in a newspaper column by Ben Stein, a former speechwriter for Richard Nixon. The column was read by ABC executive Brandon Stoddard (*Seattle Times,* February 13, 1987, p. A4), and the rest was history (or, more accurately, fiction). According to the informational flyer provided by KOMO television in Seattle,

This engrossing drama, set in the late 1990s, depicts life in the United States ten years after a takeover by the Soviet Union. The story is populated by believable characters caught in a nightmarish situation in which they and their values are tested. . . . *Amerika* serves as an early warning system, spotlighting the public and private issues Americans need to focus in on in the present. What does it mean to be an American? How important to each of us are freedom, human rights, community, democracy, patriotism, and civic-mindedness?

Amerika is based on and teaches the cold war schema. The lesson of *Amerika* is that America is to be cherished for its freedom and democracy, and the Soviet Union is to be feared for its oppression and corruption.

Amerika begins with nostalgic scenes of Americana and a voiceover, "When I had my freedom—free, free, if you say it over enough it begins to sound, mean, nothing." What follows are the worst stereotypes of Soviet-communist rule. There are lines for food and mass starvation in Amerika's breadbasket. All avenues for individual and artistic expression have been repressed. Government is corrupt, democracy a farce. Tanks and helicopters are everywhere, and masses of people are heartlessly slaughtered at the whim of power-hungry leaders. Seattle, of all unoffending places, has suffered a nuclear attack.

At one point, Colonel Andrei Denisov, a KGB administrator stationed in Amerika, cynically explains his country to the viewing audience:

In Russia, less than 5% of the people enjoy the benefits of society—the clever or lucky ones, the party members, athletes, scientists, all of whom live well in the name of and for the benefit of the other 95%. Now no one asks the 95% if they are grateful for the sacrifices the 5% are making, and of course it's all in the name of the ultimate communist man whom I'm told is still on his way.

This cold, cynical attitude is juxtaposed with the idealism of Devin Milford, a former presidential candidate whose heart-felt belief in America (with a "c") cannot be broken by years of imprisonment and torture. Milford, who captures the indomitable American spirit and is ultimately killed in an uncompromising effort to save a free America, proclaims, "If the dream of democracy cannot survive in America, it cannot survive the twentieth century."

The media debate over *Amerika* set those who accepted the fully articulated cold war schema against those who viewed anti-Soviet stereotypes as detrimental to world peace. The first side claimed that Americans must believe in America, freedom, and democracy and work to preserve these precious things. For them the film functioned as a reminder of the dangers, specifically the threat of Soviet–communist oppression. The other side claimed that the film was unrealistic and ethnocentrically biased and perpetuated misperceptions that obstructed efforts at U.S.–Soviet accommodation. Ultimately, this was an unresolved public debate over the advisability of accepting and perpetuating the fully articulated cold war schema.

On its first night, *Amerika* achieved a 43% share of television viewers. Ultimately, however, the show was a flop, not because the cold war schema had lost its power to attract Americans, but because *Amerika* was a long and excruciatingly boring production that could not compete in the free entertainment market. As with the other dramas discussed in this chapter, the cold war schema served as the backdrop for *Amerika*, as the conceptual framework that was taken for granted and made the fictional world plausible and meaningful. Against that backdrop were humanly oriented stories, and in the case of *Amerika* the story was not craftily presented. The problem with *Amerika* was not its timing, but its execution.

Nobody who remembers the heroic struggles Rocky and Bulwinkle had against the evil Boris and Natasha will contest the presence of cold war stereotypes in television cartoons. The children of the 1980s, however, received a larger dose than previous generations; the modern adventure cartoon magnified the cold war content of the video fantasy land. Hesse and Stimpson (1988) analyzed the content of twenty episodes of eight highly rated cartoon shows (*He-Man, She-Ra, Rambo, GI-Joe, Transformers, Gobots, Voltron,* and *Defenders of the Earth*). They concluded: "In sum, in the course of watching television, children are taught some of the key elements of US patriotism: the struggle for dominance among the superpowers, linked to the defense of freedom and democracy in the world" (Hesse & Stimpson, 1988, p. 11). In other words, the cold war schema was a relatively clear and consistent message in the popular cartoon adventures they analyzed.

Because of their audience, television cartoons were particularly powerful purveyors of cold war stereotypes. The children who watch cartoons are just beginning to learn about their political worlds; they have little world knowledge or experience with which to counter simple, black-and-white images. In fact, they are motivated to learn, accept, and become involved in the good-versus-evil schemata that structure the many programs they watch, for this allows them to understand and enjoy the shows. Because the cold war schema, or one very much like it, structured a number of cartoon programs, there was ample opportunity and motivation to learn it, and plenty of confirmation that the cartoon world worked that way. Through this process, children were primed for the next step: applying the cold war schema to actual world affairs.

CINEMA

It is not difficult to find American films with clear cold war messages. Rogin (1987) and Whitfield (1991) provide insightful analyses of the portrayal of cold war themes in the cinema during the heart of the cold war. In the 1980s, such films as *Rambo, Rocky IV, Red Dawn, White Knights,* and *Moscow on the Hudson* provided American moviegoers with moving entertainment that taught cold war lessons. Two of these movies, Paul Mazursky's 1984 release, *Moscow on the Hudson,* and Sylvester Stallone's 1985 film, *Rocky IV,* will be examined here.

Moscow on the Hudson is the story of Vladimir Ivanof, a Soviet saxophonist who defects while on tour with his Moscow circus in New York. The movie juxtaposes Soviet oppression with American freedom, and does so with seductive skill and grace.

The film opens in Moscow with scenes of Soviet government oppression and miserable Moscovites shivering in long lines, waiting for toilet paper and mis-sized shoes. In one scene, Vladimir meets an old friend who had been committed to an insane asylum for protesting the Soviet invasion of Afghanistan. In another, he joins his family at home, watching propaganda parade as news on television.

The New York trip has made Soviet authorities nervous, and they warn performers not to be tempted by "American decadence." Vladimir is particularly excited about the trip, because of his love for American jazz. The music scene isn't quite the same in Moscow; as Vladimir gets his family to join in on a Duke Ellington tune, his father warns, "Now we'll get arrested for sure."

The transition from Moscow to New York is abrupt and stark; New York is as joyful, energetic, and expressive as Moscow was sad, tired, and suppressed. Even the seasons change; we leave a dark, snowy Moscow and arrive in a bright, sunny New York.

The contrast between Soviet oppression and American freedom is often portrayed in visual imagery. The Soviet circus performers are shown enthusiastically peering from their "Liberty Lines" bus as it drives through New York. Although they are traveling Liberty Lines in the land of liberty, they remain imprisoned in the bus. The Soviet authorities are keeping a particularly close eye on Vladimir's closest friend, a clown who desperately yearns for freedom and is intent on defecting.

A particularly symbolic episode begins with a front view of the bus, which clearly shows the word "LIBERTY" across the grate. Focus immediately shifts to the clown, as he scrawls "FREEDOM" with his finger in the dust of his bus window. Mindful of the intimidating authorities in the seat behind them, Vladimir wipes the word out with his shirt sleeve. The authorities watch suspiciously, a bit angrily. All the while, the reflection of an American flag slowly floats by, clearly visible in the window. American freedom and Soviet oppression are skilfully and subtly juxtaposed, with no need for words or explanations.

The bus stops for a thirty-minute group indulgence in American "decadence" at Bloomingdale's department store. The wonderful assortment of clothes, jewelry, perfume, and paraphernalia found at "Bloomie's" juxtaposes nicely with Moscow's long, snowy lines for inadequate essentials.

Vladimir defects in Bloomingdale's and goes home to a "ghetto" with a black security guard. As they walk through the pleasant neighborhood, Vladimir comments, "I like it, it's nice, and the music, it's so free." "It must be pretty bad in Russia," responds the friendly guard. The discussion moves to slavery in the American South. "Sounds like Russia," observes the Russian.

The next day Vladimir goes to a Cuban-American immigration lawyer, who tells of coming to America to escape Castro, "a Cuban bullshit artist who has been taken in by Russian bullshit artists." Soon Vladimir has an Italian girlfriend who is studying to become a citizen. In one memorable scene, the two sit naked in his bath tub, framed by American flag shower curtains, studying the Declaration of Independence and the freedoms guaranteed in the Bill of Rights.

In a split second (movie time) her big day has arrived, and the scene shifts to a courtroom and a mass swearing-in ceremony. Only the most hardened cynic would not be moved by this sight of hopeful new citizens from around the world finally realizing their dreams of American citizenship. The judge proclaims, "From this day you are no longer the subject of a government, but an integral part of the government, a free man." Citizens of other nations are subjects; American citizens are free.

In predictable fashion, Vladimir loses and regains his girlfriend; he also loses and regains his faith in American freedom. His faith is shaken when he is mugged. Vladimir complains bitterly to his lawyer friend: "This is liberty? This is false liberty. What freedom? You can't walk down the street. Is that freedom?" The lawyer counters, "Do you really think you were better off before, in Russia?" Vladimir evades the question momentarily, and aggressively asks a stranger, "Hey pal, you free?" The answer is in Russian, and Vladimir translates and responds:

(Translating:) He says he's lived here for seven years and he likes it very much. He's telling me, go back to Moscow, Turk. (To the man:) In Moscow, we have to fight for a crumb of freedom. (Again translating:) He's telling me now if I want law and order I should go back to Moscow and stand in line for bread—stale bread.

Vladimir is interrupted by loud noises. "Fire crackers," his fellow Russian-American informs him, "independence day." Suddenly, the meaning of the Fourth of July fills the screen without a word or image, and Vladimir is a born-again patriot. After apologizing, Vladimir joins the other customers in the cafe in a group recitation of the Declaration of Independence: "We hold these truths. . . ."

The lesson of Vladimir's loss of faith and revival is that idealized notions of American freedom can and ought to exist alongside evidence of real restrictions. Yes, there are frustrations in America, but Russia was oppressive, therefore America is free. This is a common method for bolstering an unrealistic conception of American freedom. Americans, when faced with strong critiques of idealized notions of American freedom, will often turn to idealized notions of Soviet oppression as a point of comparison. Bringing up the Soviet Union shifts attention from the limits of freedom in America—it juxtaposes America against an image that does indeed make the home of the brave seem like the land of the free.

Idealistic expressions of American freedom are repeatedly made throughout the movie. When Vladimir defiantly declares his defection to a threatening and pleading Soviet official (who ends up happily selling hot dogs in Central Park to avoid being sent to Siberia for losing Vladimir in Bloomingdale's), one of New York's finest proclaims, "This is New York City, the man can do whatever he wants." This is an absurd statement from, of all people, a law enforcement agent, yet it somehow rings true. When asked by an FBI agent why he defected, Vladimir replies simply, "Freedom." He then runs outside and exuberantly exclaims, "I did it! I'm free like a bird!"

When they meet, Vladimir's lawyer informs him, "you can do anything in this country if you want to." His girlfriend (who, despite her heavy Italian accent, plans to be a sportscaster) proclaims, "I can do anything—is America."

In the final minutes of the movie, Vladimir is shown playing his saxophone as a giant American flag waves behind him; dollar bills are dropping into the open saxophone case next to him. A voice-over translates a letter to his family in Moscow.

> . . . I am free to do whatever I please, whenever I want to, as long as its legal. This is a free country, welcome to almost anyone, and I hope that some day you will join me here. Of course I will continue to write you every week. Yes, in America anything is possible.

In the Soviet Union, like in the United States, like anywhere in the world, citizens have always been allowed to do what has not been defined by prevailing authorities as against the rules. The United States does not come close to welcoming "almost anyone," nor is "anything possible." The idealized notions of American freedom that constitute the central political message of the movie are portrayed in this climactic letter home, and they range from trivial to absurd. The stereotypic portrayal of Soviet oppression is instrumental in conveying American freedom by contrast. And so the movie ends with a song: "Freedom, freedom, freedom. Oh, let me go. . . ."

Sylvester Stallone's popular boxing movie, *Rocky IV,* not only portrays clear cold war themes, it also supports the Reagan administration's philosophy of "peace through strength." The film opens with a head-on collision between the American and Soviet flags, each shaped like a boxing glove. Clearly, the cold war is the underlying theme and context of the movie, the meaningful framework in which the drama is played out. *Rocky IV* pits a warm and caring American philosopher/family man (Rocky Balboa) against a cold, ruthless Soviet robot/ executioner (Ivan Drago). It is a test of the relative strengths of the striving American spirit and the regimented, controlled Soviet machine. In the end, the American spirit wins not only the physical fight, but the hearts and minds of the Soviet crowd as well. The American spirit proves indomitable and irresistible. In the final scene, draped in an American flag, amid cheers from his Soviet admirers, Rocky proclaims, "If I can change, you can change, everyone can change." In his conquest, Rocky becomes a messenger for peace.

Rocky IV is a film that highlights U.S.–Soviet conflict and juxtaposed black-and-white stereotypes of the two superpowers, yet its "punch line" is that peace and understanding are possible once the Soviet Union has been shown who is number one. Rocky becomes a Reagan-like figure, and his message is "peace through strength." For peace to happen, the Soviets have to come to realize that the Americans are right and they are wrong. Thus, while *Rocky IV* is framed by and perpetuates cold war stereotypes, it provides an escape hatch: the Soviet Union does not have to be America's enemy. Like a sinner who finds religion, the Soviet Union can change; like a preacher who recognizes a convert, the United States can change too.

Cold war movies such as *Rocky IV* were popular because they were framed by familiar and deeply held cold war beliefs. Stallone did not have to explain the cold war to his audience—they shared his beliefs and biases, they understood the conflictual context of the story, and they came to the theater with complete knowledge of why Rocky Balboa was good and Ivan Drago was bad. More recently, as the Soviet enemy lost its relevance and salience in American culture, it also faded from the big screen.

ACADEMIA

Because scholarly pursuits require complex thought, critical reflection, and informed judgement, scholars are not particularly prone to simple black-and-white stereotyping. Still, scholars have not been immune to the American patriotic schema and its cold war extension. In our attempts to understand the complexities of domestic and international politics, we unfortunately are forced to accept certain basic truths as given. Preconceptions are inseparable from the research process, and scholars cannot be expected to successfully exorcise all cognitive biases they have picked up through the process of living in America. It is not surprising, then, that the cold war schema and, more often, the American patriotic schema have sometimes been integrated into frameworks of analysis. The result, however, is that scholarship has served a dual function: it has expanded understanding as it reinforced culturally predominant stereotypes, and it has educated as it indoctrinated.

For example, the work of distinguished Harvard political scientist Samuel Huntington shows strong biases that result from his belief in the American patriotic schema. Huntington's paper, "American Ideals versus American Institutions," which appeared in the Spring 1982 *Political Science Quarterly,* is a good example.

In this article Huntington makes the ironic point that the pursuit of freedom and democracy in American domestic politics limits the nation's ability to pursue freedom and democracy abroad, and vice versa. To make this claim, Huntington must assert that the United States does indeed pursue freedom and democracy abroad. To this end, Huntington claims, for instance, that the U.S. intervention in Nicaragua in the 1920s which resulted in the Somoza dictatorship was pro-democratic, that U.S. intervention in post–World War II Greece promoted democracy, and that the destruction of democracy in Chile in the 1970s was due to a lack of U.S. intervention (pp. 26–29).

In Huntington's view, the United States is, by nature, the great promoter of freedom and democracy: "The nature of the United States has left it little or no choice but to stand out among nations as the proponent of liberty and democracy" (p. 31). Huntington's logic is surprisingly simple: because the United

States is the pinnacle of freedom and democracy, U.S. involvement in the world promotes freedom and democracy.

The United States is, in practice, the freest, most liberal, most democratic country in the world with far better institutionalized protections for the rights of its citizens than any other society. As a consequence, any increase in the power or influence of the United States in world affairs generally results—not inevitably, but far more often than not—in the promotion of liberty and human rights in the world. The expansion of American power is not synonymous with the expansion of liberty, but a significant correlation exists between the rise and fall of American power in the world and the rise and fall of liberty and democracy in the world. [pp. 25–26]

One wonders what Huntington's correlation coefficient is, and at what level it is significant. One also wonders how, as a political scientist, Huntington went about measuring liberty. Did he, in order to arrive at his firm and confident conclusions, get a series of reliable readings from a "freedometer," which he strategically placed in a variety of countries around the world? According to his findings, just how much more free and democratic was the United States than, say, Switzerland?

In reality, of course, no such scientific determinations can be made, and such statements serve only to indicate and perpetuate ideological bias. It was that bias—Huntington's conviction that the United States, freedom, and democracy are inextricably bound—that led him to characterize U.S. intervention in 1920s Nicaragua, 1940s Greece, and 1960s Chile as pro-democratic.

CONCLUSION

The American patriotic schema is an important, stable, and lasting element of American political culture. It has been taught, learned, re-taught, and re-learned over the years, through both conscious and unconscious socialization processes. In the years since World War II, it was often bolstered through its appearances in American culture as part of the cold war schema. The products of a culture duplicate its prevailing beliefs and values, and the cold war was very much a part of American culture. Cold war beliefs were expressed in popular entertainment, political rhetoric, and social scientific scholarship—in all areas of American culture where they had relevance. Cold war beliefs and biases were perpetuated as they pervaded American culture, being simultaneously reinforced in a variety of realms. Fiction was created and reality interpreted in familiar cold war terms. This reinforced the cultural prominence of both the American patriotic schema and the cold war schema, as the real and fictional merged into one patriotic truth.

5

Central American Elections on Network News: Cases of Cold War Framing

Salvadorans are caught in the middle of all this. In some places, the rebels are threatening to kill them if they do vote; in others, the army is threatening to kill them if they don't.

— Correspondent Gary Shepard (CBS News, March 23, 1982)

The Salvadoran people's stunning personal commitment to the power of the democratic vision is an unanswerable repudiation of the advocates of force and violence.

— Secretary of State Haig (ABC News, March 29, 1982)

Dan, the election appears to have been a tremendous success. Unofficial estimates put the voter turnout at about one million, which means more than seventy percent of this country's eligible voters went to the polls. It amounted to a clear repudiation of the extreme left, the insurgents. . . .

— Gary Shepard (CBS News, March 29, 1982)

Many analysts see these election results as a crystal-clear rebuff of the rebels by the Salvadoran people.

— Dan Rather (CBS News, March 29, 1982)

The Salvadoran election of March 28, 1982 was a complex event with ambiguous results. Yet American television journalists followed the official American line and presented the election results as a clear and simple cold war victory for U.S.-supported democracy over antidemocratic communists. Why was this complex foreign event so easily framed by the cold war schema in the news?

This chapter demonstrates the way in which the cold war schema often framed foreign news, perpetuating itself as it molded foreign realities in its own image. What follows is a comparative case study of American network television news coverage of two Central American elections, the March 28, 1982 election in El Salvador and the November 4, 1984 election in Nicaragua. Following the Reagan administration's lead, the networks framed both in terms of the cold war schema. The heavily covered "victory for democracy" in El Salvador reinforced the belief that U.S.-supported democracy was holding off the threat of oppressive communism there. The sparsely covered election of "questionable legitimacy" in Nicaragua was dwarfed by subsequent reports that the Soviets were sending fighter jets to Nicaragua. This manufactured cold war crisis left an impression of Nicaragua as a Soviet-supported threat to American security.

Coverage of these two elections reaffirmed the perception that the United States was on the side of freedom and democracy and against Soviet-supported communist oppression. For El Salvador, Nicaragua, and U.S. policy toward these two nations to be framed as they were by the cold war schema, the biased exclusion of schema-inconsistent information was necessary. The domination of Central American news by the cold war schema created an information environment that confirmed the schema and distinguished between the American-supported good guys and the leftist bad guys in Central America. Both effects help maintain public acquiescence to and support for U.S. foreign policy, in both Central America and elsewhere.

The journalistic practice of using official sources to obtain authoritative interpretations of foreign events put the Reagan administration in the position to promote application of the cold war schema to Central American elections. Even in the case of a heavily covered story such as the Salvadoran election, the networks did not have or take the time to provide important contextual information. Instead, culturally familiar schemata were used to frame news and fill in information gaps. The officially promoted cold war schema was an ideal framework through which complex foreign events could be simply structured in a manner that was compelling and comprehensible to an ignorant public. Its use as the framework for network news presentations of these two elections reinforced the schema's prominence, both generally and in its application to Central America.

CULTURAL SCHEMATA AND TELEVISION NEWS

There are a number of reasons why relatively simple, culturally accepted schemata frame network television news renditions of foreign and international affairs. Simple, recognizable schemata are needed to make short, information-poor news reports comprehensible and compelling to the consuming public. In presenting events to a broad public united by a common culture, journalists can successfully communicate with the largest possible audience if they frame the events according to schemata that are common and well known in the society. In addition, reporters tend to use those same schemata in their own information processing; they perceive events through culturally derived schemata and communicate those perceptions to others in news reports.

Network news reports tend to be information-poor and short because of limited air time and the assumption that viewers have short attention spans. Faced with the impossible task of presenting the world's news each night in about 23 minutes, the makers of network news are forced to present brief, disjointed, scattered glimpses of complex realities. Numerous different reports on a wide variety of issues compete for that limited time, multiplying constraints and creating a need for quick, compelling, and comprehensive communication.

The journalist can fill this need through the use of simple, cultural schemata. By symbolizing and structuring reports according to familiar, recognizable schemata, reporters can leave out information that will be filled in by viewers using the correct schemata. In this way journalists can accomplish their communication goal: to present a specific, limited body of information in an interesting and comprehensible format, given constraints on message length.

The journalist will be successful only if the intended schema is used by the news viewer. For this reason it is important that the schema used in reporting is a conventional, culturally prevalent one, and preferably one that is repeatedly used in news reports and public discussions of a certain class of issues or events. The journalist, usually a product of American culture herself, is likely to have a good sense of which schemata to use.

The practice of moving journalists who cover foreign news from place to place makes reporters more likely to frame complex international realities in terms of simple American schemata. First, journalists are not permitted to "go native," to start conceiving events through indigenous schemata that the home viewers would not comprehend. Second, they are less likely to become excessively knowledgeable of the events and contexts on which they report, and so remain themselves dependent on their own culturally based schemata in the absence of sufficient information.

Even a journalist who might herself utilize some exotic or overly sophisticated schema in processing a news event is likely to search out the proper storyline that will make a short, information-poor report comprehensible and interesting to the non-exotic, unsophisticated viewer. Ready-made storylines—stock scripts that are well known and routinely used in the presentation of particularly common sorts of newsworthy events—are well known in the journalism profession and are repeatedly called upon. Such behavior is habit-forming, and seasoned reporters, in observing events, may personally come to frame them according to the stock storylines in terms of which news reports are framed. In the absence of a stock storyline, it is the job of the journalist to find a cultural schema that will be effective in presenting a given event sequence. Those schemata are often suggested by government officials, or other interested elites, in attempts to frame situations to their own advantage.

Schematic framing also tends to limit and define what events and entities are presented in the news, and it does so in a way consistent with cultural and political forces. Events that are not significant in terms of culturally prevalent schemata and are not promoted by elites will not be considered newsworthy and will not appear on the evening news. Thus cultural schemata play an important role in the agenda-setting process.

"Schema-setting" occurs for ongoing and related stories, in that dominant schemata tend to develop and be used by the pack of journalists covering such stories. Politicians often try, and succeed, to determine or influence schema-setting. By framing and symbolizing issues, events, and actors in certain ways, political elites can influence which schemata are cued and used in public discussion and news reporting. The White House and State Department, for instance, can promote a particular definition for a foreign event through both rhetoric and action. These bodies serve as sources for and significant actors in many politically relevant foreign news items. Because of these central roles, they are able to exert substantial influence over which schemata are applied in what ways to which events. Ongoing success at schema-setting is crucial to the accomplishment of relevant political goals.

Thus the specific schema used in a foreign news report is determined by the interplay of political and cultural forces. Political elites promote the use of politically advantageous schemata in the news and the culture generally. Journalists seek and use simple, consistent, culturally prevalent schemata in framing news reports. Politicians, journalists, and news viewers share a common set of cultural schemata. Together, these forces serve to set certain politically advantageous, culturally accepted schemata as frames for news reports. An example of this is described in the comparative case study that follows.

The task of the news viewer is to catch schematic cues and utilize the proper schemata in order to fill in the gaps in the news report with the elements of the schema that make the report meaningful. The combination of novelty (event) and familiarity (schema) makes for interest, while the combination of information (event) and cognitive structure (schema) makes for meaningful knowledge that is instantly understood. The viewer is attentive because the news is appealing and comprehensible and provides a relieving sense of order and connectedness. The viewer thus may gain a comforting and compelling sense of fast-paced, meaningful learning, and a sense that he or she knows and understands what is going on in the world.

The conceptual categories that are used predominantly—and to the relative exclusion of others—in the news report are those relevant to the schemata used in framing it. This provides economy of message length and facilitates the schema-cuing process for the news viewer. The viewer hears a particular set of concepts being used in the news report, associates them with the proper schemata, and uses those schemata to organize what is heard into a meaningful message.

Viewers who are repeatedly exposed to schematically framed news reports learn to use those same schemata to frame issues and events themselves. Thus we have a dynamic, integrated cultural system playing itself out in the news. Schemata are chosen for news reports based on their cultural prominence, yet schemata also become prominent as a result of their use in news reports. Politicians attempt to influence which schemata will frame news reports, yet they themselves process information through cultural schemata obtained through processes like those working on the news viewer. At least where television news on politically relevant foreign events is concerned, this system is information-poor and schema-dominated, and the schemata that dominate tend to be highly influenced by political forces.

Culturally dominant schemata serve to simply and comfortably organize cognition. Elements of dominant schemata fill in for missing information. Cognitive slots that might have been filled with information about actual events and entities are, instead, filled in with default options provided in the schema. This satiates minds and thus inhibits further information search-and-gathering activities on the part of journalists and their viewers. Schematic stereotypes are a satisfying substitute for knowledge, as a feeling of knowing accompanies relative ignorance. The domination of culturally prevalent and politically advantageous schemata thus excludes information that may hold the potential for cuing alternative, perhaps more appropriate, schemata.

FOREIGN CONFLICT AND THE COLD WAR SCHEMA

Human conflicts are as complex as they are troubling; extensive knowledge and extreme compassion are required to understand and evaluate conflicts in ways that do not rely on stereotyping and biased side-taking. For example, some knowledge and understanding of Salvadoran history and the complex social, economic, and political problems that have plagued that nation is necessary to a relatively accurate conception of the situation in El Salvador. U.S. involvement must be understood within the context of an equally complex set of policy considerations and nuances.

Because of the nature of network television news, however, adequate explanation and context are not provided to the viewer. While dramatic events and dynamic conflicts are often shown on television news, the static conditions that may have precipitated them receive secondary and fleeting mention. Deep background on complex political, economic, and social issues is difficult or impossible to portray in brief visual reports (Epstein, 1973; Graber, 1980). In addition, as Graber adds, "most reporters are ill-equipped to understand, let alone describe" complex social problems (p. 259). From the reporter's (Marvin Kalb) perspective, "It has to do with synthesizing a mass of very complicated material, and you almost know there is a kind of censorship process that takes place. . . . They don't really want a talking head to describe nuances of policy, because there are no pictures of nuances" (Kalb, Koppel, & Scali, 1982, pp. 44–45). Even if there was the time and ability to present important contextual information, such material is of a form that is assumed to lack audience appeal, and so tends not to be presented on the evening news programs.

Lack of a factual context for conflict creates the need for a schematic context. Generally, the reporting of conflict involves reducing complexity and narrowing the picture to a simple, familiar, dichotomous struggle (Epstein, 1973). According to Arno (1984), "the necessity of being intelligible to his audience" forces the reporter to frame conflicts in terms of culturally based storylines (p. 9). The ideal schema for conflict news, then, is simple, clear, dichotomous, and culturally familiar. The cold war schema fits this bill.

Using the cold war schema to frame foreign news reports has had a number of advantages in terms of attracting American viewers. It is well known culturally, and has been heavily used by American politicians. It defines and explains conflict in a clear and dichotomous way, and allows for the illusion of understanding devoid of historical, social, economic, or political detail.

Through the cold war schema, foreign conflict becomes relevant to the United States, and so of interest to Americans. Because viewers tend to be strongly on the side of the United States, freedom, and democracy, and against communism and oppression, the cold war schema allows them to take sides and, thus, to take an interest. Like a football game, a police show, or a Sylvester Stallone movie, news of foreign conflicts can be entertaining if the audience is given a simple, black-and-white basis for taking sides.

THE SALVADORAN AND NICARAGUAN ELECTIONS

The March 28, 1982 Salvadoran election and the November 4, 1984 election in Nicaragua were two important and complicated events worthy of interpretation and comparison. Both were initial attempts by Central American governments to achieve the benefits of democratic legitimacy by holding elections through reasonably conventional procedures. Armed insurgencies opposed both elections, and both took place within a context of fear and violence and without the participation of important political forces in the respective countries. Both armed insurgencies disrupted some voting, and the Nicaraguan Contras attacked two polling places (Cornelius et al., 1985, p. 24). Voter turnouts were relatively high for both elections, in the neighborhood of 70% of the voting-age populations (Spence, 1985, p. 85).

There were also important differences between the two elections. In El Salvador, the Christian Democratic and Arena parties competed for seats while the left was excluded; in Nicaragua, the Sandinista party easily dominated the voting, while Arturo Cruz and his Coordinadora coalition refused to participate (Cornelius et al., 1985). In Nicaragua voting was voluntary and entirely secret, but Salvadorans were required by law to vote, and transparent ballot boxes were used. While *La Prensa* served as an opposition press in Nicaragua, there was no such equivalent in El Salvador.

The most significant differences between the two elections consisted of the roles the United States played in them and the efforts the Reagan administration made to promote contrasting interpretations of the elections. The administration applied the cold war schema to both countries. In El Salvador, the Reagan administration was trying to create an image of a democratic government needing U.S. support to defend its citizens against violent, Soviet-supported communist guerrillas. According to the administration's cold war interpretation of Nicaragua, the Nicaraguan government was an oppressive, Soviet-supported communist regime, being opposed by a U.S.-supported "democratic resistance" fighting for Nicaraguan freedom.

Just as "democratic" elections in El Salvador would serve to legitimize the administration's application of the cold war schema to El Salvador, "democratic" elections in Nicaragua threatened to refute the administration's use of the cold war schema in framing Nicaragua. For this reason, the administration orchestrated and publicized the election in El Salvador, and declared it to be a successful birth of democracy when it occurred. To these same ends, according to the report of the Latin American Studies Association delegation that observed the Nicaraguan election, "the Reagan Administration used a combination of diplomatic, economic, and military instruments in a systematic attempt to undermine the Nicaraguan election process and to destroy its credibility in the eyes of the world" (Cornelius et al., 1985, p. 38).

Interpretations of the two elections on television news and in the print media were consistent with administration interpretations (Spence, 1985; Herman, 1984). Administration officials and Salvadoran politicians were given ample time and space in the media to proclaim the 1982 election to be a victory for freedom and democracy over the violent left. In 1984, brief claims by Sandinista officials that the election was legitimate were surrounded by more extensive coverage of claims by the Reagan administration and by opposition leader Arturo Cruz that the election was not democratic.

The Salvadoran election was promoted by the Reagan administration and became a major news story. The Nicaraguan election was sabotaged and hidden by the Reagan administration and was almost ignored in the American media. The sparse coverage of the Nicaraguan election was immediately followed by heavy coverage of the unfounded U.S. claim that the Soviet Union was shipping fighter jets to Nicaragua. This reasserted the cold war schema for Nicaragua and all but erased the election from memory.

THE COLD WAR SCHEMA AND EL SALVADOR

Figure 5.1 shows the number of reports about El Salvador that appeared on the evening news programs of ABC, CBS, and NBC each month, from January 1980 to December 1982. During 1980, El Salvador was sparsely covered by the networks, appearing only when particularly notable acts of violence took place. Thus television news viewers learned of the March murder of Archbishop Romero and the December murder of four U.S. churchwomen, but they were left ignorant of the social and political context in which such violence was taking place.

FIGURE 5.1
Monthly Network News Reports on El Salvador (1980–1982)
Compiled from the Vanderbilt Television News Archives' *Television News Index and Abstracts.*

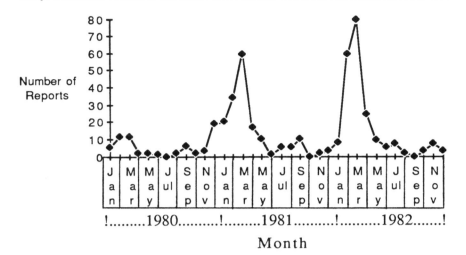

Upon entering the White House, the Reagan administration began dedicating resources to stopping revolution in El Salvador and overturning it in Nicaragua. This was accompanied by a campaign to promote an interpretation of Central American conflict in terms of the cold war schema.

The White House and State Department put El Salvador forcefully onto the network news agenda in early 1981 through cold war pronouncements and a White Paper, "Communist Interference in El Salvador." By publicizing arms links between the Salvadoran revolutionaries and the Soviets and Cubans through Nicaragua, the Reagan administration was casting the revolutionaries as oppressive communists. This set the stage for the framing of U.S. involvement as anticommunist support for freedom and democracy. As Bernard Gwertzman wrote in *The New York Times,* "When Secretary of State Alexander Haig . . . ordered an information blitz on Congress and the press, his purpose was to expose what he said was Soviet-bloc support for the leftist insurgents in El Salvador and to gain sympathy for further United States countermoves" (March 14, 1981, p. 1).

The United States actively supported the Salvadoran government. By identifying the revolutionaries as Soviet-backed communists, the Reagan administration placed both salient sides in the conflict into roles in the cold war schema, and made the schema appear to be an appropriate framework for understanding the situation. News reports tended to concentrate on U.S. aid for the Salvadoran government and communist support for the revolutionaries, rather than on the oppressive reign of the Salvadoran army. In this context, the cold war schema could fill in information gaps, making the Salvadoran government appear to be on the side of freedom and democracy. Instances of official repression, terror, and murder seemed to be anomalies that could either be ignored or explained by *individual* corruption, moral deprivation, or lack of proper training.

Lack of information concerning the Salvadoran government, the army, and their activities thus allowed a repressive dictatorship to be fit into the cold war schema on the side of freedom and democracy. Public inattention to and ignorance of the ongoing realities within El Salvador was the result of the extremely sparse coverage of El Salvador that preceded the media blitz of early 1981 (see Figure 5.1). Coverage previous to February 1981 had concentrated on selected violent crises. This had created a confusing image of strife with a cold war flavor, lacking in historical, social, political, or economic context. The general public ignorance that resulted from sparse coverage made the public particularly open to a familiar schema being applied to an unfamiliar situation, and so made the administration's promotional task easier.

Bennett (1983) articulated these connections among news coverage, popular ignorance, susceptibility to simple schemata, and political influence:

Events that unfold rapidly and dramatically are made to seem relevant because they are urgently reported; permanent but unchanging conditions become invisible and, for all practical purposes, irrelevant. Thus the decades of grinding poverty, exploitation, and oppression suffered by the people of El Salvador were scarcely reported by the American news media. Then, suddenly, there was guerrilla warfare, and the drama of revolution made the news. Why, the American people must have wondered, was there such a sudden explosion in El Salvador? Officials in San Salvador and Washington pronounced the trouble the result of communist infiltration from Nicaragua, Cuba and Russia—nations bent on importing revolution into peaceful, democratic countries. The credibility of such an absurd explanation depended in large part on the virtual absence of prior coverage of the decades of poverty, misery, and government terrorism that led to popular uprising. [p. 126]

In February and March of 1981, the administration was simultaneously placing El Salvador on the news agenda and promoting the culturally prominent cold war schema. Thus the administration created a need for a simple, familiar, salient schema to structure the new big agenda item and, at the same time, supplied the perfect schema for that purpose. The authoritative voice of the White House convinced members of the news media to go along with the application of the cold war schema to El Salvador, even when there was recognition of its distortions. According to Ike Seamans of NBC, "Anyone who'd been to Salvador as much as the people who normally cover it knew it was a pretty simplified view of the situation. But if the leader of the Western world makes a statement, it's policy almost. You've got to follow it up. . . . There's always a thing in your mind, 'Well, maybe there is something to it'" (Hallin, 1983, p. 5).

Much to the young Reagan administration's anguish, however, the cold war rhetoric for El Salvador led some in politics and the press to begin to associate and compare El Salvador with Vietnam (Hallin, 1983; *The New York Times,* March 14, 1981). President Reagan was later to complain of media interference with "the efforts we'd made in El Salvador, to try to convince the American people that what we're having is an infiltration into the Americas that is really directed by the other superpower. . . . There has been a kind of editorial slant that has something, almost, of the Vietnam syndrome, which challenges what we're doing there" (Weisman, 1982, p. 8). Increasingly vocalized concerns that Reagan was creating "another Vietnam" were politically dangerous to the new administration, and it was forced to retreat, ease El Salvador off the news agenda, and find another way to dramatize the battle between democracy and communism there.

SALVADORAN ELECTION COVERAGE

The Salvadoran election of March 28, 1982 served as an ideal vehicle for promoting the cold war schema in a context that did not lend itself readily to a Vietnam comparison. First, as long as the election appeared to be legitimate and supported by "the Salvadoran people," it clearly established the United States and the Salvadoran government (particularly the one to be elected) on the side of democracy. Second, the election provided a battleground on which the fight between democracy and communism could be clearly, if symbolically, fought. In the context of the cold war schema, opposition by leftist guerrillas to a fair and free election appeared to be an attempt by violent communists to suppress freedom and democracy. Framed by the cold war schema, the elections served to reinforce the schema and dispel doubts about its applicability to El Salvador.

The election was to be the showcase of democracy, and the administration made a concerted and successful effort to call it to the attention of the news media. Since a large proportion of Americans depend on network television news for their views of the world, the nature of the extensive network coverage of the elections was important to the administration's framing efforts. Like other American news organizations, the networks put El Salvador back into the spotlight for the elections (see Figure 5.1). According to Spence (1984), "The networks' nightly news featured the Sunday, March 28, elections from the Wednesday before through the Wednesday after with twenty-two stories averaging just under five minutes (out of twenty-two minutes per show). Election day and day after stories averaged over eight minutes, surpassing coverage of any recent foreign election" (p. 29).

This section consists of a case study of the March 29 ABC post-election segment. The purpose is to show how and why the cold war schema provided an overarching framework into which the election story was placed. ABC's March 29 coverage lasted a full nine minutes and consisted of contributions by five reporters. An initial report on the voter turnout was followed by one on the results and their political implications. This was followed by a report on the armed struggle and a description of events in Usulutan Province. The election was proclaimed a success, and speculations were made concerning prospects for the future. Finally, the Reagan administration's reactions to the election were reported from Washington. The CBS and NBC election segments for that night, though shorter (both ran about six minutes), were strikingly similar in structure and content to the ABC version.

Despite the serious problems and ambiguities associated with the election, it was clearly and enthusiastically presented on March 29 by ABC as the birth of democracy in El Salvador. This put the U.S.-supported Salvadoran government clearly on the side of freedom and democracy in the cold war schema. According to anchor Frank Reynolds, "one message has come through loud and clear" from the election. That message was, as Richard Threlkeld told us, "let's see if this thing called democracy really works." The viewers were not disappointed, as Threlkeld later proclaimed the election "the biggest and best election El Salvador has ever had, and apparently the most honest." Obviously impressed, Reynolds added that "this exercise in democracy there in El Salvador has been gratifying, even inspiring." As ABC news portrayed it, democracy, with all its meaning, was budding in a foreign land. American viewers needed few additional details; they were quite familiar with democracy (that is, they had schematic notions of its idealized U.S. version).

On ABC news, Salvadoran electoral politics began to fit relatively neatly into the American democratic process script which elaborates the American patriotic schema (see Chapter 2). Thus, according to Threlkeld, Roberto d'Aubuisson, of death squad fame, could "set about being the leader of the responsible opposition, now that the voters of a healthy fraction of Salvadorans have made him legitimate." The newly elected politicians would have to learn "all those democratic compromises known as politics as usual." Although most political scientists would be hard-pressed to describe "politics as usual," Threlkeld's viewers knew what he meant: politics American-style.

The criterion used to determine who won the battle between U.S.-supported "democracy" and the oppressive "leftist guerrillas" was a clear and simple one: voter turnout. Since the army and government were trying to get people to vote while the revolutionaries were trying to get them not to, voter turnout appeared to be the logical measure of victory in this battle for democracy.

Thus the voting was interpreted by the networks as a popular "referendum" in which Salvadorans chose between democracy and the extreme left that opposed it. As Threlkeld told it, the "guerrillas" tried "not to participate in the election, tried very hard to stop it, and find out that what appears to be a record turnout of voters transpired, and they have to be looking to see how much support they have now really. This has been a kind of electoral referendum on their support."

The rebels had lost, democracy had won. As Threlkeld described it, "They climbed the wall, they walked for miles, they stood for hours in the hot sun, they braved the bombs and the bullets just to vote." The image was one of brave citizens, driven by a commitment to democracy, defying threats of death by violent communists and flocking to the polls.

On February 26, one month before the election, Threlkeld had painted a dismal picture of the election, and of the sorts of calculations that Salvadorans would have to make when deciding whether or not to vote.

Threlkeld: The great mass of Salvadorans who live in misery in the villages or the barrios would just as soon sit this election out—like the unemployed waiter, we'll call him Louis, they're afraid to vote, and afraid not to.

Louis: If you didn't go to vote you will have problems, maybe you will be killed or something like that.

Threlkeld: Will you be killed maybe if you do vote?

Louis: Aha, maybe also because if you go to the elections, walking on the street you can have a bullet in your body.

Fear and intimidation, the message was, would motivate decisions concerning voter participation. Army rule by intimidation, terror, and murder continued through election day. Citizens were required by law to vote, and identification cards—which had to be carried at all times—were stamped upon voting. Salvadoran Defense Minister General Jose Guillermo Gacias proclaimed a week before the election that not voting would be "an act of treason" (Spence, 1984, p. 42). Given these facts and considerations, a high voter turnout is reasonably interpreted as an indication of the relative power of army intimidation as compared to that of the rebels. In this context, it would be difficult to interpret a high voter turnout as a victory for freedom and democracy.

Yet this is exactly what the networks did (free of this context). On March 26, Charles Krause of CBS made a remarkable, yet accurate prediction. "Whether as a result of conviction or intimidation, those who go to the polls will be judged pro-government and those who don't, pro-left." Krause was saying that it did not matter to those who were interpreting the turnout what the actual motives of those voting were; voters would be interpreted as choosing sides, regardless of the intent of their behaviors.

An enthusiastic Threlkeld summed it up at one point: "The voters came in droves and proved that, given a free chance, they'd do the right thing." Freedom and democracy together triumphed. Good, acculturated American news viewers knew what Threlkeld meant by "do the right thing"—what they did not know was how dubious that "free chance" was. One wonders if Threlkeld had forgotten his friend "Louis."

Why did experienced journalists like Threlkeld (or Gary Shepard of CBS), who knew of coercive efforts by the army to get out the vote, report the event as if citizens were freely flocking to the polls, like salmon struggling upstream to spawn, expressing their basic human instinct for democracy?

One explanation is based on the professional objectives of television journalists. Despite the confusing and complicating factors that set the meaning of the election in doubt, journalists were faced with the difficult task of making the outcome of the election interesting, compelling, and comprehensible to the distracted viewer. Oversimplification, information exclusion, and assumption of the democratic process script from American culture made it possible for reporters to describe a Salvadoran election in terms that American television news viewers could relate to.

Regardless of doubts cast in the preelection coverage, the actual voting and its results were the climax of a major, ongoing network news story, and so were treated as such. Reporters might have said that the voter turnout was required by law and was as much a measure of army intimidation as anything else. They might have said that it is hard to call votes in the midst of a civil war a "mandate." They might have said that it was difficult to determine fraud or the accuracy of figures on election eve in El Salvador and that it was not clear that the army would relinquish much power to an elected body. To do so, however, would have been to destroy the climax, to present a confusing, uninspiring, unappealing, and uninteresting portrayal of the high moment of a major story. It would have been to present an ostensibly important event as unimportant.

In fact, in their attempt to pump upbeat clarity into a confusing, indecisive reality, the ABC team mistakenly claimed that Duarte's Christian Democrats had "won" the election, and divined meaning into that "victory" (neither CBS nor NBC was guilty of this error). According to Jack Smith, "This was clearly a vote against the extremes of both sides, and the violence they have inflicted against this country." The message was that democracy had clearly spoken and moderation had won the day. The ongoing saga of Salvador's bid for democracy had a happy ending.

The fact that the election occurred during a civil war was not used to evaluate the democratic legitimacy of the election. Rather, the armed struggle was used to further symbolize a democratic victory in the cold war. In the absence of background knowledge on the history and objectives of the rebels, they were portrayed on the ABC stage as antidemocratic leftists. Hillary Brown began her description of the hot mini-cold war with, "Since January the guerrillas have been saying they would stop the elections—they did not, and this is the price they paid for it." A truckload of bodies was shown, implying that just punishment had come to those who attempted to stop democracy by force.

Fighting was not particularly intense leading into the election, and on election day civilian deaths were not higher than average (Spence, 1983). Still, the rebels had objected to an election that they could not safely participate in, and this led American journalists to interpret fighting as leftist attempts to suppress democracy by disrupting the election (Spence, 1984). News reports on battles became reports on battles over democracy.

Another more important factor contributing to the cold war interpretation of the election was the use of official sources in news reporting (Sigal, 1973; Gans, 1979; Fishman, 1980); the sources included leaders of the Christian Democratic and Arena parties, and U.S. embassy and State Department officials. In their

March 29 segments, all three networks allowed Duarte's deputy, Julio Rey Prendes, to speak. CBS and NBC gave U.S. Ambassador Dean Hinton a chance to speak, while ABC presented the embassy's perspective. Secretary of State Haig spoke on both ABC and NBC, and Dan Rather quoted him for CBS. All these official sources had it in their interests to promote the interpretation that the election was not only democratic, but a victory for the side of democracy in a cold war battle. That is what they did.

For ABC, Jack Smith allowed Rey Prendes to give his interpretation of the outcome: "In every ballot places [sic], crowds that we have never seen before in the history of this country. The people in the first place went to vote against violence, went to vote against the extreme left." This explanation was accepted, and no alternative was suggested.

Barry Dunsmore gave Secretary of State Haig his chance to speak: "The Salvadoran people's stunning personal commitment to the power of the democratic vision is an unanswerable repudiation of the advocates of force and violence." This repudiation theme was echoed by network reporters.[1]

Dunsmore closed ABC's election segment with Haig's cold war interpretation of the continued conflict in El Salvador: "But having proclaimed the guerrillas' political and military defeat, Haig pointedly noted that the civil war goes on, due to external support. And so Cuban and Nicaraguan involvement in El Salvador continue to be a Washington preoccupation."

The networks, as professional journalists often do, turned to official sources for the simple, authoritative interpretations they needed to frame a major news story in a manner that was compelling and comprehensible to their American viewing public. Thus they enthusiastically proclaimed the Salvadoran election a clear cold war victory for democracy. Reporters may not have needed much coaxing to do so. As Americans, they were used to using the cold war schema in interpreting and reporting on foreign conflicts, and they were used to interpreting and reporting on elections in terms of the generic democratic election script. In this case, they presented a complex and ambiguous event to an ignorant public in a manner that clearly and simply portrayed it as a cold war victory for U.S.-supported democracy over the threat of oppressive communism.

NICARAGUAN ELECTION COVERAGE

The contrast between coverage of the 1982 Salvadoran and 1984 Nicaraguan elections is as stark as it is instructive. The Salvadoran election appeared as a heavily covered "victory for democracy," the Nicaraguan election appeared as an almost uncovered election of "questionable legitimacy," and each appeared as the U.S. government wanted it to (Spence, 1985; Herman, 1984).

In contrast to the extensive pre-election coverage in El Salvador, there was no buildup for Nicaragua's November 4, 1984 election. Nicaragua was simply not an agenda item for the networks, which were concentrating on the American election at home. ABC did not report on the Nicaraguan election the day before it happened, while CBS and NBC provided two-minutes of coverage each. The CBS report questioned the election's legitimacy and mentioned U.S. criticisms of it, while NBC reported on criticism of the election by opposition leaders.

On election day, ABC and CBS spent two minutes each reporting on the election. Both showed opposition leader Arturo Cruz criticizing the election. For ABC, Sam Donaldson began by mentioning the high voter turnout. Unlike in El Salvador, however, this did not become the basis for enthusiastic celebration about democracy's victory in Nicaragua. Instead, the election's democratic legitimacy was seriously questioned. First, President Reagan was quoted denouncing the election. Then Sandinista leader Sergio Ramirez was allowed to claim that the election had endowed Nicaragua with democratic legitimacy. Cruz was given the chance to disagree. The opposition's perspective was discussed. Another opposition leader, Enrique Bolanos, was shown claiming that people had voted out of fear of reprisal. This claim, unsubstantiated in the Nicaragua case (see Cornelius et al., 1985, pp. 34–36), would have been entirely appropriate with reference to the Salvadoran election.

The day after the election, ABC added a two-minute report in which Peter Jennings recounted the U.S. State Department's interpretation of the election. Cruz was again given the chance to dismiss the election as illegitimate, and President Ortega's view of the election outcome was mentioned. On the following day, NBC and CBS informed the American people of U.S. intelligence reports indicating that the Soviets were shipping fighter jets to Nicaragua.

Was the "Mig scare" a clever scheme by which the Reagan administration was able to drown the Nicaraguan elections in cold war panic, or was it dumb luck? Regardless of the answer to this question, this whole episode demonstrates the administration's strong effect on the foreign and international news agenda, and on interpretations attached to foreign and international events (real and fictional) in the news. In the days that followed, all three networks devoted substantial news time to the Mig scare. ABC spent four minutes or more covering the scare on November 7, 8, and 9. By November 9, the networks duly reported administration admissions that Soviet fighter jets bound for Nicaragua did not exist.

Although only a few days elapsed between the initial scare and its resolution, this was enough time to divert attention from the Nicaraguan election and refocus it on military connections between Nicaragua and the Soviet Union. Thus Nicaragua was returned to its proper place in the cold war schema. Even after it was clear that the planes were fictional, the networks continued for a number of days to report on Soviet arms shipments to Nicaragua. News also included U.S. concerns about Nicaragua's military capability due to Soviet aid, as well as U.S. naval exercises which sparked Nicaraguan fears of a U.S. invasion. Nicaragua, solidly in the context of the cold war schema, was suddenly a major agenda item. The sparsely covered election was no competition for the salient, heavily covered cold war "crisis" and its aftermath.

CONCLUSION

The extreme contrast between coverage of the March 28, 1982 Salvadoran election and that of the November 4, 1984 Nicaraguan election forcefully demonstrates the effects of official promotion of the cold war schema on U.S. foreign news coverage. The Reagan administration highlighted the Salvadoran election and downplayed the Nicaraguan election, interpreting the first as a cold war victory and drowning the second with a cold war scare. The "birth of democracy" in El Salvador was a major news story, while the Nicaraguan election was all but ignored, presented as an insignificant attempt to appear democratic. Thus news coverage of these two elections helped to confirm the cold war schema and guard against its refutation. Journalists, whether they liked it or not, helped the administration to promote the cold war schema and its application to Central America.

While coverage of the 1982 Salvadoran election left the impression of a U.S.-supported democracy winning the battle against the violent left, coverage of the 1984 Nicaraguan election and the Mig scare left the impression of a Soviet-supported armed camp threatening the United States. Both impressions are structured by the cold war schema in the manner prescribed by the U.S. government. Thus Secretary of State Shultz could feel confident in his speech of April 22, 1985:

Our goals in Central America are clear: we seek peace, security, economic progress, and the growth of freedom and democracy in every country . . . the transition to democracy is succeeding everywhere in Central America—everywhere, that is, except Nicaragua, where a small group of Marxist–Leninists who call themselves "Sandinistas," backed by the Soviet Union and Cuba, are in the process of imposing a brutal tyranny. . . . With Soviet and Cuban help, the Sandinistas are still working to consolidate their power and turn Nicaragua into a full-fledged communist state . . . the first casualty of a communist consolidation in Nicaragua would be the freedom and hopes for democracy of the Nicaraguan people. . . . And the results of our failure to stop the spread of communism in this hemisphere will be clear for all to see, in the millions of refugees who will escape to freedom from tyranny, just as others have before them—from Eastern Europe and Afghanistan, from Cuba and Indochina. . . . The Congress will vote tomorrow on funds for the Nicaraguan democratic resistance. . . . How can we say to those Salvadorans who stood so bravely in line to vote: "We may give you some economic and military aid for self-defense, but we will also give a free hand to the Sandinistas to undermine your new democratic institutions"? . . . Tomorrow, Congress will choose whether to support the President in his determination to stop Soviet encroachment right here in this hemisphere. If Congress fails this test, the message will go worldwide—to freedom fighters in Afghanistan, Southeast Asia, Africa, and elsewhere where the spark of freedom still glows. . . . We in this country must stand firmly in the defense of our interests and principles and the rights of peoples to live in freedom. Nicaragua's democrats deserve our support. [Shultz, 1985]

In 1990 another election was held in Nicaragua, but this time the Sandinistas lost. From the mainstream American perspective, this was the birth of democracy in Nicaragua, its first "free" election. Few Americans remembered the 1984 election, and fewer still saw it as anything but a Soviet-style sham. According to the cold war schema, the election of "communists" cannot constitute democracy, as communism and democracy are mutually exclusive. The 1990 election in Nicaragua, like the 1982 election in El Salvador, was a cold war victory: The election became democratic as the "communists" lost. From the cold war perspective, the picture was clear: with America's help, democracy beat communism in Central America, just as it did in Eastern Europe.

NOTE

1. ABC was not the only network to echo Haig. This chapter opens with a series of quotes that demonstrate the conversion of Gary Shepard and Dan Rather of CBS to the Haig line.

PART II

COGNITIVE EFFECTS
OF THE COLD WAR SCHEMA

6

Common Meanings
for Cold War Concepts

Interviewer: How about the word "democracy," what does that mean?

Judith: Democracy . . . oh. Well, democracy is really a kind of—well, what the people have—well, I can't explain it!

I: Say the words that come to your mind.

J: Well, democracy is sort of what the people should have . . . well, you should have democracy and be . . . well, it's like . . . uh!

I: You're not exactly sure what it is?

J: I'm not exactly sure but in a way I am—it's what the people should have, they should have democracy, like be a good citizen, or something like that—I can't explain it.

I: Uh huh—it's something good at any rate.

J: Yes.

I: You're not completely sure about the details.

J: No, I'm not.

I: Did I ask you what sorts of things you thought of when you heard the word "communism"?

J: Communism? No, you didn't.

I: What does it mean to you offhand?

J: Well, communism is sort of—it's a different way of people: well, sort of like . . . to me it's *bad*. I can't explain it, just like democracy—it's sort of the opposite.

(Greenstein, 1969, pp. 25–26)

Judith was ten years old during this 1957 interview. At that time, she knew very little about democracy and communism, but she knew they were opposites, and that democracy was good and communism bad. Later in life, she no doubt accumulated a more sophisticated body of knowledge about democracy and communism, a body of knowledge that most likely serves to bolster and explain the basic black-and-white structure she acquired early in life. Our knowledge tends to be consistent with our simple attitudes and stereotypes, not only because we seek out information that reinforces our preconceptions, but also because our knowledge and stereotypes are acquired within a cultural system that tends to enforce their consistency. It may be that the adult Judith believes that her attitudes about democracy and communism derive from her knowledge. It may be that her views did change as she gained sophistication. Still, the basic preconceptions that each of us learned early in life remain within our psyches, framing our realities even when we would rather they did not. Because Americans learn their political preconceptions within a common cultural context, there is a tendency for certain preconceptions to become pervasive among the population.

These preconceptions affect how Americans tend to interpret and respond to political stimuli. If the adult Judith can be convinced that a policy serves to promote democracy or counter the threat of communism, then she is likely to support that policy. She also may find counter-attitudinal events, such as communists being elected through democratic processes, to be incomprehensible contradictions. This makes Judith susceptible to the sorts of cold war interpretations used to justify U.S. interventions in Guatemala, Vietnam, Chile, El Salvador, and Nicaragua.

In Chapter 2 it was argued that cultural schemata are held in the memories of members of society and perpetuated when they structure individual or collective information processing or behavior. Chapter 3 discussed the persistence of the cold war schema in America, as evidenced by official interpretations and public opinion. Chapter 4 provided examples of cold war culture in America. The use of the cold war schema in framing news was demonstrated in Chapter 5. Thus far it has been shown that elements of the cold war schema have been used by politicians, entertainers, scholars, journalists, and the public as they play their particular social roles. It has not, however, been directly shown that the cold war schema is actually stored in American minds. This chapter and the next take on that task.

When individuals think about a given word or phrase, they do not recite a dictionary definition to themselves. The functional meaning of a word is a set of associations that the word carries with it into an individual's mind. A stimulus word will elicit an array of associated images, feelings, other words, and so forth. While there is variation across contexts and individuals, some associations are sufficiently strong and pervasive within a culture that they occur repeatedly for a given word. These associations comprise the common meaning that is actually experienced by mainstream members of the culture.

The free-association study presented in this chapter is designed to find culturally common meanings of the following seven words and phrases: the United

States, freedom, democracy, the Soviet Union, communism, capitalism, and dictatorship. These seven words were chosen because they were the elements of a hypothesized cold war schema that differs somewhat from the schema presented in Chapter 2. In the early stages of this research project, it was suspected that the cold war schema consisted of the United States, freedom, democracy, and capitalism, on the one side, opposed to the Soviet Union, communism, and dictatorship on the other.

This early, hypothesized cold war schema was based on theory, knowledge, observation, and guesswork: it was bound to profit from testing and refinement. This word-association study has allowed for the testing and refining of the hypothesized cold war schema and yields a more accurate and defensible conception of the schema. Capitalism and dictatorship were included in the list of words because it was hypothesized that they were important elements of the cold war schema. Findings, as we will see, tended to confirm five of the seven hypothesized schematic elements. Strong associations were found among the United States, freedom, and democracy, on the one side, and the Soviet Union, communism, and oppression, on the other.

Because neither capitalism nor dictatorship came to subjects' minds when they thought of the United States, freedom, democracy, the Soviet Union, or communism, these two concepts were dropped from the central formulation of the cold war schema.[1] Oppression was not included in the list of words because its importance to the schema was realized when the data were analyzed, not when the study was designed. Thus this free-association study did more than just reaffirm the obvious: it provided strong evidence for a reformulated notion of the cold war schema.

This study provides evidence that many of the cognitive links hypothesized in the cold war schema are indeed found in the memories of mainstream Americans: since subjects were given no cues to elicit specific associations, their own minds were the only possible sources of the associations they made. The study also provides a sense of what the elements of the cold war schema mean to Americans. By finding out what other words tend to be associated with elements of the cold war schema, we achieve a more elaborated understanding of how the world looks through schematic lenses. The cold war schema is strewn with meaning, as each word and phrase elicits a number of associations. This study provides a greater understanding of what that meaning is for Americans by identifying the most common associations elicited by elements of the cold war schema.

METHOD

Subjects were students in an introductory course in political science at the University of Washington. During the month of January 1987, 40 to 45 students began class on Tuesdays and Thursdays by spending between five and ten minutes responding to "the word for the day," one of the seven stimulus words. The order in which the words were presented to subjects was determined through a random process, and the delays of at least 48 hours between words served to minimize contamination across trials. In order to minimize effects of course content on responses, the study was conducted at the beginning of class and at the outset of the academic quarter.

Subjects were instructed to provide up to three 1-word responses to each of four word-association tasks. The four separate tasks were designed to tap visual, verbal, emotional, and semantic associations with each word or phrase. Thus the study was not biased in favor of any one association process. First, subjects were instructed to close their eyes for about 30 seconds, let images that they associated with the stimulus word appear in their minds, and then write down their first three images. This tapped visual associations. Next they were instructed to repeat the word to themselves in their minds, think of other words that they associated with it, and write down the first three words that came into their minds. This tapped verbal associations. Then they were instructed to think about the word and pay attention to how it made them feel. The three feelings they were instructed to write down showed the subjects' emotional associations. Finally, subjects were instructed to complete a sentence of the form "(stimulus word) is. . . ." The three responses to this task tapped semantic associations.

After the four weeks of word associations were over, each subject was asked to write a one-page essay on one of the stimulus words. The titles of the essays were of the form, "What (stimulus word) means to me." Excerpts from some of these essays are used below to enrich the discussion of the word-association findings.

The numbers of subjects giving particular responses to each stimulus word or phrase were counted. When responses were different forms of the same word or two words with essentially the same meaning they were considered as the same response. For instance, responses of "freedom," "liberty," and "free" were counted as the same. The response referred to below as "United States" included responses of "America" and "USA," the "Soviet Union" response included responses of "Russia" and "USSR," "communism" included "communist," and so on. Since the point of the study was to identify common conceptualizations, it was important to avoid hiding clearly common meaning behind slightly different expressions of it. On the other hand, liberal use of response categories would have organized the data around the conceptualizations of the researcher, not the subjects. For this reason, decisions concerning what responses would be considered equivalent were made conservatively according to the above-stated criteria, and based on agreement between the researcher and an assistant. So, for example, while "afraid" and "scared" were considered to be the same response, "threatened" was considered different.

For each stimulus, the percentage of subjects giving each response was calculated. Responses made by 30% or more of the subjects were considered to be frequent responses and are presented in Tables 6.1 through 6.7. It is likely that those who responded with a given word represent only a subset of the total number of subjects who actually associate that word with the stimulus. In addition, words with similar, but not essentially the same, meanings were counted as different responses, and this tended to keep the percentages giving any one response low. Given the open-ended nature of the tasks subjects engaged in, and given the conservative coding techniques, a response made by 30% or more of the subjects is reasonably impressive.[2]

The findings presented here are not intended to be a conclusive demonstration of the meanings these concepts have to Americans. They are, however, useful indicators of the types of things Americans, or at least the subjects of this study, think about when the United States, freedom, democracy, capitalism, the Soviet Union, communism, and dictatorship come to mind. For each stimulus word there was at least one response that was made by about two-thirds of the subjects. Given such impressive numbers, it is reasonable at least to conclude that these response words are central to the functional American definitions of the stimulus words.

FINDINGS AND DISCUSSION

Frequent responses to each stimulus word are presented and discussed below. In addition, illustrative passages from the essay task show how the associations operate in the structure of political thinking.

The United States

Words associated with the United States by 30% or more of the subjects are listed in Table 6.1. It is not surprising that "freedom" came to mind for 65% of the subjects. Americans have been taught—by political elites, journalists, educators, advertisers, entertainers, and artists—to make the U.S.–freedom association. Almost from birth, Americans learn that they live in the "land of the free," a nation that stands above the rest in its ability and willingness to grant personal freedom to its citizenry. According to the mythology, repressed people from around the world have come to the American shores in search of liberty. The Statue of Liberty stands beside Ellis Island to symbolize American freedom and to welcome new immigrants to it. Like American school children, immigrants who seek to become citizens learn that freedom is a uniquely American gift. For example, the *Federal Textbook on Citizenship* (*Our Constitution and Government*, by Seckler-Hudson), which serves as the main text for those seeking to pass the citizenship exam, has a clear and simple lesson: "The people of the United States are more free than in any other country. We are free to work and to play, to think and to talk. We are free to make plans to improve our lives and our families" (1973, p. 181)

The subjects in this study had been exposed throughout their lives to countless similar messages, and the result was a strong tendency to think "freedom" when they thought about their country. One student wrote:

TABLE 6.1
Words Associated with the United States by 30% or More of the Subjects

Freedom	65%
Flag	53%
Proud	40%
Democracy	38%
Powerful	35%
Reagan	33%

Primarily, to me, the United States means freedom. Freedom of choice, speech, religion, and freedom of the press. You may choose the religion of your choice without reservation. People may assemble and worship in whatever way they wish. Americans vote for their leaders and elect those whose views reflect those of the country's. It is the people of the United States that dictate the policies of the government. The politicians of this country are held accountable for their actions. If the people are unhappy about the state of the union, they may vote those people in who they feel would do a better job. U.S. citizens are free to speak to whomever about whatever they choose. They may organize and bond together to achieve common political goals without fear of reprisal. People are also free to pursue those things which they find pleasurable. They can raise their families wherever they choose to do so. . . . They are free to make choices about the occupation they desire. It is easy to receive grants to colleges if that college wants you. Freedom of choice is what the United States means to me.

Lerner (1957) wrote of this common view held by Americans about their nation:

The most elusive word in the political vocabulary, "freedom" is also one of the most important in the American consciousness. It is the first image the American invokes when he counts the blessings of his state. The inheritor of the English and French revolutions, as well as of his own, he has gazed so long into the pool of freedom that he has fallen half in love with his own reflection in it. [p. 181]

Because freedom implies the absence of being controlled, the strong cognitive link between the United States and freedom creates a tendency to overlook the role of power and control in America. Despite frustrating daily reminders that they are unable to study, work, or live wherever they choose, despite constant contact with the economic inequalities, power differentials, legal restrictions, and social pressures that restrict their freedoms, Americans maintain a strong sense of their own freedom. Ironically, the strong and pervasive belief in American freedom makes it difficult for Americans to recognize ways in which they are being controlled, and thus ultimately restricts their freedom.

The general view of the United States as the land of the free makes the suggestion that U.S. foreign policies are designed to spread freedom around the globe easy to accept. In the context of the cold war, such suggestions were made by countless American leaders. Because of the strong U.S.–freedom link, U.S. intervention is easily interpreted as liberation.

The American Flag is the principle iconic symbol of the United States, so one would expect a good proportion of the subjects to associate the United States with the flag. For 53% of the subjects, images of the flag came to mind as they thought about the United States. National pride was another common response to the United States. Forty percent of the subjects reported that thinking about the United States made them feel proud. Americans learn that the United States is a democracy, and that its democratic nature is part of what sets it apart. Democracy was associated with the United States by 38% of the subjects.

Thirty-five percent of the subjects responded to the United States with the word "powerful." Given the U.S. role as a superpower in world politics, this is not surprising. Finally, it is interesting, but not surprising, that a third of the subjects associated Ronald Reagan with the United States. Reagan had been president of the United States for the six years prior to January 1987 (when this study was administered to subjects in their late teens and very early twenties); thus Reagan had personified the United States for most of the subjects' politically attentive lives.

Freedom

Words associated with "freedom" by 30% or more of the subjects are listed in Table 6.2. The United States was the most frequent association with freedom, and two-thirds of the subjects responded in this way. Not only does the United States tend to bring freedom to mind, but freedom tends to bring the United States to mind. The visual images described by one subject portray not only the depth at which the U.S.–freedom association is felt, but also its cultural origins: "I see freedom as a bald eagle on the flame of the Statue of Liberty's torch. I see the American freedom as certain beer commercials."

TABLE 6.2
Words Associated with Freedom by 30% or More of the Subjects

United States	67%
Flag	45%
Happy	43%
Good	33%

The close association between freedom and the United States is further indicated by the fact that 45% of the subjects mentioned the iconic symbol of the United States, the flag, in response to freedom. This finding is particularly impressive in light of the fact that only 25% mentioned what might be expected to be the main iconic symbol of American freedom, the Statue of Liberty.

Subjects clearly felt positively toward freedom: 43% reported that it made them feel happy, and a third of the subjects associated freedom with "good." For 28%, freedom made them feel "lucky." Thus freedom is highly valued and highly associated with the United States, and this contributes to the degree to which the United States is valued and citizens feel pride in their country. It also creates a mind-set that is prone to supporting U.S. foreign policy, which, almost by definition, promotes freedom worldwide.

Democracy

Words associated with "democracy" by 30% or more of the subjects are listed in Table 6.3. The United States and freedom were each mentioned by two-thirds of the subjects. Most subjects, when they thought of democracy, thought of the United States and freedom, which are highly associated with each other. Americans are taught that democracy is the American way and is an important safeguard of the freedom that makes America great. Given this strong mutual link between democracy and the United States, American interventions appear to be, by definition, prodemocratic, even when democratic institutions are bypassed or destroyed in the process.

Since the electoral process is central to democracy, some association with elections would be expected, and 37% of the subjects associated democracy with "voting." The idea of democracy, Americans are taught, is that the people rule; 30% of the subjects associated democracy with "people." Finally, democracy, like freedom, is a highly valued state of affairs, and a third of the subjects associated it with "good."

The essays subjects wrote on democracy were particularly interesting, in that they often seemed to be essays on freedom in America. Some examples will illustrate this:

Democracy . . . means such things as freedom, equality, and opportunity. Freedom is a given right that all people in America have. It is not a given right in other countries, including Russia. We all have the right to choose things and do things as we wish.

Democracy gives the ultimate authority in political affairs to the people. Democracy means freedom, the freedom to do what you want to do within the bounds of the morality of social relations in my country. Democracy allows me to make my own decisions in life. Without democracy the world would be a different place. Taking into account the world powers of today, if the United States was not a democracy it would probably be ruled by a communist dictatorship; in which case I'd rather be dead.

In a truly free and democratic system, people will be allowed to think as they please and worship without governmental interference. The Bill of Rights insures these and other

TABLE 6.3
Words Associated with Democracy by 30% or More of the Subjects

United States	67%
Freedom	67%
Voting	37%
Good	33%
People	30%

freedoms, essential to any true democracy. . . . I believe that the Unites States is a truly blessed nation. With the right men as our representatives, we have the ability to be a country free from tyranny and truly mindful of the individual citizen. This is what democracy means to me.

I believe democracy, although not perfect, is taken for granted by many of us. We have the right to not go to Siberia when we break a law, we can choose our own occupations, where we would like to reside, when many in other countries do not share these choices. Democracy is the United States of America.

Such perceptions of freedom in democratic America tend to be vague, general, and either exaggerated or trivial. They tend to lack empirical reference and to rely heavily on the dogma taught in American schools and citizenship textbooks and taken for granted by most Americans. Unfounded, overblown, or meaningless comparisons with presumably unfree and undemocratic, and definitely un-American, countries are often made. For example, to the last subject, for whom "Democracy is the United States of America," democracy also means "the right to not go to Siberia when we break a law." No thought is given to where law breakers *are* sent in democratic America. To this subject, democracy means that Americans are free (presumably even in jail), and that Soviets are not.

As the above examples suggest, the most common bases for comparisons were stereotyped notions of the Soviet Union and communism. The Soviet Union and communism jointly served for years as the assumed aggressive threat against which U.S. foreign policy was presumably forced to respond. As these examples show, they often also served as the assumed oppressive alternatives to the United States, freedom, and democracy. Juxtaposed against stereotyped Soviet communism, the United States, not just U.S. foreign policy, looked great. General support for status quo America, as well as support for American involvement in world affairs, was promoted through this contrast.

Capitalism

Words associated with "capitalism" by 30% or more of the subjects are listed in Table 6.4. Seventy-nine percent of the subjects associated capitalism with money, the medium of exchange, and chief symbol of capitalist economics; 30%

TABLE 6.4
Words Associated with Capitalism by 30% or More of the Subjects

Money	79%
United States	60%
Freedom	47%
Business	30%

mentioned business. These responses reflect the subjects' perceptions of capitalism as an economic system.

Sixty percent of the subjects associated capitalism with the United States, and 47% mentioned freedom. Like democracy, capitalism is more than just a way of doing things, it is the American way of doing things, the path of "free enterprise." This perspective is expressed well in the writings of two subjects:

As good Americans we learn to pride ourselves on our capitalistic society. For centuries America has been regarded as the "land of opportunities." Immigrants come to this land with a dream of success and prosperity. In fact, there's no better place on earth to fulfill this dream than America, a nation which opens its arms to all who want to be free, a world power which controls a major portion of the world's resources, and a perfect model of capitalism.

In my mind, capitalism is closely associated with nationalism. When someone starts criticizing capitalism, I get this almost patriotic feeling and start getting defensive. It's almost as if someone was directly criticizing my country. Capitalism, in my mind, has been made into sort of a nationalistic symbol. . . . It has attained a status of one of those things that "sets America apart" and "makes America great." It is one of the great morally right things that Americans should protect at all costs (like freedom and liberty).

The Soviet Union

Words associated with "the Soviet Union" by 30% or more of the subjects are listed in Table 6.5. The Soviet Union, as the rival superpower, was the communist country that was most salient to Americans. It was pointed to as the prototypical communist country, and Soviet-supported communist expansionism was said to be the threat against which U.S. foreign policy must guard. In the American consciousness, the Soviet Union and communism were defined in terms of each other. Thus 70% of the subjects responded to "the Soviet Union" with the word "communism."

Given the Soviet Red Army, Red Square, and the red Soviet flag, one would expect the Soviet Union to have brought red to mind, and it did for 35% of the subjects. As they did to the United States, 35% of the subjects responded to the

TABLE 6.5
Words Associated with the Soviet Union by 30% or More of the Subjects

Communism	70%
Red	35%
Powerful	35%
Oppressive	30%

Soviet Union with the word "powerful." The two superpowers elicited the same response patterns in this regard, no doubt due to the immense power each had wielded since World War II. Finally, the Soviet Union tended to be viewed as an unfree, undemocratic, oppressive place, and 30% of the subjects mentioned oppression in response to the Soviet Union. One subject's essay incorporated a number of these themes:

When I imagine the Soviet Union I see a cold place, uninviting, boring, and repressed. A land of people who cannot speak out against the government and who are forced to live under a Marxist umbrella so that no other "Western" ideas rain down on them. I also feel threatened to a certain extent. Not by the people necessarily but just the fact that they're the "other" World Power and if we screw them over in any way it's inevitable that we're going to get the same medicine.

Communism

Words associated with "communism" by 30% or more of the subjects are listed in Table 6.6. It is not at all surprising that two-thirds of the subjects associated communism with the Soviet Union. The Soviet Union was the most salient communist country in American eyes, the prototype in terms of which communism was perceived and according to which communism was judged.

One student wrote, "I've noticed that every time that I say communism I automatically say Russia." Another subject noticed the same thing, and put communism into a cold war context that brought on patriotic feelings:

For some reason the first thing that comes to mind when I hear the word communism is war. Why I don't know but I see images of soldiers and missiles. In a way the word itself

TABLE 6.6
Words Associated with Communism by 30% or More of the Subjects

Soviet Union	67%
Red	30%

makes me feel more patriotic, makes me think of how great this country is. . . . One thing I just realized is that whenever someone says "communism" people (or at least I do) immediately think of Russia. Why is that? China is just as communist and many times larger than Russia. What about all the other communist countries in the world. Why is Russia so special?

When communism brings the Soviet Union to mind, governments or movements branded as communist do as well. The communist label tends to elicit stereotyped notions of Soviet oppression, which are often applied to perceived communists in the absence of actual knowledge of their aims or actions. Before the demise of the Soviet Union, the label also brought with it the assumption that "communists" were supported or controlled by the Soviet Union, that their success would be a Soviet cold war victory, and that they therefore were a threat to U.S. national security. From this perspective, hostile or repressive American acts against those believed to be communists were justified, since communists, by definition, sought a Soviet-style order and constituted a threat to the United States.

Thirty percent of the subjects saw red, the communist team color that was also associated with the Soviet Union, in response to communism. Twenty-seven percent of the subjects mentioned oppression (30% did in response to the Soviet Union), 24% responded that communism was a threat, and 24% said that it made them angry. One subject wrote:

My picture of communism is that of which I had been told of during the days of Hitler. With that strict control hanging over the people's head at all times. Not knowing if you'll live until the next day or not. I know that this seems exaggerated but it is what I was taught. That's a scary feeling.

This subject expressed the sort of frightening image of communist oppression that many Americans have come to know. It *is* a scary picture. For those who hold similar views of communism, an "anticommunist" U.S. foreign policy is both necessary and comforting.

Dictatorship

Words associated with "dictatorship" by 30% or more of the subjects are listed in Table 6.7. Sixty percent of the subjects associated dictatorship with Hitler, 42% associated it with power, 31% mentioned control, and 29% said it made them feel angry. Nazi Germany, not the Soviet Union, remained the prototypical dictatorship, and Hitler stood out as dictatorship's most salient symbol. Communism was mentioned by only 13% of the subjects, and Stalin (11%) and the Soviet Union (7%) were mentioned about as often as were Castro (13%) and Cuba (9%).

Contrary to expectations, neither communism nor the Soviet Union were strongly associated with dictatorship. It is likely that most subjects thought that the Soviet Union was a dictatorship, but it was not *the prototypical* dictatorship.

TABLE 6.7
Words Associated with Dictatorship by 30% or More of the Subjects

Hitler	60%
Power	42%
Control	31%

Communism entails dictatorship, but perhaps not vice versa. The strong semantic links between the Soviet Union and communism, and between the United States and freedom, indicate that the words in question are defined in terms of each other. Democracy and capitalism are defined in terms of the United States and freedom. Dictatorship is not defined in terms of communism or the Soviet Union, but it is defined in terms of Hitler, extreme terms indeed.

The United States and the Soviet Union

A comparison of responses to the two superpowers (see Table 6.8) provides a sense for common American preconceptions of the two major cold war participants.

Subjects clearly recognized both the United States and the Soviet Union as superpowers; "powerful" was a response of 35% of the subjects to each. Visual symbols (the American flag and the color red) were also frequently mentioned. While many subjects (40%) reported pride in response to the United States, no single emotional response to the Soviet Union was reported by 30% or more of

TABLE 6.8
Contrasting Association with the United States and the Soviet Union

	Superpower	
	United States	*Soviet Union*
Ideology/System:	Democracy (38%)	Communism (70%)
Human Condition:	Freedom (67%)	Oppression (30%)
World Stature:	Powerful (35%)	Powerful (35%)
Emotion Response:	Pride (40%)	(none at 30% level)
Visual Symbol:	Flag (53%)	Red (35%)

Note: The percentages of subjects who gave these responses to the superpowers are given in parentheses.

the subjects. The most common emotional responses to the Soviet Union were anger, fear, and sadness.

Findings showed strong mutual associations between the United States and democracy, on the one hand, and the Soviet Union and communism, on the other. As our ten-year-old expert, Judith, explained, democracy and communism represent opposite ways of people, one good, the other bad. In general, it appears that each superpower was thought of as having a particular ideological perspective and as setting up, at home and abroad, a corresponding sociopolitical system. One subject (also quoted above) put it in a nutshell: "Taking into account the world powers of today, if the United States was not a democracy it would probably be ruled by a communist dictatorship; in which case I'd rather be dead."

Why "better dead than red"? Each superpower, with its associated ideology and system, tends to be thought of as providing those under its power with certain conditions of life. American democracy provides freedom, Soviet communism yields oppression.

As the findings and discussion presented above establish, freedom is clearly central to American conceptions of America. About two-thirds of the subjects thought of freedom in response to both the United States and democracy. Thirty percent of the subjects mentioned oppression in response to the Soviet Union, and 27% responded to communism that way. Had responses such as "totalitarian," "tyrannical," "domination," "unfree," and "restricted" been included in a category with "oppressive," these figures would have been more impressive. Even so, a 30% rate is high in free association, and it is likely that many subjects who did not mention oppression in the word association would have agreed that Soviet communism was oppressive.

Like democracy and communism, freedom and oppression are perceived as opposites. While both are vague, badly defined terms, freedom generally means being able to do what one wants without being harmed, while oppression is the opposite. Given that freedom elicits associations of "happy" and "good," it is clear which human condition is preferred. Thus the United States is associated with democracy and freedom, which are good, while the Soviet Union is associated with communism and oppression, which are bad.

Do Americans perceive the Soviet Union and communism to be in opposition to the United States, freedom, and democracy? Although this word association study cannot conclusively answer this question, the findings presented in Chapter 7 indicate that the answer is yes.

The essays subjects wrote provide some anecdotal evidence of perceived opposition as well. Essays on democracy (quoted above) contrasted American freedom with the Soviet Union and communism. Another essay clearly set communism in opposition to the United States and freedom: "Communism is that dirty word you were brought up to hate. It opposes everything America stands for: freedom, liberty and happiness."

Yet another subject referred to that same opposition in discussing freedom and its abuse:

Our freedom must be used in a way that does not jeopardize the freedom of others. An example is people using the Constitution to promote communism. . . . The Constitution states freedom of speech and freedom of press, which communism does not believe in. Americans have lived with freedom for some time, and I believe we all like it. If other countries were able to experience this freedom we know so well without government intervention people would be happier, because they could choose their destiny.

For another subject, "the Soviet Union represents a way of life that I find appalling and a threat to our current way of life." These negative feelings were increased by the perception that Soviet communist expansionism was forcing the United States to take costly and unsavory action to save democracy:

The Soviet Union is obviously a major threat to the United States. I resent them for causing us to spend (waste) so much money on weapons. It seems we have no choice because we have to keep up with them so that they do not take us over. They also seem to be forcing us to lower our standards on acceptable behavior and methods to prevent the spread of communism. I hope we don't lose sight of the purpose, which is to preserve the democratic way, as we struggle with the Soviet Union.

For these subjects, and other like-minded Americans, there was a clear and deep opposition between American freedom and democracy on the one side, and Soviet communism and oppression on the other. World politics collapsed into a dichotomous, black-and-white struggle between two internally consistent opposites. It made sense from this perspective that the United States was fighting for freedom and democracy, and the inclusion of the oppressive Soviet communist antithesis naturally and convincingly rounded out the picture.

CONCLUSIONS

Common meanings of key concepts have been identified in this word-association study, and they fit the cold war schema. Strong associations were found among the United States, freedom, and democracy, on the one side, and the Soviet Union, communism, and oppression, on the other. Democracy and freedom were both associated with good, while communism and oppression were their functional antitheses.

These associations constituted powerful preconceptions that predisposed Americans to perceive international affairs and their nation's foreign policy in conventional cold war terms. This has often led to biased interpretations of international realities and to quick support for policies that might otherwise have received closer scrutiny.

This has occurred in a number of ways. Because of the preconceived associations among the United States, freedom, and democracy found in the American patriotic schema, U.S. motives and behaviors tend to be interpreted as the promotion of freedom and democracy. Because of this same association, the assumption has often been that governments and movements supported by the United

States promote freedom and democracy, while enemies of the United States oppose freedom and democracy. Because Americans are proud of their country and consider freedom and democracy to be good, they tend to be supportive of U.S. foreign policy, particularly if they are convinced that freedom and democracy are being promoted.

Because of the strong association between the Soviet Union and communism in the Soviet schema, Americans tended to consider Soviet allies to be communist, or to consider governments or movements labeled as communist not only to be Soviet allies, but also Soviet clones. Because of the associations of the Soviet Union and communism with oppression (the antithesis of freedom), "pro-Soviet" or "communist" governments or movements were perceived in a negative light, and U.S. policies and actions against them tended to be supported on both moral and security grounds.

The claim is not that all Americans, under all conditions, will respond to international relations in these ways. Preconceived associations are not the only influences affecting perceptions of and reactions to U.S. foreign policy. For instance, the ways in which political actors and journalists frame events and policies strongly influence how the public will perceive things.

The facts are, however, that many Americans, under many conditions, have behaved and do behave in exactly these ways. A great many U.S. interventions around the globe have been interpreted in one or more of the ways just described. For example, despite U.S. preferences for a puppet government in the South over free elections to reunify Vietnam, many Americans believed their country to be fighting for freedom and democracy in Vietnam. It was seen as necessary to fight against "the communists" because their victory would have meant both oppression in Vietnam and a cold war defeat for the United States.

The point is not that these interpretations of U.S. involvement in Vietnam were wrong, but that the preconceived associations revealed in this study make such interpretations "easy to think." If we are concerned, for instance, with understanding why it is that so many Americans supported the Vietnam War for so long, we cannot ignore evidence that Americans were cognitively predisposed to do such things.

NOTES

1. What this word-association study shows is that capitalism and dictatorship do not come to mind as readily as the other five concepts do in relation to each other. This should not be taken to mean that capitalism and dictatorship are not elements of a more elaborated conception of the cold war schema. In fact, capitalism clearly is. Findings here show that capitalism brings the United States and freedom to mind, and findings from the word-pair study (Chapter 7) placed capitalism clearly on the side of the United States, freedom, and democracy, against the Soviet Union and communism.

2. Obviously, the 30% level was somewhat arbitrarily chosen, as there was no rigid rule by which it was selected over 20% or 40%. A much lower percentage would have

allowed the inclusion of more, richer data, but would have lengthened and diluted this work without adding substantially to its lessons. A much higher percentage would have limited findings to the one or two most frequent responses for each stimulus. In fact, those responses made by 60% or more of the subjects are emphasized in the discussion below, but this emphasis did not make it necessary to ignore other important results. The 30% cut-off proved to be an effective middle ground.

7

Balance, Stability, and Change in the Cold War Schema

Heider's (1958) notion of structural balance has, over the years, proved to be a useful tool for understanding beliefs and attitudes about international relations (Harary, 1961; Scott, 1965; Jervis, 1976). In the human mind, the family of nations is often divided into opposing camps, one virtuous, the other malevolent. It is assumed that members of each camp support one another, that they oppose members of the other camp, and that they remain true to their benevolent or evil natures. Usually, such balanced belief systems easily simplify international reality, imposing perceptions that justify national chauvinisms. Occasionally, however, complex and changing international realities create pressures for inconsistency and change in the belief systems used to interpret them. Cognitive counter-pressures work to protect balanced belief structures from the threats of inconsistency and change, and to restore balance once it has been lost. New beliefs emerge from this process of conflicting pressures.

According to the cold war schema, the United States and its "free world" allies stand opposed to the Soviet Union and its communist comrades. Salient U.S.–Soviet animosity, along with reports of Soviet and communist oppression, bolstered the cold war schema over the years. Popular American use of the cold war schema structured the world in a clear and balanced way that fostered patriotism while justifying national policies and chauvinisms.

International relations, however, are not nearly as simple as the cognitive structures used to understand them. Occasionally complex and changing international realities create pressures for inconsistency and change in the belief systems used to interpret them. Changes in the Soviet Union, and in its relations with the United States, created the sorts of pressures that ignite and power the process of belief system change. As the Soviet Union's image among Americans improved, those simple, balanced cold war preconceptions were disrupted. Cognitions were thrown off-balance as perceptions and evaluations of the Soviet Union became strewn with contradictions. Unbalanced perceptions of the Soviet Union had to be temporarily tolerated during this unstable stage of belief system flux. In the event of renewed cold war hostilities, balance would have returned as the Soviet Union fell back into its enemy role. As it happened, the downfall of the Soviet Union and communism in Eastern Europe finally closed the book on the cold war. Balance is reestablished, as what is left of the Soviet Union is increasingly dissociated from communism and superpower rivalry.

This chapter provides additional evidence of the cold war schema in American minds and examines the role of structural balance in the process of belief system change. Following a description of the methodology, a number of findings will be presented. Those findings generally support the notion that Americans used a balanced cold war schema to evaluate relevant stimuli. The vast majority of subjects were found to believe in most aspects of the cold war schema, and to hold balanced cognitions for most of the conceptual triads in the schema. However, a tendency for some subjects to have unbalanced perceptions of the Soviet Union was also detected. This tendency was a result of increasingly positive evaluations of the Soviet Union and its relations with the United States, accompanied by continued perceptions of the Soviet Union as unfree, undemocratic, and communist. However, even among those subjects who held unbalanced cognitions concerning the Soviet Union, cognitive pressure toward balance was evident, serving to moderate unbalanced responses. Findings show that unbalanced sets of responses proved to be less extreme than balanced ones. It appears that, in 1990, American perceptions of the Soviet Union were in an unbalanced state of flux. Since that time, the disintegration of the Soviet Union and the fall of communist parties in Eastern Europe have guided perceptions toward a new balance outside the cold war schema.

METHOD

This study was designed both to examine whether the positive and negative relationships hypothesized in the cold war schema could be found in American minds, and to explore subjects' propensities for balanced and unbalanced cognitions. The pervasiveness of each cognitive link in the cold war schema (excluding those involving "oppression"[1]) was tested in the simplest of ways: subjects were presented with pairs of words and asked how positive or negative they thought the relationship between each pair of words was.

If subjects overwhelmingly indicated, for instance, that they perceived a positive relationship between the United States and good, or a negative relationship between the Soviet Union and democracy, then it could be concluded that these schematic relationships were prevalent in the sample of mainstream American university students. If, on the other hand, a substantial portion of the sample negatively evaluated the relationship between the United States and good, or viewed the relationship between the Soviet Union and democracy as positive, then the predominance of the hypothesized schematic relationship had to be challenged.

To detect stability or change in the pervasiveness of schematic relationships, the study was conducted twice: in January 1988 (41 subjects) and again in January 1990 (191 subjects). A comparison of results from the two separate years identified those schematic relationships that were strong and stable, as well as those that appeared to be weakening over time. The data were also analyzed to determine the extent to which subjects' responses were structurally balanced. Finally, balanced and unbalanced responses were compared to determine whether pressure toward balance made unbalanced attitudes less extreme than balanced ones.

Relevant word-pairs included various combinations of the following seven elements of the cold war schema: the United States, you, good, freedom, democracy, the Soviet Union, and communism.[2] The word "you" was used to indicate the self. Aside from the "you–good" pair (which was excluded), all of the possible combinations among those seven elements of the cold war schema were included in the questionnaire. Subjects evaluated twenty relevant word-pairs in all (there were an additional forty-five word-pairs in the questionnaire).

The meanings of "positive" and "negative" relationships among stimuli depend upon the sorts of stimuli under consideration. The stimuli in this study consisted of nation states (the United States and the Soviet Union), concepts (freedom, democracy, communism, and good), and the subjects themselves (you). To facilitate responses, subjects were instructed to think about the positive–negative dichotomy in terms of three other contrasting dichotomies: friendly–hostile, supporting–opposing, and compatible–incompatible.

The friendly–hostile and supporting–opposing dichotomies were emphasized because they are generally used to describe positive and negative relationships among nations and individuals. Friendly relations among nations tend to include affirming rhetorical exchanges and symbolic acts by leaders, trade, and other cooperative behaviors. In contrast, hostile relations are typified by aggressive or cold rhetoric and/or interaction. Support by a nation or individual for another nation may consist of approving of its principles, policies, or behaviors, or acting in a way beneficial to that nation or its government. Opposition may consist of disapproval or conflictual behavior.

The compatible–incompatible dichotomy was emphasized because of its suitability to relationships among concepts. Concepts that go together well, that fit together harmoniously, are viewed as compatible. Incompatible concepts contrast and clash.

Each of these three dichotomies was presented to the subjects and explained in terms of examples irrelevant to the content of the study. Subjects were instructed to think of a "positive" relationship as friendly, compatible, and/or supporting, and to think of a "negative" relationship as a hostile, incompatible, and/or opposing one.

Subjects indicated their responses to each word-pair on a 7-point scale ranging from +3 to –3, with 0 as a neutral midpoint. Subjects were instructed to circle +3 or –3 if they viewed the relationship between the stimuli as extremely positive or negative, +2 or –2 if the relationship seemed moderately positive or negative, +1 or –1 if it was slightly so, and 0 if they felt the relationship was neither positive nor negative. Subjects practiced on five irrelevant word-pairs. They were then given twenty seconds to respond to each of the sixty-five word-pairs on the questionnaire. Pairs were presented in random order, and no two consecutive word-pairs contained the same word.

Both the 1988 and 1990 studies were conducted in early January, during the first week of Winter Quarter at the University of Washington. Both samples consisted of students enrolled in "Political Science 101" at the university. For both samples, the average exposures to the front section of a daily newspaper and to network television news were between three and four times per week. Both samples contained more liberals than conservatives (by margins of 59% to 32% in 1988, and 51% to 36% in 1990). In 1988, subjects who preferred the Republican Party outnumbered those preferring Democrats 49% to 39%, while in 1990 Democratic sympathizers were more numerous by a margin of 45% to 41%. In both years the mean age was twenty. Thus the two samples were obtained in the same fashion and were demographically alike. Demographics did not explain any of the difference between 1988 and 1990 findings.

FINDINGS

The results are presented and discussed in three sections. In the first section, 1988 and 1990 responses are reported and compared with the cold war schema. Findings show that, except for word-pairs containing the Soviet Union, responses were overwhelmingly consistent with the cold war schema. The 1988 and 1990 responses are then compared with each other, in order to gauge stability and change in the schema's prevalence over that two-year period. With the exception, again, of those word-pairs containing the Soviet Union, there were few significant differences between the 1988 and 1990 findings. Compared with the 1988 findings, those of 1990 indicated a relative drift by the Soviet Union out of its conventional role in the cold war schema. Thus relationships involving the Soviet Union were not as stable and strongly held as those among the other conceptual elements of the cold war schema.

The analyses of structural balance utilize the data from the more recent and larger (191 subjects) 1990 study. In the second section, the 1990 responses are directly tested for structural balance. Overall, responses tended to be balanced. Not surprisingly, however, conceptual triads that included the Soviet Union were unbalanced for up to a third of the subjects. It appears that increasingly positive perceptions of the Soviet Union led to unbalanced cognitions. Changing political realities resulted in a shock to the belief system, knocking beliefs, at least temporarily, off balance.

The third section examines the effects of pressures toward cognitive balance on unbalanced responses to triads containing the Soviet Union. It was predicted that unbalanced responses would be less extreme than balanced responses, because pressures toward balance function to moderate unbalanced cognitions. Findings fit this hypothesis and thus demonstrated the moderating effect that pressure toward balance has on unbalanced cognitions.

Word-Pair Responses, 1988 and 1990

In both 1988 and 1990, the American patriotic schema was almost unanimously held (see Tables 7.1 and 7.2). The weakest finding was still strong: in 1990, 83% positively evaluated the relationship between the United States and good, while 9% judged it to be negative. Aside from that, over 90% of the subjects positively evaluated each of the relationships among the United States, freedom, democracy, good, and themselves in both years. Thus findings show a strong and stable consensus around the American patriotic schema.

Consistent with the cold war schema, subjects in both years showed extremely strong tendencies to negatively evaluate the relationships between communism and the five elements of the patriotic schema (see Table 7.3). In addition, the vast majority of subjects positively related communism with the Soviet Union: in 1988, 88% judged the Soviet–communist relationship to be positive and 10% considered it negative, while evaluations were 78% positive and 19% negative in 1990. In the vast majority of responses, communism clearly continued to hold its place in the cold war schema.

The same cannot be said for the Soviet Union (see Table 7.4). Responses to the Soviet Union showed a good deal of consistency with the cold war schema, but

TABLE 7.1
Positive and Negative Evaluations of the Relationships among the United States, Freedom, Democracy, Good, and You (January 1988)

	Good	You	Democracy	Freedom
United States	Pos: 93% Neg: 2%	Pos: 98% Neg: 2%	Pos: 100% Neg: 0%	Pos: 100% Neg: 0%
Freedom	Pos: 100% Neg: 0%	Pos: 100% Neg: 0%	Pos: 98% Neg: 2%	
Democracy	Pos: 95% Neg: 0%	Pos: 98% Neg: 2%		

TABLE 7.2
Positive and Negative Evaluations of the Relationships among the United States, Freedom, Democracy, Good, and You (January 1990)

	Good	You	Democracy	Freedom
United States	Pos: 83% Neg: 9%	Pos: 92% Neg: 5%	Pos: 96% Neg: 4%	Pos: 95% Neg: 4%
Freedom	Pos: 95% Neg: 1%	Pos: 96% Neg: 1%	Pos: 96% Neg: 2%	
Democracy	Pos: 93% Neg: 2%	Pos: 95% Neg: 2%		

they also showed some movement away from it. In 1988, subjects were almost unanimous in negatively relating the Soviet Union to democracy (98%) and freedom (95%). The U.S.–Soviet relationship was also deemed negative by most subjects (78%) in 1988. Still, only half of the subjects negatively evaluated the Soviet Union's relationships with good and themselves, and a third judged those relationships to be positive.

TABLE 7.3
Positive and Negative Evaluations of the Relationships between Communism and: the United States, Freedom, Democracy, You, and Good (January 1988 and 1990)

	1988	1990
United States	Pos: 0% Neg: 98%	Pos: 3% Neg: 95%
Freedom	Pos: 7% Neg: 88%	Pos: 4% Neg: 89%
Democracy	Pos: 12% Neg: 81%	Pos: 6% Neg: 86%
You	Pos: 7% Neg: 85%	Pos: 6% Neg: 83%
Good	Pos: 12% Neg: 73%	Pos: 14% Neg: 69%

TABLE 7.4
Positive and Negative Evaluations of the Relationships between the Soviet Union and: the United States, Freedom, Democracy, You, and Good (January 1988 and 1990)

	1988	1990
United States	Pos: 20% Neg: 78%	Pos: 48% Neg: 39%
Freedom	Pos: 2% Neg: 95%	Pos: 17% Neg: 71%
Democracy	Pos: 0% Neg: 98%	Pos: 16% Neg: 76%
You	Pos: 32% Neg: 49%	Pos: 46% Neg: 26%
Good	Pos: 34% Neg: 54%	Pos: 41% Neg: 47%

These findings are consistent with the public opinion data, which show anti-Soviet sentiments waning during the period surrounding January 1988, when the questionnaire was administered (Yatani & Bramel, 1989). For instance, a NORC survey of March 1988 found that half the public had negative attitudes toward the Soviet Union and 44% felt favorably toward the rival superpower (Niemi et al., 1989, p. 61). These results make sense, given that this was a time of diplomatic optimism, a period in which anti-Soviet sentiments were being downplayed in the United States. Indeed, given the accommodative diplomatic context, the fact that only 20% of the subjects perceived a positive relationship between the United States and the Soviet Union is testimony to the cold war schema's stubborn resistance to change.

Caution was used in comparing the 1988 and 1990 samples, since they did not include the same subjects. It was impossible to be certain how much of the differences between responses in 1988 and 1990 were due to the idiosyncrasies of the samples. Still, an effort was made to replicate the 1988 study as exactly as possible in the 1990 version. The two samples consisted of students from the same course at the same university, they had basically the same demographic profile, and the same questionnaire was administered during the same week of the same term. Thus it is probable that the two samples were extremely similar and that a careful comparison of their responses is valid.

In 1990, cognitions concerning the Soviet Union continued to stray from the cold war schema (see Table 7.4). Forty-one percent positively related the Soviet Union with good, while 47% did so negatively. The relationship between the Soviet Union and the self was given positive evaluations by 46% of the subjects and seen as negative by only 26%. Forty-eight percent judged the U.S.–Soviet relationship as positive, while 39% viewed it as negative. These findings, too, are generally consistent with national Gallup findings at the time: in August 1989, the public held favorable attitudes toward the Soviet Union by a 51% to 40% margin (*Gallup Poll*, 1990, p. 180), and that gap had spread to 55% to 32% by May 1990 (*Gallup Poll*, 1991, p. 53).

Although most subjects negatively evaluated the Soviet Union's relationship with freedom (71%) and democracy (76%) in the 1990 word-pair study, these findings are a far cry from the near unanimous results from 1988. In fact, *t*-tests yielded significant differences between 1988 and 1990 responses on almost all word-pairs containing the Soviet Union (see Table 7.5).

While demographics tended to have no effect on responses, conservatives and Republicans tended to be more patriotically pro-American and anti-Soviet than liberals and Democrats. Table 7.6 show mostly mild but significant tendencies for the more conservative and Republican 1990 subjects to evaluate more positively the relationships between the United States and the other elements of the

TABLE 7.5
Mean Differences between 1988 and 1990 Responses to Word-Pairs Containing the Soviet Union

Other Word	Mean 1988	Mean 1990	t value	deg. of freedom	2-tailed prob.
United States	-1.2	+0.1	-5.4	225	<.0005
Freedom	-2.2	-1.1	-4.8	226	<.0005
Democracy	-2.3	-1.2	-4.3	228	<.0005
You	-0.5	+0.3	-3.2	228	.02
Good	-0.3	-0.1	-0.9	229	.4
Communism	+2.0	+1.3	2.0	228	.04

TABLE 7.6
Effects of Party and Ideology on Responses to Word-Pairs Containing the United States (January 1990)

	Party	Ideology
You	tau=-.23, p<.0005	tau=-.21, p<.0005
Good	tau=-.27, p<.0005	tau=-.24, p<.0005
Freedom	tau=-.32, p<.0005	tau=-.28, p<.0005
Democracy	tau=-.21, p<.0005	tau=-.22, p<.0005

patriotic schema (freedom, democracy, good, and the self). While liberals and Democrats showed strong pro-American tendencies, they were not as extreme as conservatives and Republicans. For instance, 92% of all Democrats positively evaluated the relationship between the United States and freedom, and 30% judged that relationship to be extremely positive. By comparison, 100% of the Republicans positively evaluated the U.S.–freedom relationship, and 62% chose the most extreme response. Thus, while the American patriotic schema is strongly and stably held regardless of party and ideology, conservatives and Republicans tend to be more extreme in their patriotism.

Conservatives and Republicans also tended to evaluate the relationships between the Soviet Union and elements of the patriotic schema more negatively than did liberals and Democrats (see Table 7.7). For example, slightly over half

TABLE 7.7
Effects of Party and Ideology on Responses to Word-Pairs Containing the Soviet Union (January 1990)

	Party	Ideology
You	tau=.17, p=.002	tau=.20, p<.0005
Good	tau=.14, p=.007	tau=.25, p<.0005
Freedom	tau=.09, p=.07	tau=.11, p=.03
Democracy	tau=.18, p=.001	tau=.16, p=.003

of all liberals (53%) and Democrats (52%) positively related the Soviet Union with themselves, and only about 20% negatively evaluated the Soviet–self relationship. By comparison, conservatives and Republicans were both evenly split between positive and negative (about 40% on each side) on that word-pair. By a 55% to 34% margin, liberals tended to positively relate the Soviet Union with good. By an even greater margin, 63% to 25%, conservatives judged the Soviet–good relationship to be negative. Liberals positively evaluated the U.S.–Soviet relationship by a 53% to 33% margin, while conservatives tended to negatively view the relationship between the two superpowers by a 52% to 43% margin. In general, then, conservatives and Republicans showed a greater tendency to cling to the notion of a Soviet enemy, while liberals and Democrats showed a relative tendency to embrace friendly U.S.–Soviet relations.

This may have been due to a tendency, relative to conservatives and Republicans, for liberals and Democrats to emphasize international cooperation over competition. In addition, Republican politicians have often been particularly insistent in their cold war rhetoric, and conservatives hold ideological perspectives that tend to be less tolerant of socialism. For a variety of reasons, then, it appears that the new tolerance of the old enemy was found particularly among liberals and Democrats.

Triadic Balance in Responses

Balance is tested by grouping the word-pairs into sets of three. Each of the three word-pairs shares one word with each of the other two pairs. The three word-pairs in the triad thus share the same three words among them. For instance, the communism–democracy–you triad is made up of three word-pairs: communism–democracy, democracy–you, and you–communism. It is a simple matter to discover whether a subject's responses are balanced for a given triad: the responses to the three word-pairs are multiplied by each other. If the result is zero, then one or more of the word-pair responses was zero (neutral), and the triad cannot be said to be either balanced or unbalanced. Otherwise, the product's sign indicates whether the triad is balanced or not. If it is positive, then either one or all (but not two) of the three responses are positive (see Figure 2.1), and the triad is balanced. If the product is negative, then either one or all of the responses are negative (see Figure 2.2), and the triad is unbalanced.

Using this technique, it was possible to discover the extent to which 1990 responses tended to be balanced. As Table 7.8 shows, triads that made up the American patriotic schema were balanced for the overwhelming majority of the subjects. For example, 93% of the subjects responded in a balanced fashion to the three word-pairs containing the United States, freedom, and democracy, and only 3% had unbalanced responses to these word-pairs. There is nothing shocking about these strong results: given that responses to all of the word-pairs in the patriotic schema were overwhelmingly positive, the triads had to consist overwhelmingly of three positive responses.

TABLE 7.8
Balance and Imbalance in the American Patriotic Schema, by Conceptual Triad (January 1990)

Triads containing Freedom, Democracy and:

United States	You	Good
Bal: 93%	Bal: 92%	Bal: 90%
Unbal: 3%	Unbal: 1%	Unbal: 2%

Other triads containing the United States and:

	Freedom	Democracy
You	Bal: 89%	Bal: 89%
	Unbal: 5%	Unbal: 5%
Good	Bal: 85%	Bal: 82%
	Unbal: 5%	Unbal: 7%

Note: Bal = Balanced triad. Unbal = Unbalanced triad.

When communism is added to the picture, it remains overwhelmingly balanced. Table 7.9 shows findings for triads that link communism with two elements from the patriotic schema. Depending on the triad, from 66% to 86% of the responses were balanced, and imbalance ranged from 6% to 12%. This too makes sense: responses overwhelmingly tended to combine positive evaluations of the relationships among elements of the patriotic schema with negative evaluations of the relationships between them and communism. Thus there tended to be one positive and two negative evaluations in each triad.

As an inspection of Table 7.10 reveals, triads containing the Soviet Union showed a much weaker tendency to be balanced. This is not to say that there was no tendency toward balance in triads containing the Soviet Union. Seventy percent of the responses to the Soviet Union–freedom–democracy triad were balanced, and only 12% were not. For the triad containing the Soviet Union, the United States, and the self, only 17% gave unbalanced responses. In no triad did more than a third of the subjects display unbalanced cognitions, and approximately half (or more) of the subjects gave balanced responses to most of the triads containing the Soviet Union.

TABLE 7.9
Balance and Imbalance in Conceptual Triads Containing Communism and Elements of the Patriotic Schema (January 1990)

Triads containing Communism and:

	United States	Democracy	Freedom
You	Bal: 81% Unbal: 8%	Bal: 76% Unbal: 8%	Bal: 77% Unbal: 7%
Good	Bal: 68% Unbal: 12%	Bal: 66% Unbal: 12%	Bal: 68% Unbal: 11%
Freedom	Bal: 86% Unbal: 6%	Bal: 80% Unbal: 7%	
Democracy	Bal: 84% Unbal: 8%		

Note: Bal = Balanced triad. Unbal = Unbalanced triad.

TABLE 7.10
Balance and Imbalance in Conceptual Triads Containing the Soviet Union (January 1990)

Triads containing the Soviet Union and:

	United States	Communism	Democracy	Freedom
You	Bal: 47% Unbal: 17%	Bal: 32% Unbal: 31%	Bal: 33% Unbal: 32%	Bal: 36% Unbal: 26%
Good	Bal: 51% Unbal: 23%	Bal: 47% Unbal: 25%	Bal: 49% Unbal: 30%	Bal: 50% Unbal: 25%
Freedom	Bal: 47% Unbal: 31%	Bal: 61% Unbal: 19%	Bal: 70% Unbal: 12%	
Democracy	Bal: 48% Unbal: 34%	Bal: 60% Unbal: 24%		
Communism	Bal: 48% Unbal: 34%			

Note: Bal = Balanced triad. Unbal = Unbalanced triad.

Although cognitions concerning the Soviet Union were more balanced than unbalanced, they were nonetheless unbalanced for sizable minorities. In particular, a quarter to a third of the subjects positively relate the United States, good, and/or themselves with the Soviet Union, which they positively relate with communism or negatively relate with freedom and/or democracy. Such cognitions, accompanied by positive relationships among the elements of the patriotic schema and their negative relationships with communism, create imbalance. Thus, for instance, responses to the Soviet Union–you–communism triad and the Soviet Union–you–democracy triad were one-third balanced, one-third unbalanced, and one-third neither balanced nor unbalanced.

Pressures toward Balance in Responses

While most responses were balanced, then, many involving the Soviet Union were not. If balance theory is correct, then balanced cognitions are mutually reinforcing while there is pressure pushing those unbalanced cognitions in the direction of balance. Eventually, attitude change is expected to reestablish cognitive balance where it has been lost, either through a return to the previously balanced belief system (in this case the cold war schema), or by the emergence of a new one. Until that happens, however, pressure toward balance functions to moderate unbalanced cognitions, keeping them from becoming extreme and drawing them in the direction of neutrality.

Unbalanced cognitions tend to moderate each other, while balanced cognitions tend to bolster each other, and this is one reason why unbalanced cognitions tend to be less extreme than balanced ones. For example, if an individual thinks of the Soviet Union as good, communism as bad, and the Soviet Union as communist, the combination of these three cognitions is likely to moderate the strength of one or more of the separate cognitions. Individuals may think that the Soviet Union is good, but believing that the Soviet Union is communist and that communism is bad puts a damper on their enthusiasm for the Soviet Union. They may view communism as bad, but if the Soviet Union is communist and the Soviet Union is good, then they may think that communism isn't that bad after all. They may know that the Soviet Union is communist, but if communism is bad and the Soviet Union is good, then they may wonder just how communist the Soviet Union really is. Thus imbalance among the three cognitions may function to moderate one or all of them.

The effect is quite the opposite for balanced cognitions: each cognition may be bolstered by its inclusion in a balanced triad. If one views the Soviet Union as bad, communism as bad, and the Soviet Union as communist, cognitions fit together in gratifying harmony. Soviet depravity serves as evidence of the evils of communism, and the fact that the Soviet Union is communist makes it seem that much worse. Thus balanced cognitions are mutually confirming, and may serve to counter external pressures toward moderation.

Extreme beliefs and attitudes function to inhibit the change that is necessary to transform cognitions from balance to imbalance. For example, a person who views the United States as extremely good and the Soviet Union as extremely bad will have trouble viewing U.S.–Soviet relations as positive. Harmony between polar opposites (in this case extremes of good and bad) does not sit well in the psyche. Individuals can be expected either to resist the idea that U.S.–Soviet relations have become positive, or to moderate their views about the virtues of the two superpowers until a positive relationship between them seems possible. Either way, balanced cognitions will tend to be more extreme than unbalanced cognitions because extreme cognitions form a barrier to the belief or attitude change that yields imbalance.

For these reasons, all else being equal, balanced responses should be more extreme (farther from neutrality), on average, than unbalanced responses. This prediction is tested with respect to triads containing the Soviet Union, since they are the triads that tended to elicit relatively large proportions of unbalanced responses.

Responses to word-pairs ranged from extremely positive or negative (+3 or –3), to moderately positive or negative (+2 or –2), to slightly positive or negative (+1 or –1), to neutral (0). Thus the extremity of each response is indicated by its absolute value. This being the case, the extremity of a subject's responses to each triad is operationalized as the sum of the absolute values of each of the subject's responses to the three relevant word-pairs. In other words, where Exyz is the measure of response extremity for the triad x-y-z and Rxy is the response to the word-pair consisting of x and y:

$$Exyz = |Rxy| + |Ryz| + |Rzx|$$

For each triad containing the Soviet Union, the extremity of balanced responses is compared to the extremity of unbalanced responses (see Table 7.11). For all fourteen triads, balanced responses were, on average, more extreme than unbalanced responses. In some cases the differences were substantial: for instance, balanced responses to the communism–democracy–Soviet Union triad tended to be a good deal more extreme than unbalanced responses. On the other hand, the difference was negligible for the freedom–you–Soviet Union triad. Overall, balanced responses were consistently more extreme than unbalanced responses, and *t*-tests show these differences to be significant at the .05 level for ten of the fourteen triads. Thus the findings generally support the hypothesis. It appears that pressure toward balance does moderate unbalanced cognitions.

DISCUSSION

Findings show the American patriotic schema to be a strong, stable, and widely held belief structure among a sample of American university students. While there was also broad agreement that communism is opposed to the United

TABLE 7.11
Mean Differences in Extremity between Balanced and Unbalanced Responses to the Word-Pairs in Triads That Contain the Soviet Union (January 1990)

Other Words In the Triad	Mean (frequency) Balanced	Unbal.	t value	deg. of freedom	1-tailed prob.
the United States and You	5.75 (n=88)	5.28 (n=32)	1.8	118	.03
the United States and Good	4.97 (n=94)	4.70 (n=43)	1.1	135	.15
the United States and Freedom	5.85 (n=88)	5.26 (n=58)	2.4	144	.008
the United States and Democracy	5.93 (n=89)	5.52 (n=63)	1.7	150	.04
the United States and Communism	6.22 (n=90)	6.03 (n=64)	0.8	152	.2
Communism and You	6.47 (n=60)	5.88 (n=59)	2.3	117	.01
Communism and Good	5.94 (n=88)	5.32 (n=47)	2.2	133	.01
Communism and Freedom	6.62 (n=114)	5.58 (n=36)	3.2	148	.001
Communism and Democracy	6.89 (n=114)	5.33 (n=45)	5.3	157	<.0005
Democracy and You	6.16 (n=63)	5.78 (n=60)	1.4	121	.08
Democracy and Good	5.88 (n=92)	5.46 (n=56)	1.7	146	.04
Democracy and Freedom	6.43 (n=132)	5.68 (n=22)	2.1	152	.02
Freedom and You	6.32 (n=68)	6.29 (n=49)	0.2	115	.4
Freedom and Good	6.29 (n=94)	5.72 (n=46)	2.7	138	.004

States, freedom, democracy, good, and the self, this was not the case with respect to the Soviet Union. By 1990 it was clear that the Soviet Union was not, for most subjects, the enemy. For many subjects, cognitions concerning the Soviet Union were in an unstable state of flux.

As beliefs and attitudes about the Soviet Union changed, some cognitive imbalance had to be tolerated, at least for a limited period of time. Pressure toward cognitive balance does not mean that cognitions never become unbalanced: it means that human minds seek to maintain balanced cognitions when possible and to regain balance once it has been lost. Evidence of pressure toward balance in unbalanced cognitions was found in the fact that unbalanced responses tended to be less extreme than balanced ones. Thus the existence of unbalanced responses does not refute balance theory: while balance is the more stable cognitive state, imbalance is a common and often necessary part of cognitive change. Changing realities often create cognitive inconsistencies, and they take a while to sort themselves out. Such periods of change may bring on cognitive dissonance, discomfort felt when unbalanced cognitions come into conflict in the psyche. Dissonance may subconsciously motivate the reestablishment of consistency among cognitions, while more conscious reasoning processes work to find an old or new framework that is both internally and externally consistent.

Belief system change is far from the instantaneous reprogramming portrayed in George Orwell's (1949) fictional "Oceana." In Orwell's novel, *1984*, the citizens of Oceana shift their hatred back and forth between Eurasia and Eastasia in instant obedience to governmental cues. The masses appear to have no memories, no lasting sentiments; they are thoroughly socialized and entirely responsive to official declarations of national enemies. Orwell's exaggerated vision ignores a crucial aspect of cognitive change: it is often a slow and gradual process. Changes in real relations and governmental rhetoric do lead to changes in public sentiments, but the transition takes time and entails temporarily unbalanced attitudes. Changes in underlying beliefs take place gradually, as beliefs move in the direction of some old or new balanced structure.

Most elements of the cold war schema continue to be stored in the individual memories of millions of Americans, and such cognitive structures do not simply disappear when events change the world. Significant mass change in cold war predispositions must consist of a combination of political, cultural, and psychological processes that take years to complete. The interweaving workings of politics, culture, and cognition create a lag between changing political realities and changing cognitive structures for interpreting those realities. The process of belief system change tends to be a slow and uncertain one in which pressures toward cognitive balance play an important role.

In the context of overall schematic stability, change in cognitions concerning the Soviet Union created, at least temporarily, unbalanced cognitions. These unbalanced cognitions did not constitute a stable state: there was pressure for change in some direction that would restore balance. Had it survived, the Soviet Union would eventually have either returned to its role in the cold war schema or left the schema completely. Until one of these things happened, Americans would have experienced the discomfort of imbalance.

Had friendly U.S.–Soviet relations continued uninterrupted for many years, anti-Soviet cognitions would have continued to fade and might eventually have been all but forgotten. Positive U.S.–Soviet relations and pro-Soviet rhetoric were inconsistent with notions of Soviet opposition to the United States, good, and the self. This created pressure for change in conceptions of the Soviet Union, the sort of change that eventually leads to schematic restructuring. Had the Soviet Union survived, prolonged U.S.–Soviet harmony promised to ease the Soviet Union slowly out of its enemy role. Balance would have been restored, and the Soviet Union would have been positively related to good things and negatively related to bad things.

The political and economic reforms that went on in the Soviet Union provided the perfect opportunity for an image shift; the Soviet Union could be viewed as in the process of transition from communist oppression toward increased freedom and democracy. To the extent that the Soviet Union could be dissociated from communist oppression and associated with the United States, freedom, and democracy, Americans could feel comfortable with positive feelings toward the Soviet Union. Perceived progress away from communist oppression and toward freedom and democracy need not have been completed to allow for pro-Soviet sentiments; the perceived direction of change was enough to allow for the correct symbolic associations.

On the other hand, had souring of U.S.–Soviet relations led to renewed pressure to dislike the Soviet Union, it would have been a simple matter to refocus upon Soviet communism and oppression in order to regain balance. Reform in the Soviet Union allowed for comfortable pro-Soviet attitudes, but it did not cause them. What went on in the Soviet Union was not as important to American beliefs as how those events were interpreted, and American interpretations were made in a manner consistent with attitudes based on U.S.–Soviet relations. The reemergence of hostilities would have motivated negative interpretations of developments within the Soviet Union, and this would have revitalized the Soviet role in the cold war schema.

In addition, events that indicated a return of the Soviet Union to its oppressive communist days could have quickly rekindled old stereotypes and reinvigorated the cold war schema. Had the coup that temporarily deposed Gorbachev succeeded, the anti-Soviet aspects of the cold war schema would have been reactivated. Balance would have been regained with the return of the Soviet Union to its proper enemy role in the cold war schema.

This possibility that the pro-Soviet trend might have been halted or reversed is demonstrated by findings concerning China (Hirshberg, 1992). In 1988, responses to word-pairs containing China reflected relatively friendly relations between the United States and China, but unpopular actions by the Chinese government (the crackdown against protesters in Tiananmen Square) rekindled images of oppressive communism and elicited very different responses from the

1990 sample. In 1988, subjects held the same sorts of unbalanced perceptions of China as the 1990 subjects held with respect to the Soviet Union: they tended to positively relate China with the United States, good, and themselves, but to negatively associate the People's Republic with democracy, and to positively link it with communism. Like perceptions of the Soviet Union, views of China were in an unstable state of transition in the late 1980s, and imbalance resulted from some perceptions changing more quickly than others. The Tianamen Square massacre of June 1989 interrupted the transitional process and sent perceptions of China shooting back toward the balanced cold war schema. The massacre set the Chinese government in a clear symbolic struggle against freedom and democracy. This rekindled latent cold war images of China and elicited disapproving rhetoric from American leaders. The result was a quick reversion to negative perceptions of China, structured by the lingering cold war schema. Thus 1990 subjects tended to place China squarely in the communist enemy role, opposed to all elements of the American patriotic schema. While the Soviet Union appeared to be slipping out of the cold war schema in the period between January 1988 and January 1990, the People's Republic was returning to it.

For instance, in 1988, only 17% negatively evaluated the relationship between China and the United States, and 68% judged it positively. In 1990, 47% negatively evaluated the Sino–American relationship and 37% gave positive responses. Events in China and official reactions in the United States clearly changed perceptions of Sino–American relations, resulting in a significant difference between the 1988 and 1990 findings ($t = 4.38$, $df = 226$, $p < .0005$). Similarly, 22% negatively related themselves with China in 1988; 52% did in 1990 ($t = 4.14$, $df = 226$, $p < .0005$).

Historically, American beliefs and attitudes about the Soviet Union followed diplomatic and rhetorical developments (see Chapter 3). When U.S.–Soviet relations soured and anti-Soviet rhetoric flowed, beliefs and attitudes moved in the direction of the fully balanced cold war schema, complete with the Soviet Union in its "proper" role as the evil empire. When U.S.–Soviet relations improved and rhetoric was more accommodative, attitudes moved in the direction of a new structure which removed the Soviet Union from its enemy role. As long as relations and rhetoric remained relatively mixed and unstable, attitudes did not come to rest at this new point, as the cold war schema received enough use to keep it alive in American minds.

As it was, the dissolution of the Soviet Union made the Soviet component of the cold war schema irrelevant to present-day reality. Thus the demise of the Soviet Union quickened the pace of belief system change. The inheritors of the Soviet legacy have already lost many of the stigmas associated with the evils of communism. Assuming they can overcome their domestic problems without excessive oppression and bloodshed, they will increasingly be viewed as free and democratic.

Still, the American patriotic schema persists, as does its assumed opposition to the evils of communism and oppression. What villains will accompany these evils in future American schemata are matters for speculation. As long as there exist leftist revolutionaries and regimes who can be labeled as communists, it is unlikely that communism will disappear from American minds. In the absence of the Soviet threat, the United States will continue to exert its power in the name of freedom and democracy. The negative image of communism, which became so prominent during the cold war, is likely to retain its power as a condensational symbol, and it will continue to play a role in maintaining the American patriotic schema in the context of American interventionism.

NOTES

1. "Oppression" was not included in this study because its importance to the schema was not yet realized when the questionnaire was created.

2. A number of other words and phrases were also included in word-pairs on the questionnaire. Those words included China, Iran, South Africa, the Nicaraguan government, the Nicaraguan Contras, and capitalism. Aside from some of the findings concerning China, the responses to pairs containing these words are not discussed in this chapter.

8

Attributions
for Superpower Interventions

Why did the United States drop hydrogen bombs on Japanese cities? Was the United States "forced" to do so by Japan's refusal to agree to unconditional surrender? Was it a typical, inhumane act by a cruel, callous, imperialist power?

Why did the same nation shower Western Europe with economic aid? Was the United States "forced" to do so in order to prop up Western European capitalism against impending socialist revolution? Was it a typical, generous act by a heroic, unselfish world leader?

Attribution biases in interpreting the behaviors of actors are rooted in, and help perpetuate, biased conceptions of those actors. If one thinks of the United States as good, then one will assume good, helpful behavior by the United States to be natural and voluntary; bad, harmful behavior will seem unnatural and it will be assumed that some outside influence forced the United States to do it.

In the context of international relations, attribution biases involve the simplification of complex international interactions in which the leaders of nations, in particular situations, direct their nations to act in particular ways. In general terms, the interaction between the nation and the situation yields the behavior. Were a nation to act in basically the same manner in all situations, then it would be reasonable to attribute all its actions to its nature. Were all nations to respond in the same general way to a certain sort of situation, then it would be fair to attribute their actions to situational forces.

Things are rarely so simple, and it is usually necessary to take both the nature of the nation and the pressures of the situation into account in accurately attributing causes to national behavior. It is typical, however, for humans to simplify things in order to understand, evaluate, and respond to complex realities. Not only is there a tendency to emphasize either a nation's nature or situational forces, and to de-emphasize the other, but this tendency is strongly determined by stereotyped preconceptions concerning the nation in question.

Citizens, like political scientists, seek to understand what nations are like and why they act in the ways they do. Like political scientists, they use what they know about the nation, the situation, the act, and the interrelationships among the three in order to understand the nation and attribute causality to its actions.

Some of that knowledge is extremely simple. Citizens know that their nation is good: that is part of their patriotic national self-image. They tend to consider allies of their own nation to be good, while enemies of their nation are not. In addition, they are able to tell a helpful act, such as airlifting relief supplies, from a harmful act, such as dropping tons of incendiary bombs. They know that helpful acts are characteristic of good nations, but that they are sometimes forced to do harm. Finally, they know that harmful acts are characteristic of bad nations, but that they are sometimes forced to be helpful. This sort of general knowledge exists without reference to particular situations, and so it is possible for citizens to make judgements about nations and their actions without knowing the situation.

Regardless of the situation, then, patriotic Americans know that it is the nature of their nation to aid others, but that the United States is sometimes forced to use its military might in an immediately destructive, though ultimately (it is assumed) constructive, manner. Thus one would expect a tendency for Americans to explain the Marshall Plan in terms of U.S. generosity and leadership, while the bombings of Hiroshima and Nagasaki were made necessary by an intransigent and dangerous Japan.

American political scientists may also be prone to this sort of dynamic. For example, the orthodox interpretation of the origins of the cold war fits this framework (see Schlesinger, 1967; Spanier, 1985) (see also Chapter 2). The United States is viewed as forced into confrontation by the inherently aggressive and expansionist Soviet Union. This one-sided view is based in the perception of "our country" as good and the enemy therefore as both bad and the cause of the conflict. The extreme revisionist alternative, that the Soviet Union was forced into confrontation by the inherently aggressive and expansionist U.S. imperialists, manifests opposite biases.

From the American point of view, the United States is good, it is the nature of the United States to give aid, and the United States does not drop bombs unless it is forced to. Americans did not feel the same way about the other superpower. Because the Soviet Union was both America's rival and summit partner, Americans had mixed feelings about the Soviet Union in the late 1980s, and those mixed feelings were reflected in their attributions for Soviet behavior. This chapter presents experimental evidence of these assertions.

Findings from the word-pair study in Chapter 7 show a strong tendency to positively relate the United States with good. In this chapter we see how this preconception creates a tendency to consider helpful behavior to be "natural" to the United States but harmful behavior to be something that America was "forced" to do. As a result of these attribution biases, helpful behavior serves as further evidence of American virtue, while harmful behavior is discounted as something forced upon the nation and thus does not adversely affect notions of American greatness.

Word-pair findings with respect to the Soviet Union and good were mixed: about half of the subjects evaluated the relationship negatively and somewhat over a third did so positively. Consistent with these results, attribution findings were also mixed. However, when liberals (who show a greater tendency to be pro-Soviet) were excluded, anti-Soviet attribution tendencies emerged among the remainder of the sample.

These attribution findings show one way in which the in-nation favoring found in the cold war schema biased perceptions of international events. Due to attribution biases, Americans are more likely to judge their country by its positive acts, not its negative acts. This reinforces positive perceptions of the United States and its leaders, which serve as the basis for further biased perceptions. The same process operated in reverse for those holding negative views of the Soviet Union. Thus elements of the cold war schema led to attribution biases that perpetuated those elements of the schema.

ATTRIBUTION THEORY AND RESEARCH

Attribution theory generated massive amounts of research in social psychology, particularly in the 1970s (see Harvey & Weary, 1981; Hewstone, 1983; Jaspars, Fincham, & Hewstone, 1983). Attribution scholars have examined the causes that subjects tend to attribute to specific types of behavior by particular sorts of actors under certain conditions. Traditionally, the stimulus actor has been an individual, but attribution theory has also been extended to the group and nation-state levels. While early work concentrated on evaluatively neutral behaviors, research spread to distinguish between "good and bad," "effective and ineffective," "friendly and unfriendly" behaviors. The general approach relevant here is succinctly described by Regan, Strauss, and Fazio (1974):

Liking for the actor should strongly affect the observer's assignment of causality for the action. As Heider (1958) suggested, we expect good people to perform good actions, and bad people to perform bad actions. Thus when liked actors do good things or disliked actors do bad things, we can readily understand the action as caused by the characteristics of the actor. We provide an internal attribution (Jones & Nisbett, 1971) for such expected actions, we regard them as typical of the actor, and we expect more of them in the future. However, when the action is seen as out-of-character—when good actors do bad acts, or bad actors do good acts—we are unable to understand the action as internally caused, and instead provide an external attribution. We see the action as atypical of the actor, as caused by some external or situational factor, and do not expect similar actions in the future . . . these attributional biases act to maintain the stability of existing levels of liking. [p. 386]

Regan et al. found that pro-social behavior was attributed internally to liked actors and externally to disliked actors. This same sort of attributional bias links ethnocentric attitudes and stereotypes with perceptions of behavior (Deaux & Emswiller, 1974; Mann & Taylor, 1974; Taylor & Jaggi, 1974; Duncan, 1976; Stephan, 1977; Greenberg & Rosenfield, 1979). Taylor and Jaggi, for instance, found a tendency for Hindus to attribute socially desirable behaviors by Hindus internally and socially undesirable behaviors externally. They found the opposite tendency when the actor was a Muslim. Attributional biases often indicate the functioning of social stereotypes (Tajfel, 1981) and serve to maintain them through perceptual distortion.

The same sorts of biases that affect attributions about the behaviors of individuals also affect attributions about the behaviors of nations. Stereotyped notions of nations yield attributions for national behavior which, in turn, bolster those stereotypes. Two studies (Rosenberg & Wolfsfeld, 1977; Heradstveit, 1979) that examine attributional biases in the Arab–Israeli conflict are relevant.

Rosenberg and Wolfsfeld (1977) presented an "attributional consistency model," in which balance theory (Heider, 1958) plays a prominent role. Both nations and national acts can be evaluated as positive (good, successful, etc.) or negative (bad, unsuccessful, etc.). Cognitive consistency involves a good nation performing a good act or a bad nation performing a bad act. If a good nation does something bad or a bad nation does something good, that is inconsistent. Consistency creates a good Gestalt in which elements fit together harmoniously, while inconsistent cognitions create pressure for cognitive change or reorganization. Given that a nation behaves in a certain manner, and that the individual maintains stable evaluations of the nation-state and the sort of behavior in question, if inconsistency is to be reconciled it must be through the attribution process.

Internal attribution to the nature of the nation strengthens the nation-behavior link and is gratifying given nation–behavior consistency. External attribution to the situation relieves the nation of responsibility for the behavior, thus weakening the nation–behavior link and alleviating inconsistency. Thus consistency elicits internal attribution while inconsistency elicits external attribution (see Figure 8.1).

The "attributional consistency model" synthesizes predictions based on balance theory with the "fundamental attribution error" (Jones & Nisbett, 1971). Rosenberg and Wolfsfeld tested the predictions of their model against the attributional responses of Arab, Israeli, and American subjects with varying orientations toward the Arab–Israeli conflict. Findings generally supported their hypotheses.

Heradstveit (1979) stressed the relationship between attribution and responsibility (or credit) for behavior. An internal, dispositional attribution holds the actor responsible for the behavior, while an external, situational attribution does not. Internal attribution implies freedom of choice on the part of the actor, while external attribution implies that the situation forced the behavior. Given the

FIGURE 8.1
Attribution and Cognitive Consistency

		Behavior	
		Good	Bad
Actor	Good Nation	Internal	External
	Bad Nation	External	Internal

desires of national elites to protect both their own egos and their negative views of their enemies, Heradstveit predicted a tendency among elites to attribute the good behavior of their own nation and bad behavior of their enemy to internal causes, and to attribute bad behavior by their nation and good behavior by the enemy to the situation (see Figure 8.2). His findings were generally consistent with expectations.

Sande, Goethals, Ferrari, and Worth (1989) conducted a set of experiments that were very similar to the one presented in this chapter. American students read news articles in which either the United States or the Soviet Union was depicted engaged in either "positive" or "negative" behavior. In separate questions, subjects were asked to what extent they attributed the action they read about internally (to the nation's "nature, character, traits, etc.") and externally (as "a response to the situation that faced them") (p. 96). Sande et al. did not find either internal or external attribution biases favoring the United States over the Soviet Union. Their lack of significant findings is particularly noteworthy, since the nation–action interaction effects they failed to find in their study are indeed found in the present one.

Their weak findings in this regard may well be due in large part to the nature of the descriptions of the "negative" acts. The two negative acts chosen for the

FIGURE 8.2
Attribution and National Enemies

		Behavior	
		Good	Bad
Actor	Own Nation	Internal	External
	Enemy Nation	External	Internal

experiments—building nuclear-powered submarines and sending military aid—are not unambiguously negative. Indeed, in the face of real external threats, nuclear submarines and military aid could well be life-savers. The submarine article included claims that the subs were a threat to the security of the other side, but it also included justifications of the action. The military-aid article included a statement by the acting country which justified the aid. Thus both articles supplied subjects with alternative interpretations that allowed so-called negative actions to be perceived as positive. This made internal and external attribution biases unnecessary. The American action could easily be viewed as positive because it made Americans safer, while the Soviet action could be interpreted as a threat to the United States. This flaw in their stimulus materials makes their lack of findings regarding internal and external attribution biases suspect.

These problems notwithstanding, Sande et al. did come up with other interesting and important findings. Subjects did view the positive acts (saving a whale and sending humanitarian aid) to be much more "typical" of the United States than of the Soviet Union, and they had a greater tendency to view the American whale-rescue as altruistic and the Soviet rescue effort as self-serving. General tendencies were found for subjects to assume good motives for American acts and relatively bad motives for Soviet acts. These "valued-guided" attribution biases served, they claim,

to maintain the belief that the United States is morally good and that the Soviet Union is bad. Regardless of the nature of the actions taken by the two countries, American students more frequently imputed altruistic and positive motivations to American actions than to Soviet actions. They imputed self-serving and negative motivations more often to Soviet actions than to American actions. That is, attributions were made to particular internal characteristics in order to assimilate new information into existing beliefs. [pp. 114–115]

This is an important finding, since it points to another way in which cognition based on the cold war schema serves to reinforce and perpetuate the schema. Schema-based notions of American virtue and Soviet depravity had a greater effect on motivational attributions than the actual act had. Thus, regardless of what each superpower did, subjects assumed good motives for the United States and bad ones for the Soviet Union. This allowed schema-inconsistent behavior to be explained away, and helped to maintain the cold war schema in the face of disconfirming evidence. Ultimately, Sande et al. argue, this allowed Americans who identified closely with their nation to maintain positive, moral self-images.

Sande et al. used Canadian subjects in a replication of one of their experiments. As expected, Canadians showed much less of a tendency than their American counterparts to make attributions that favored the United States over the Soviet Union. Canadians were less motivated than Americans, according to Sande et al, "to maintain a moral self-image and a diabolical enemy image" (p. 115).

IS IT THEIR NATURE OR WERE THEY FORCED?

Some national behaviors, such as the bombing of villages, are clearly harmful. Other national behaviors, such as airlifts of relief supplies to villages, are just as clearly helpful. Helpful acts are consistent with the dispositions of good nations, while harmful acts are consistent with the dispositions of bad nations. When national behavior is consistent with the nature of the nation, that is explanation enough of the behavior, and there is no reason to assume that situational factors forced the behavior. So if subjects read of a good nation acting helpfully or a bad nation acting harmfully, they will tend to agree that it is the nature of the nation to do so, not that it was forced to.

Conversely, harmful acts are inconsistent with the nature of good nations, and helpful acts are inconsistent with the nature of bad nations. In such cases, one important way of alleviating inconsistency is by believing that the nation would not have taken such action had it not been forced to do so. Thus subjects who read of a bad nation acting helpfully or a good nation acting harmfully will agree not that it is the nature of the nation to do what it did, but that it was forced to do so.

International relations are complex and involve both conflict and cooperation. Popular sentiments regarding other nations depend upon the perceived relations between those "out-nations" and the "in-nation." Citizens tend to view their own and allied nations positively, enemy nations negatively, and nations with ambiguous or mixed relations with theirs in varied or ambivalent ways. Thus it is possible to predict whether a subject will judge a helpful or harmful act to be natural or forced, based on whether the actor is the subject's own nation, considered to be an ally, perceived as an enemy, or seen to be in a mixed or ambiguous relationship with the in-nation (see Figure 8.3).

FIGURE 8.3
Expected Attributional Responses to Helpful and Harmful Behaviors by One's Own and Other Nations

		Behavior	
		Helpful	Harmful
Actor	Own Nation	Nature	Forced
	Allied Nation	Nature	Forced
	Enemy Nation	Forced	Nature
	Ambiguous Nation	Mixed	Mixed

The United States is clearly the in-nation, but how did the Soviet Union fit into this framework in 1988, when this study was undertaken? The answer to this question is far from simple. The Soviet Union was certainly not viewed as an ally in 1988, and it was still considered an enemy by many American. Given improved U.S.–Soviet relations, however, there were also many Americans who had mixed or even positive feelings toward the rival superpower.

The specific hypotheses to be tested in this study are based on knowledge gained from the 1988 word-pair study (see Chapter 7). The word-pair study was conducted less than three months prior to the attribution study and used similar subjects. It provided crucial data on orientations toward the United States and the Soviet Union that, when combined with the framework expressed in Figure 8.3, allowed for reasonable hypotheses.

In the 1988 word-pair study, 93% of the subjects saw a positive relationship between the United States and good, and 98% viewed the relationship between themselves and the United States as a positive one. These two measures of orientation toward the United States yielded consistently positive results, and were highly correlated ($r_s = .56$, $p = .001$). In contrast, 34% of the subjects evaluated the relationship between the Soviet Union and good as a positive one, while 54% saw it as a negative relationship. Similarly, 32% viewed themselves to be in a positive relationship with the Soviet Union, while 48% viewed their relationship with the Soviet Union to be a negative one. These two measures of orientation toward the Soviet Union yield similar mixed pictures leaning slightly toward the negative. They, too, were strongly correlated ($r_s = .79$, $p = .001$). In addition, significant negative correlations were found between orientations toward the United States and those toward the Soviet Union. Those who felt positively toward the Soviet Union tended to be less extreme in their positive feelings toward the United States.

These responses also correlated with the ideological orientations of the subjects. Liberals tended to be less pro-American and anti-Soviet than conservatives. This relationship is particularly important with respect to the Soviet Union, where the variation is large and the correlation strong (for "good and the Soviet Union," $r_s = .54$, $p = .001$; for "you and the Soviet Union," $r_s = .58$, $p = .001$). Tolerance of the Soviet Union was found predominantly among those who considered themselves to be liberal. While conservatives and middle-of-the-roaders tended to view the Soviet Union as bad, liberals did not. This may be due to a relative tendency for liberals to emphasize international cooperation over competition, or because liberals hold ideological perspectives that are more tolerant of socialism.

In the 1988 word-pair study, then, evaluations of the subject's "own nation," the United States, were overwhelmingly positive regardless of ideology. For conservatives and middle-of-the-roaders, the Soviet Union remained an "enemy nation," and tended to be negatively evaluated. Among liberals the Soviet Union

FIGURE 8.4

Hypothesized Attributional Responses to Helpful and Harmful Behaviors by the United States and the Soviet Union

	Behavior	
	Helpful	Harmful
United States (for all subjects)	Nature	Forced
Actor Soviet Union (for non-liberals)	Forced	Nature
Soviet Union (for liberals)	Mixed	Mixed

was an "ambiguous other nation," and responses were positive and negative with about equal frequency.

This information can be plugged into Figure 8.3, yielding Figure 8.4. The following hypotheses are tested:

1. *The United States*   Subjects will tend to attribute helpful behavior to America's nature and to assume that the United States was forced to engage in harmful behavior.

   A. Regardless of ideology, subjects will tend to agree that it is the nature of the United States to airlift relief supplies to a village, and will tend not to agree that it is America's nature to drop bombs.

   B. Regardless of ideology, subjects will tend to agree that the United States was forced to bomb a village, and will tend not to agree that they were forced to airlift relief supplies.

2. *The Soviet Union*   Attribution tendencies will be mixed with respect to the Soviet Union, and only very weak biases will be found for the entire sample. However, when liberals are excluded the remaining subjects will tend to attribute harmful behavior to the nature of the Soviet Union and to assume that the Soviets were forced to engage in helpful behavior.

   A. Conservative and middle-of-the-road subjects will tend to agree that it is the nature of the Soviet Union to bomb a village, and will tend not to agree that it is the Soviet Union's nature to airlift relief supplies. Liberals will not show this tendency.

   B. Conservative and middle-of-the-road subjects will tend to agree that the Soviet Union was forced to airlift relief supplies to a village, and will tend not to agree that they were forced to drop bombs. Liberals will not show this tendency.

3. *Overall*   Subjects will tend to show attribution biases that favor the United States over the Soviet Union. These biases will be particularly strong among nonliberals.

METHOD

Stimulus Materials

The experiment was carried out in late March, 1988. Each subject was presented with a 79-word fictional news report. All subjects read of the village of "Bamora" which, caught in the middle of a civil war, was surprised by aircraft one morning. For half of the subjects the aircraft were "American," while the other half read of "Soviet" aircraft. In addition, half of the subjects read that the aircraft dropped "tons of incendiary bombs," causing "panic" and "horror" among villagers, while the other half read that "tons of relief supplies" were dropped, spreading "joy" and "glee" among the villagers. The texts were identical in all other ways, taking the following general form:

BAMORA—The village of Bamora had an unexpected surprise this morning at dawn. (American/Soviet) aircraft sent hundreds of civilians scurrying with (joy/panic) as they dropped tons of (relief supplies/incendiary bombs) throughout the area. Witnesses said that children were seen running about the streets with unrestrained (glee/horror) as the aircraft circled overhead. The village, which has been caught in the middle of this country's protracted civil war, has been without fresh supplies of food and medicine for at least two months.

Thus the experiment was based on a 2×2 factorial between-subjects design. In the four experimental conditions each superpower was depicted as behaving in a harmful or helpful manner: Americans dropped bombs, Soviets dropped bombs, Americans dropped supplies, and Soviets dropped supplies.

Questionnaire

The text was followed by a questionnaire. First, subjects were instructed to indicate their agreement or disagreement (on 7-point scales) with two statements. The statement, "It is the nature of the United States/Soviet Union to do what it did in Bamora," tested whether the subject felt that the reported superpower behavior was consistent with what the subject perceived to be the disposition of that superpower. The other statement, "The United States/Soviet Union would probably not have taken such action had it not been forced to do so," tested the extent to which subjects believed the cause of the superpower's behavior to be something beyond its control. The order of the two statements was reversed on half of the questionnaires.

Subjects were also asked to describe, in one or two words, the probable motive for the superpower behavior. They were then asked how helpful or harmful they thought the supplies or bombs were to the villagers. This tested whether subjects did, in fact, view the behaviors as truly helpful or harmful. Questions concerning ideological and party preferences, news consumption habits, and other demographics followed.

Subjects

The subjects, 98% of whom were U.S. citizens, were 104 students in an introductory political science course at the University of Washington. Subjects were randomly assigned to the four conditions and given as much time as they needed to complete the questionnaire. There were 26 subjects in each condition. There were as many conservatives as liberals, and somewhat more Democrats than Republicans. Almost all the subjects read newspapers and watched television network news, but there was substantial variation in how much. The mean age was 20, and 85% of the subjects were between the ages of 18 and 21; 53% of the subjects were female.

FINDINGS

Subjects indicated how helpful they thought the supplies were or how harmful they thought the bombs were on a scale ranging from 0 ("not at all") to 6 ("extremely"). Responses overwhelmingly tended to fall on the higher end of the scale. The mean evaluation of the helpfulness of the supplies was 4.9, while the mean evaluation of the harmfulness of the bombs was 4.6. Analyses of variance showed no significant main or interaction effects involving the identity of the superpower, what was dropped on the village, or the ideology of the subject. These strong, stable responses indicate that the subjects were presented with unambiguously helpful and harmful superpower behaviors.

There was a negative correlation ($r_s = -.44$, $p = .001$) between agreement with the statement, "It is the nature of the United States/Soviet Union to do what it did in Bamora," and agreement with the statement, "The United States/Soviet Union would probably not have taken such action had it not been forced to do so." Those who thought the behavior to be consistent with the nation's nature tended not to think the nation had been forced to act as it did, and vice-versa. Overall, fewer subjects agreed than disagreed with each statement.

Agreement with the "nature" and "forced" statements was measured on 7-point scales ranging from −3 (disagree) to 3 (agree). In the analyses that follows, responses are sometimes collapsed into dichotomous (agree/disagree) categories to facilitate clarity in the presentation of findings. Where this has been done, neutral (neither agree nor disagree) responses are excluded from the analysis. Findings are presented in 2 × 2 tables (response by action), and the likelihood ratio chi-square statistic is used to evaluate the significance of the findings relating to the first two hypotheses.[1] Analyses of variance are used to test the third hypothesis.

The United States

The first hypothesis predicts a tendency to attribute the helpful behavior to America's nature, and to assume that America was forced to engage in the

TABLE 8.1

Agreement with the Nature Statement in Response to Acts by the United States

		Response		
		Agree	Disagree	
	Airlifted	2 0	3	2 3
Act	Supplied	(77%)	(12%)	(89%)
	Dropped	1 0	1 3	2 3
	Bombs	(38%)	(50%)	(89%)
		3 0	1 6	4 6

Note: There were 26 subjects per condition. Neutral responses were excluded from this table. Chi-square = 10.1, $df = 1$, $p = .001$.

harmful act. Findings fit this hypothesis well with respect to the helpful behavior, but not so well with regard to the harmful act. Still, the differences between the responses to the two conditions were highly significant for both the nature and forced statements.

Of the subjects who read of the helpful U.S. behavior (airlifting supplies), 77% agreed that it was America's nature to do so, and 12% disagreed (see Table 8.1). In contrast, half as many subjects (38%) who read about harmful U.S. behavior (dropping bombs) agreed that it was consistent with America's nature to do so, and more subjects (50%) disagreed. This highly significant difference (chi square = 10.1, $df = 1$, $p = .001$) demonstrates a far greater tendency to make internal attributions when the United States helps others, as compared to when the United States causes harm to others.

Similar findings were obtained with regard to external attributions (see Table 8.2). Only 8% of the subjects agreed that the United States had been forced to

TABLE 8.2

Agreement with the Forced Statement in Response to Acts by the United States

		Response		
		Agree	Disagree	
	Airlifted	2	2 3	2 5
Act	Supplied	(8%)	(89%)	(97%)
	Dropped	1 5	8	2 3
	Bombs	(58%)	(31%)	(89%)
		1 7	3 1	4 8

Note: There were 26 subjects per condition. Neutral responses were excluded from this table. Chi-square = 18.7, $df = 1$, $p = .00002$.

airlift the relief supplies, while 89% disagreed. In contrast, 58% agreed that the United States had been forced to drop the bombs, while 31% disagreed. This difference was also highly significant (chi square = 18.7, $df = 1$, $p = .00002$), and shows a far greater tendency to attribute destructive U.S. action externally, as compared to constructive U.S. behavior. In general, then, it can be concluded that the first hypothesis was supported by the findings.

While the attribution bias was extremely strong with respect to helpful U.S. behavior (airlifting supplies), it was less powerful with respect to harmful U.S. behavior (dropping bombs). This may be due in part to the fact that liberals are not quite so prone to letting their government off the hook for destructive behavior. Among conservatives and middle-of-the-road subjects, U.S. bombing behavior did tend to be interpreted as something inconsistent with its nature that the United States was force to do. Liberal subjects, however, showed no such tendency.

Among both liberals (75%, $n = 12$) and nonliberals (77%, $n = 13$), about three quarters of the subjects agreed that it was America's nature to airlift supplies, and only 8% of each group agreed that the United States had been forced to do so. Among conservatives and middle-of-the-roaders ($n = 17$), 29% agreed that it was America's nature to drop the bombs (65% disagreed), while 65% agreed that the United States was forced to do so (24% disagreed). Among liberals ($n = 9$), however, 56% thought it was America's nature to drop the bombs (only 22% disagreed), while 44% felt that the United States had been forced to do so (the same number disagreed). While liberals did not differ with the others in their responses to U.S. helping behavior, they were less prone to view harmful behavior as inconsistent with America's nature or to assume that the United States was probably forced to drop the bombs. Due to the small sample size, t-tests did not show these differences between liberals and others to be significant at the .05 level (for the "nature" question, $t = 1.7$, $df = 24$, two-tailed, $p = .11$; for the "forced" question, $t = 1.1$, $df = 24$, $p = .3$). Obviously, these particular findings are far from conclusive, and they cannot be taken as refutation of the prediction that there would be pro-American attribution biases regardless of ideology. Still, they do suggest the interesting possibility that liberals tend to view destructive U.S. behavior with less pro-American bias.

Liberals, like conservatives and middle-of-the-roaders, tend to maintain an image of the United States as, by nature, a doer of good. It appears that they may be, on the whole, more willing and able than nonliberals to tolerate the inconsistency involved in the generally good United States committing harmful acts. This is consistent with recent conservative support for and liberal opposition to U.S. military interventions. From the more liberal perspective, although the United States is by nature helpful and ideally only becomes destructive when necessary, recent U.S. interventions in Southeast Asia and Latin America have been unnecessary and destructive. From the more conservative perspective, those interventions have been necessary responses of a peaceful nation to dangerous provocations. Liberals have often been prone to rejecting this perspective and to

TABLE 8.3
Agreement with the Nature Statement in Response to Acts by the Soviet Union

		Response		
		Agree	Disagree	
Act	Airlifted Supplied	4 (15%)	1 7 (65%)	2 1 (80%)
	Dropped Bombs	9 (35%)	1 3 (50%)	2 2 (85%)
		1 3	3 0	4 3

Note: There were 26 subjects per condition. Neutral responses were excluded from this table. Chi-square = 2.5, $df = 1$, $p = .11$.

placing the blame for "out of character," destructive U.S. behavior internally, on presidential regimes which they oppose.

The Soviet Union

The second hypothesis predicted that anti-Soviet attribution biases would only show up once liberals had been excluded from the sample. Findings lend partial support to this hypothesis.

As expected, overall results concerning the Soviet Union showed only weak, insignificant attribution biases. Table 8.3 shows a tendency not to attribute helpful behavior to the Soviet Union's nature (by a 65% to 15% margin), but it also shows a slight tendency not to attribute harmful behavior to the Soviet Union's nature either (by a 50% to 35% margin). The difference between these two response tendencies was not significant (chi-square = 2.5, $df = 1$, $p = .11$).

TABLE 8.4
Agreement with the Nature Statement in Response to Acts by the Soviet Union, Liberals Excluded

		Response		
		Agree	Disagree	
Act	Airlifted Supplied	1 (8%)	1 1 (85%)	1 2 (93%)
	Dropped Bombs	7 (47%)	6 (40%)	1 3 (87%)
		8	1 7	2 5

Note: Neutral responses were excluded from this table. Chi-square = 6.5, $df = 1$, $p = .01$.

TABLE 8.5
Agreement with the Forced Statement in Response to Acts by the Soviet Union

		Response		
		Agree	Disagree	
Act	Airlifted Supplied	9 (35%)	14 (54%)	23 (89%)
	Dropped Bombs	9 (35%)	15 (58%)	24 (93%)
		18	29	47

Note: There were 26 subjects per condition. Neutral responses were excluded from this table. Chi-square = 0.01, $df = 1$, $p = .9$.

These findings do not demonstrate that there is no anti-Soviet attribution bias, but merely that the bias is too weak to achieve statistical significance. This was expected due to softening anti-Soviet attitudes. In addition, it was predicted that, because more accommodative attitudes were predominantly found among liberals, excluding them from the sample would produce clear and significant anti-Soviet attribution biases among the remaining conservative and middle-of-the-road subjects. This prediction also turned out to be accurate.

Table 8.4 shows the pattern of responses by nonliberals to the nature statement for conditions involving the Soviet Union. It shows an overwhelming tendency (by an 85% to 8% margin) not to attribute helpful action to the nature of the Soviet Union. A significantly different (chi-square = 6.5, $df = 1$, $p = .01$) pattern emerged in responses to harmful Soviet behavior: 47% agreed that it was the Soviet Union's nature and 40% disagreed. No such relationship was found among liberals (chi-square = 0.3, $df = 1$, $p = .6$).

TABLE 8.6
Agreement with the Forced Statement in Response to Acts by the Soviet Union, Liberals Excluded

		Response		
		Agree	Disagree	
Act	Airlifted Supplied	5 (39%)	6 (46%)	11 (85%)
	Dropped Bombs	3 (20%)	11 (73%)	14 (93%)
		8	17	25

Note: Neutral responses were excluded from this table. Chi-square = 1.6, $df = 1$, $p = .2$.

As Table 8.5 indicates, there was no overall relationship between what the Soviet Union did and whether subjects assumed that it had been forced to do so. In both conditions, 35% agreed with the forced statement and somewhat over half of the subjects disagreed. When liberals are excluded from the sample, a very weak, insignificant relationship emerges (chi-square = 1.6, $df = 1$, $p = .2$; see Table 8.6). Although nonliberals showed a strong tendency not to think the Soviet Union had been forced to drop the bombs (by a 73% to 20% margin), they did not tend, as expected (hypothesis 2-B), to assume that the Soviets had been forced to airlift the supplies. While excluding liberals strengthened the relationship, it did not produce significant findings for the forced statement.

Results of t-tests support the notion that liberals tend to view the nature of the Soviet Union somewhat differently from more conservative Americans. Nonliberals tended to view the Soviet airlifting of relief supplies to be inconsistent with its nature significantly more than did liberals ($t = 1.9$, $df = 24$, one-tailed, $p < .05$). They also tended to agree with the notion that the bombing of Bamora was consistent with the nature of the Soviet Union significantly more than liberals ($t = 1.9$, $df = 24$, one-tailed, $p < .05$). The t-test results were weaker with respect to the forced statement. Liberals were somewhat less prone to rejecting the idea that the Soviets were forced to bomb Bamora than were nonliberals, but this difference was only of marginal significance ($t = 1.5$, $df = 24$, one-tailed, $p < .08$). There was no significant difference in their tendencies to agree that the Soviet Union had been forced to airlift supplies. Thus, removing liberals from the analysis did not serve to alter greatly findings regarding external attributions for Soviet behavior.

Overall

The third hypothesis predicted overall attribution biases that favored the United States over the Soviet Union, particularly among nonliberals. Analyses of variance support this hypothesis. Given pro-American and anti-Soviet attribution biases, superpower identity (the United States or the Soviet Union) is expected to show an interaction effect with superpower behavior (the dropping of bombs or supplies). The helpful act is expected to elicit more agreement with the "nature" statement and disagreement with the "forced" statement when the superpower is the United States, while the harmful act is expected to elicit more agreement with the "nature" statement and more disagreement with the "forced" statement when the superpower is the Soviet Union.

Overall, analysis of variance indicated the expected interaction effect between the superpower involved and its behavior, both for agreement with the "nature" statement ($F = 13.2$, $p = .001$) and for agreement with the forced statement ($F = 8.0$, $p = .006$). Analyses of variance were also done separately for the liberal and nonliberal subsamples. As expected, for both the "nature" and the "forced" responses, the superpower–behavior interaction effect remained strong among nonliberals ($F = 19.4$, $p = .001$; $F = 9.3$, $p = .004$), but was not found among liberals ($F = 0.1$, $p = .8$; $F = 0.4$, $p = .5$). Liberals did not tend to exhibit the same pro-American and anti-Soviet attributional tendencies shown by nonliberals.

In summary, then, subjects tended to perceive the airlifting of relief supplies as an extremely helpful act, and to view the bombing of the village as extremely harmful. Overall, subjects tended to consider behavior they perceived to be consistent with the nature of the actor to be voluntary, and behavior that they viewed as inconsistent with the actor's nature as something it was forced to do. Subjects who read of the United States behaving in the helpful manner viewed it as a voluntary act consistent with the nation's nature. Conservatives and middle-of-the-roaders who read of harmful U.S. behavior tended to view it as uncharacteristic behavior that the United States had been forced into. Liberals did not show this second tendency, but the sample was too small to make firm conclusions on this matter. Conservatives and middle-of-the-roaders tended to exhibit the reverse tendencies with regard to the Soviet Union, while liberals, again, did not. Overall findings show pro-U.S. attributional tendencies and mixed tendencies with respect to the Soviet Union.

DISCUSSION

Why was airlifting relief supplies considered to be a voluntary, naturally American act while dropping bombs was not? It is not because Americans know that their nation sometimes airlifts relief supplies, but do not know that America often drops bombs as well. Given the many wars and interventions the United States has participated in and America's heavy use of aerial bombings over the last half-century, Americans cannot help being conscious of their country's fondness for air attacks. Hiroshima and Dresden are famous legends of devastation. The saturation of Southeast Asia with American bombs is not only historical record, it is also frequently reenacted on television and in the cinema. More recent events, from the bombing of Khadafi's tents to the latest Gulf War, provide further knowledge of America's use of aerial bombing. The United States is the greatest aerial bomber of all time, and the American university students who served as subjects in this experiment must at least have had some consciousness that the United States often resorts to such behavior.

Because of this awareness, about a third of the subjects saw bombing as consistent with America's nature. Yet despite the American propensity to bombing, more subjects did not perceive such destructive behavior to be consistent with America's nature. Instead, they showed a tendency to attribute American bombing behavior (destructive action by a benevolent nation) to outside forces: The United States does not respond in a destructive manner unless forced to do so.

As a result of this attribution process, the stereotype of a peace loving, benevolent America can persist in the presence of intermittent destruction on the part of agents of U.S. foreign policy. The stereotype of a benevolent America is further maintained, in a more straightforward way, by attributions about instances of American aid: apparently voluntary, generous aiding behavior is seen as quintessentially American, and knowledge of it serves to reinforce the stereotype of a benevolent America.

Americans tend to view their country as a generous, helpful nation. In this context, acts of giving need no further explanation. Thus there is a tendency to overlook situational pressures that motivate U.S. "giving" behavior. Aid has been an important part of U.S. foreign policy, an effective policy tool which has allowed a rich nation to control the lives of others. As Edelman (1974) points out, "helping" language and behavior often functions to disguise and justify domination.

The line between helping and hurting often becomes blurred: not only are situational motives for helpful acts ignored, but harmful acts by what is assumed to be a benevolent nation are interpreted as ultimately helpful. Thus the United States destroyed villages in Vietnam in order to "save" them, and "helped" the Nicaraguan people by sending "humanitarian aid" to counterrevolutionary guerrillas. The public image of the United States as a generous (perhaps even too generous) helper serves to facilitate public support for interventions that can be framed as helping missions. Most interventions, even violent attacks on villages, can be framed in this manner. Ironically, then, harmful acts are often justified as helpful. Alternatively, aggression can be attributed to an outside force and justified as a necessary response to danger or provocation. Ultimately, the self-image of the attacking nation is not sullied by the blood that may flow in the wake of its bombs.

As was shown in Chapter 3, there were fluctuations both in U.S.–Soviet relations and public perceptions of the Soviet Union during the post–World War II period. The Soviet Union's enemy status varied with U.S.–Soviet relations, but this did not happen in a uniform manner throughout the American populace. Easing of anti-Soviet feelings began among liberals and spread right, while renewed anti-Sovietism began among conservatives and spread left.

Anti-Soviet attribution biases were dependent on the anti-Soviet stereotypes they perpetuated. In the late 1980s, increasingly positive attitudes toward the Soviet Union were accompanied by a decreased tendency to discount helpful Soviet behavior or use harmful Soviet behavior as a basis for dispositional attributions. Attribution biases no doubt continued to bolster anti-Soviet sentiments for some, but for others pro-American attribution biases remained strong in the absence of an anti-Soviet counterpart.

NOTE

1. Analyses using Kendall's tau on the uncollapsed ordinal response data were also done, and they yielded the same results as the dichotomous chi-square analyses presented in this chapter.

9

Cold War Goals
in American Foreign Policy:
Nicaragua and the World

This chapter provides additional evidence for the cultural predominance of two relationships in the cold war schema: the positive relationship between the United States and democracy, and the negative relationship between the United States and communism. It also provides evidence that the two beliefs (that the United States supports democracy and that it opposes communism) are tied together in the same belief system. Finally, this chapter provides evidence that many who held the cold war schema as a general stereotype applied it to U.S. intervention in Nicaragua, a specific case about which they were ignorant.

In these ways, this chapter provides additional evidence of Americans using the cold war schema and shows one way in which the schema has been manifested in perceptions of a specific case. The cold war schema produced a particular set of general perceptions of U.S. foreign policy goals, which were used to draw conclusions concerning actual foreign policies and realities about which little was known. In the absence of substantive information, Americans used schema-based perceptions to make sense of Nicaragua and U.S. objectives there. The application of the general schema to specific instances reinforced and reified the patriotic schema as it produced patriotic perceptions of important events.

"Scripts" are schemata for stereotyped event sequences; they are the schemata we use to make sense of events and actions. Schank and Abelson (1977) identified a number of components that scripts have, including settings, props, plans, roles, goals, and actions. When the general cold war schema is used to interpret international events and behaviors, it takes on a scripted form. Roles include the United States, freedom fighters, and democratic governments, as well as the

Soviet Union, communist guerrillas, and oppressive communist governments. The goals of the United States, freedom fighters, and democratic governments include defending freedom and democracy, and opposing communism and oppression. The Soviets and their communist friends have opposite goals according to the schema. To the extent that the cold war schema was relevant and applied to a particular world event or foreign policy behavior, the various plans and actions undertaken were interpreted in terms of actors in cold war roles being guided by cold war goals.

In this way, perceptions of the goals of U.S. foreign policy strongly affect interpretations of U.S. involvement in world affairs. In this chapter, findings from a study of beliefs about U.S. foreign policy goals are presented. The study tests the validity of a number of assumptions that go with a culturally predominant cold war schema.

First, an important claim being made and supported in this book is that elements of the cold war schema have pervaded American culture. If this is the case with respect to the positive link between the United States and democracy and the negative link between the United States and communism, then most subjects should agree that defending democracy and opposing communism are important U.S. foreign policy goals. In fact, subjects in the study tended to have such beliefs.

Second, even if these beliefs are generally accepted, that does not mean that they are linked together in one schema. Are "U.S. Goal = Defending Democracy" and "U.S. Goal = Opposing Communism" independent beliefs, or are they parts of the same belief system (the cold war schema), joined as "U.S. Goals = Defending Democracy and Opposing Communism"? If these two beliefs are linked in a common belief system, then there should be strong correlations between the two. Such correlations are found.

Third, schemata and scripts are general cognitive frameworks that are used to process the specific information to which they are applied. It is one thing to show that subjects believe that defending democracy and opposing communism are important foreign policy goals, and it is another to show that they actually use these beliefs when interpreting American objectives in specific instances. This study shows, not only that Americans believe in aspects of the cold war schema, but that they apply them in interpreting specific U.S. involvement in the world.

Subjects were asked about their beliefs concerning general U.S. foreign policy goals, and concerning U.S. objectives in Nicaragua. If the general beliefs were being applied to the specific case by the subjects in this study, then there should have been strong correlations between believing that defending democracy or opposing communism were general foreign policy goals, and believing that they were objectives of U.S. involvement in Nicaragua. Such correlations were found, suggesting that Americans often used general cold war beliefs to interpret American objectives in specific cases like Nicaragua.

THE PRELIMINARY STUDY

Results from a preliminary, open-ended questionnaire administered to students in an advertising course at the University of Washington were used as the basis for the statements that were presented to subjects in the main questionnaire. Both studies (preliminary and main) were conducted during the month of May in 1986. In the preliminary questionnaire, 29 subjects were asked, "What do you think are the main goals of U.S. foreign policy?" The goal of opposing communism was mentioned by 52% of the subjects, while the promotion of democracy and economic goals were each mentioned by 41% of the subjects. Fifty-nine percent of the subjects mentioned at least one of the following: peace, understanding, communication, justice, U.S. ideals, rights, freedom, and morality. These responses were placed in a single "peace/moral" category. Thus there were four main types of goals mentioned by the respondents: opposing communism, and promoting democracy, economics, and peace/morality.

To ascertain whether those subjects who mentioned one type of goal tended to (or not to) mention another type of goal, cross-tabulations were run on the six possible goal-pairs. For four of the goal-pairs no relationship was found. However, it was found that only 2 respondents mentioned both economics and peace/morality, and that the negative relationship was significant to the .02 level. More significant (both statistically and substantively) was the strong positive relationship between mentions of opposing communism and promoting democracy. A chi-square of 13 and a significance level of .001 lend strong support to the notion that these two are joined in a common, culturally predominant schema. Inspection of a few responses adds anecdotal support to the idea that the cold war schema resided in the minds of many. America's main foreign policy goals were, according to selected subjects:

"To protect democracy or something like protect freedom of people and rights, to stop spread of communism."

"To keep the world free of Communism; to increase Democracy where possible."

"To keep our allies, to protect democratic nations (whether they want to be or not) to stop communism's spread."

"Preserve democracy, stop the spread of communism."

THE MAIN STUDY

Method

The main questionnaire was administered to 76 student subjects from an intermediate-level communications course at the University of Washington. Subjects were presented with a series of statements, and were instructed to express their agreement or disagreement on a 5-point scale. The eight goal statements included on the questionnaire applied the four goal-types (opposing communism, promoting democracy, economics, and peace/morality) generally to U.S. foreign policy, and specifically to U.S. involvement in Nicaragua:[1]

1. "Stopping the spread of communism is the goal of U.S. foreign policy."
2. "Promoting democracy around the world is the goal of U.S. foreign policy."
3. "Protecting U.S. economic interests overseas is the goal of U.S. foreign policy."
4. "Keeping peace and improving understanding between nations is the goal of U.S. foreign policy."
5. "The purpose of U.S. actions toward Nicaragua is to stop the spread of communism."
6. "The purpose of U.S. actions toward Nicaragua is to establish democracy in Central America."
7. "The purpose of U.S. actions toward Nicaragua is to protect U.S. economic interests."
8. "The purpose of U.S. actions toward Nicaragua is to bring peace to the region."

General statements were presented first, in a randomly selected order, followed by a few buffer statements and then specific (Nicaragua) statements, also in randomly selected order. Other statements not discussed here were interspersed among the goal statements.

Finally, subjects were given six descriptions of important Nicaragua-relevant people, places, and groups and were asked to identify them. The questions varied in difficulty and were intended to measure levels of knowledge on Nicaragua.

Findings and Discussion

The knowledge test asked subjects to identify current Nicaraguan President Ortega, pre-revolutionary President Somoza, Managua as the capital of Nicaragua, Honduras as the primary base of the Contras, the Contadora group, and the Miskito Indians. The fact that 68% of the subjects were unable to answer *any* of the six questions correctly testifies to the widespread ignorance concerning Nicaragua among the subject pool.

Table 9.1 shows the percentage of subjects who agreed, disagreed, or were neutral with respect to each of the eight goal statements. There is a clear tendency to agree, rather than disagree, with all eight statement. This indicates that the four goals of U.S. foreign policy are reasonably well accepted by the subjects.

However, the number of subjects willing to take a stand (in agreement or disagreement) is consistently less for the Nicaragua statements as compared to the general statements. An average of 21% of the subjects were neutral in response to the general statements, while 38% did not choose sides in response to statements regarding U.S. involvement in Nicaragua. Some subjects were appar-

TABLE 9.1
Percentage of Subjects Agreeing and Disagreeing with the Eight Goal Statements

Goal Statement	Response		
General: U.S. Foreign Policy	Agree	Disagree	Neutral
Opposing Communism	63%	17%	20%
Promoting Democracy	5 7	2 5	1 8
Economics	7 0	1 3	1 7
Peace	5 5	2 2	2 3
Specific: Nicaragua			
Opposing Communism	54%	12%	34%
Promoting Democracy	4 2	2 0	3 8
Economics	4 3	1 6	4 1
Peace	3 7	2 5	3 8

ently willing to declare a general schematic notion, but unwilling to simply apply their general beliefs to a specific case about which they knew little or nothing.

Since the vast majority of the subjects knew little or nothing about Nicaragua, that still left a significant portion who were willing to simply apply general beliefs to a specific case about which they were ignorant. Figure 9.1 displays the seven relationships among the various responses that were significant at the .005 level or better (using Kendall's tau). For the goals of opposing communism (tau = .37, $p = .0001$), promoting democracy (tau = .28, $p = .002$), and bringing peace (tau = .32, $p = .0007$), there were strong correlations between believing that the United States was pursuing the goal in general and believing that the United States was doing so in Nicaragua. American intervention was being publicly framed in cold war terms, and, in the absence of knowledge on Nicaragua, cold war schema users tended to instantiate the general cold war schema when called upon to interpret the specific case of Nicaragua. The schema provides the answer, making actual

FIGURE 9.1
Highly Significant Correlations in Responses to Goal Statements

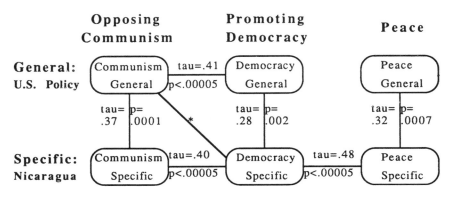

knowledge about Nicaragua unnecessary to opinion formation. The result of this phenomenon is that Americans who had no referential knowledge concerning the conflict, its actors, or history tended to believe that the United States was trying to save democracy from communism down there. It is likely that this same dynamic applied to interpretations of and opinions about similarly framed interventions, most notably those in Greece, Guatemala, Vietnam, Chile, and El Salvador.

Given elite use of the cold war schema to frame the situation in Nicaragua, a situation the American public knew very little about, it was not unreasonable that the schema was a primary basis for mass interpretations of U.S. objectives in Nicaragua. News biases such as those demonstrated in Chapter 5 aided the White House and State Department in their efforts to promote the cold war schema as the proper framework for interpreting Nicaraguan and U.S. intentions there. In turn, the tendency to perceive U.S. intentions in Central America as anticommunist and prodemocratic made Americans more likely to accept cold war schema–based portrayals of reality there. The predominance of the general schema allowed it to be cued and used in specific cases such as Nicaragua, and its use in specific cases reinforced and perpetuated its cultural predominance.

This relationship between the general and the specific is crucial to cultural knowledge and its use. The pervasive belief in the general schema and its repeated use in specific instances are interdependent: neither will happen without the other. The general schema is a culturally accepted cognitive tool for processing a set of specific instances, and it is expressed and reinforced through its application. This relationship between the general schema and its specific applications is crucial both to the maintenance of the American patriotic schema and to the ongoing perpetuation of patriotic perceptions and behaviors.

Figure 9.1 also shows an extremely strong relationship between agreement that the United States is working to oppose communism and agreement that the United States is promoting democracy. Both in general (tau = .41, $p < .00005$) and with respect to Nicaragua (tau = .40, $p < .00005$), perceptions of U.S. goals as opposing communism and promoting democracy went together. This finding indicates that the beliefs that the United States promotes democracy and opposes communism are not independent. The cold war schema has bound these two beliefs together in a common belief system. The findings of this study are further evidence of the schema's presence in American minds and of its impact on American perceptions of international affairs.

NOTE

1. The reader will notice that each statement specifies "*the* goal of U.S. foreign policy" rather than *a* goal, "*the* purpose of U.S. action in Nicaragua" rather than *a* purpose. This strong language was used intentionally in order to identify subjects who truly thought the goal in question was an important one. The strong wording was used in the interest of validity, and the percentages of subjects agreeing with the statements are subsequently less than they might have been. More subjects would have agreed with statements referring to "*a* goal" or "*a* purpose": subjects who disagreed because they did not think that the goal in question was centrally important enough to be called "*the* goal of U.S. foreign policy" might have opted for the weaker characterization of "*a* goal of U.S. foreign policy."

10

Choosing Sides
with the Cold War Schema

We're for the good guys. . . . I know who the good guys and the bad guys
are.

—Secretary of State George Shultz
(*The New York Times,* February 28, 1986, p. A6)

How do we know who the good guys and the bad guys are? Americans have at
their disposal an array of criteria for determining which side to support in a
foreign or international conflict. The cold war schema provides a number of
particularly important criteria, many of which Secretary of State Shultz used to
arrive at the above conclusion about Nicaragua.

According to the cold war schema, the side of the United States, freedom,
and democracy is the good side, and the side of the Soviet Union, communism,
and oppression is the bad side. When a cold war schema user chooses side
in a foreign or international conflict, associating one or both of the protagonists
with one or more of these six elements of the schema is likely to affect side-
taking. If balance theory is correct, there should be a tendency for cold war
schema users to favor whoever is positively associated with the United States,
freedom, or democracy, or negatively associated with the Soviet Union, communism, or oppression.

In the experiment presented in this chapter, subjects were presented with news
reports of a foreign conflict in which one side was either supported by the United
States, supported by the Soviet Union, referred to as "democratic," or referred to
as "communist." As cold war schema users would have been expected to do,

subjects tended to support the side in conflict which was believed to be either democratic or supported by the United States, and to oppose the side which was believed to be communist or supported by the Soviet Union.

These findings demonstrate how the cold war schema served as a basis for choosing sides in international conflicts. Because the schema has guided side-taking, it has been rare for Americans to believe that their country has intervened on the wrong side in a conflict. Americans have often objected that an intervention involved unnecessary cost or risk, but they have tended to believe tautologically that the United States is on the right side because they favor the side associated with the United States. Objections to interventions, then, tend to be limited to disagreements over their costs and benefits, rather than fundamental challenges concerning whether the United States has intervened on the correct side. Official rhetoric has often magnified the benefits of an intervention by framing the American-supported side as democratic, or the American-opposed side as communist or Soviet-supported. Thus these side-taking effects of the cold war schema have served to facilitate public support for U.S. interventions.

METHOD

This chapter and the one to follow report on different sorts of findings from the same experiment. Subjects in the experiment were presented with information in the form of a newspaper article. In the article, a superpower intervened on behalf of a government besieged by rebels. The original text was about 240 words in length and taken from an article on Soviet intervention in Afghanistan that appeared in *The New York Times* (February 18, 1986, p. A8). This article was chosen because it was a clear example of superpower intervention in a conflict with clearly drawn sides, and it did not include incidents that were very salient or recognizable. The report was general enough to permit it to be used as a generic case of intervention, and to permit the United States or the Soviet Union, democracy or communism, to characterize actors interchangeably without seeming out of place.

Dates were removed, figures altered, and names changed for presentation to subjects. In various conditions of the experiment, the superpower was identified as either the United States, the Soviet Union, or "UVW." In some of the conditions either the government of "XYZ" or the rebels opposing it was labeled as either "democratic" or "communist." In other conditions, neither was given any ideological label. The superpower was identified eight times in the text, and the government or rebel ideology, when specified, was identified four times. The general form of the text was as follows:

{United States / Soviet / UVW} forces were sent into XYZ at the time of a coup that installed the {democratic / communist / (no ideology)} Government of Philip Barnon, which said it needed {Washington's / Moscow's / UVW's} help to fight a growing {democratic / communist / (no ideology)} insurgency.

The fighting between {democratic / communist / (no ideology)} rebels and {democratic / communist / (no ideology)} Government soldiers, which began after an earlier coup, continued after the {U.S. / Soviet / UVW} forces moved in. The level of fighting has gradually lessened, and the war seems to have reached something of a deadlock as more than 80,000 {U.S. / Soviet / UVW} soldiers help the Government forces confront a stubborn and elusive guerrilla army.

{Democratic / Communist / (no ideology)} rebel forces report a pattern: they press in on an outpost or harass a major garrison town. {The Americans / The Russians / UVW} send(s) a tank column to the beleaguered area, bringing relief supplies and scattering the rebels. The tank column then withdraws, and a few months later, the cycle is repeated.

The cost for the rebels has been great. Schools, hospitals, and factories have been destroyed and thousands of refugees are estimated to flee the country each month. But rebel leaders say they will fight on.

{The United States / The Soviet Union / UVW} has said repeatedly that it will negotiate with the {democratic / communist / (no ideology)} Government in XYZ on a withdrawal of {U.S. / Soviet / UVW} soldiers only after outside aid to the {democratic / communist / (no ideology)} rebels is cut off.

Rebel leaders insist that {the United States / the Soviet Union / UVW} withdraw to the last man and say they will not accept any formula that would keep the {democratic / communist / (no ideology)} Government in place.

Thus different combinations of elements of the cold war schema were found in the fifteen different conditions of the experiment (see Table 10.1). In the control condition (number 1), no elements of the cold war schema are present. In six conditions (numbers 2, 3, 4, 7, 10, and 13), one element of the schema is found. These are the conditions that were used to test the side-taking effects of the cold war schema. Two elements of the cold war schema (one superpower and one ideology) are present in the remaining eight conditions (numbers 5, 6, 8, 9, 11, 12, 14, and 15), which were used to examine memory effects of the cold war schema (see Chapter 11).

The experiment was administered to students in introductory-level political science courses at the University of Washington on October 7, 1986. It took place during the second week of the academic year in order to minimize possible biases caused by political science courses. Half of the subjects had previously taken at least one university-level political science or history course, and one in ten had taken four or more. Almost all paid some attention to news, although there was a good deal of variation in how much. Average exposures to the front section of a daily newspaper and to network television news were both about four times per week. Subjects were evenly divided between liberals and conservatives, and between those preferring the Democratic and Republican parties. The mean age was 20, and 92% of the subjects were between the ages of 17 and 24; 46% of the subjects were female.

Subjects were randomly assigned to conditions, and the number of subjects per condition ranged from 24 to 31 (most conditions had 28 or 29 subjects). They were told that the text they were about to read was taken from an actual past news

TABLE 10.1
The Fifteen Conditions of the Experiment: Superpower Identity by Government or Rebel Ideology

Government or Rebel Ideology	Superpower Identity		
	UVW	USA	USSR
No Ideologies	1	2	3
Govt. = Democratic	4	5	6
Govt. = Communist	7	8	9
Rebels = Democratic	1 0	1 1	1 2
Rebels = Communist	1 3	1 4	1 5

Cond. #	Condition used to test side-taking (Chapter 10)
Cond. #	Condition used to test recall (Chapter 11)

report, and that some details had been altered. They were instructed to read the article as they would any article concerning an important issue.

Each subject was presented with the appropriate version of the article and given two minutes to read it. This was enough time to read the article at a leisurely pace but not enough to study or reread substantial portions of it. They then spent four minutes involved in an interference task, reading a short, irrelevant article. This was intended both to simulate a normal news-consumption situation and to increase schematic effects on recall (Fass & Schumacher, 1981) (see also Chapter 11).

Subjects were then presented with a questionnaire and given ten minutes to complete it. In that questionnaire, subjects were instructed to choose which side (the government or the rebels) they would rather see win the conflict.

HYPOTHESES

Cold war schema users consider themselves to have positive relationships with the United States and democracy, and negative relationships with the Soviet Union and communism (see Figure 10.1). All else being equal, a cold war schema user is expected to support a side in conflict which is believed to be either

FIGURE 10.1
Relationships between the Self and Other Elements of the Cold War Schema

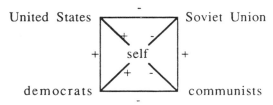

democratic or supported by the United States, and to oppose a side which is believed to be communist or supported by the Soviet Union. All else, of course, is not equal, and other criteria go into taking sides in a conflict. Still, a strong tendency to choose sides in accordance with the cold war schema is expected.

The text of the article presents a balanced triadic relationship among a super-power, the government of "XYZ," and the rebels (see Figure 10.2). The super-power and government are in a positive, supporting relationship with each other, and each is in a negative, opposing relationship with the rebels.

Hypotheses concerning which side subjects will tend to choose in reaction to schema-relevant versions of the text are derived by combining the relationships described in the text (Figure 10.2) with relevant relationships specified in the cold war schema (Figure 10.1), and assuming pressure toward cognitive balance. The six hypotheses specify expected tendencies to support one side or the other, given one schematic element in the text. They are listed below and graphically portrayed in Figure 10.3.

The Superpower

1. *Superpower = United States → Support for Government*

   When the superpower is the United States, subjects will tend to support the government because the subjects support the United States and the United States supports the government.

2. *Superpower = Soviet Union → Support for Rebels*

   When the superpower is the Soviet Union, subjects will tend to support the rebels because the subjects oppose the Soviet Union and the Soviet Union supports the government.

The Government

3. *Government = Democratic → Support for Government*

   When the government is democratic, subjects will tend to support the government because the subjects support democratic actors.

4. *Government = Communist → Support for Rebels*

   When the government is communist, subjects will tend to support the rebels because the subjects, like the rebels, oppose communists.

The Rebels

5. *Rebels = Communist → Support for Government*

When the rebels are communist, subjects will tend to support the government because the subjects, like the government, oppose communists.

6. *Rebels = Democratic → Support for Rebels*

When the rebels are democratic, subjects will tend to support the rebels because the subjects support democratic actors.

FINDINGS

These hypotheses were tested through comparisons of the percentages of subjects supporting each side in conditions in which only one schematic element (either the United States, the Soviet Union, democrats, or communists) was present. Findings are presented in Table 10.2. Effects of the superpower's identity were isolated by comparing conditions in which no ideologies were specified for the government or rebels. When the United States supported the government, 76% of the subjects did too, while 8% supported the rebels. When it was the Soviet Union that intervened, 18% supported the government and 67% supported the rebels. Thus superpower identity strongly determined the sides subjects supported (chi square = 18.2, $df = 1$, $p = .0001$).

Effects of the government's ideology were examined through a comparison of conditions in which UVW was the superpower and no ideology was specified for the rebels. When the government was democratic 62% supported it and 17% supported the rebels, while when the government was communist 18% supported it and 63% supported the rebels. Thus government ideology also had a strong effect on the side chosen (chi square = 11.7, $df = 1$, $p = .001$).

Finally, effects of the rebel's ideology were pinpointed through a comparison of conditions in which the superpower was UVW and the government was not given an ideology. When the rebels were communist 24% supported them and 62% supported the government, while 56% supported the democratic rebels and 22% supported the government they opposed. Thus rebel ideology affects the side supported by subjects as well (chi square = 6.1, $df = 1$, $p = .01$)

In the control condition (which does not refer to any of the cold war schema elements), 42% sided with the rebels, 23% took the government side, and 35%

FIGURE 10.2
Relationships between Actors in the Text

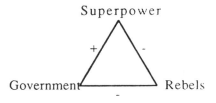

declined to choose sides. Only 14% to 22% of the subjects who read texts containing a schematic element declined to choose sides. This suggests that the addition of schema-relevant information provided an additional basis for side-taking. The pro-rebel tendency in the control condition may be due to a number of factors, including subtle biases in the article, the nature of the events described, a tendency to support the underdog, and the fact that the rebels were mentioned first on the questionnaire.

FIGURE 10.3
Hypotheses Concerning the Choosing of Sides
The relationships in parentheses—"(–)" or "(+)"—are hypothesized as based on the combination of the other, text-based and schema-based relationships and the assumed impositions of cognitive balance.

The Superpowers-

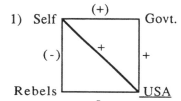 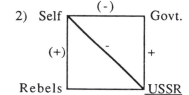

Government Ideology-

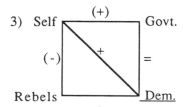 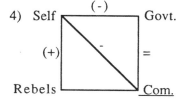

Rebel Ideology-

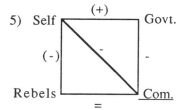 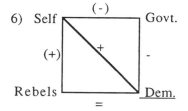

TABLE 10.2
Percentage of Subjects Supporting Each Side, by Condition

Condition	Side Supported	
	Government	Rebels
Superpower Identity:		
United States (n=24)	76%	8%
Soviet Union (n=27)	1 8	6 7
Government Ideology:		
Democratic (n=29)	62%	17%
Communist (n=27)	1 8	6 3
Rebel Ideology:		
Democratic (n=27)	22%	56%
Communist (n=29)	6 2	2 4

DISCUSSION

Findings indicate that Americans tend to be able to choose sides in foreign and international conflict on the basis of who they think is involved. Subjects tended to support the United States, whoever was supported by the United States, or an actor or entity that was presented to them as "democratic." They also tended to oppose the Soviet Union, whoever was supported by the Soviet Union, or an actor or entity that was presented to them as "communist." These findings are consistent with the idea that Americans often applied the cold war schema when choosing sides in foreign and international conflict.

It may be that schematic effects were particularly strong here because the text did not provide much detailed information about the unfamiliar situation in "XYZ." More information on the conflict might have lessened the effects of the schema on side-taking. It is probable that the extent to which Americans tended to lack knowledge and detailed information on foreign and international conflicts increased their dependency on the cold war schema when they chose sides.

This suggests that while the cold war schema created a tendency to support the policies and actions of the United States and its allies, additional information could potentially break down stereotypes and supply reasons to oppose the United States or support the enemy. In response to this danger, it is important for government officials and other interested elites to frame additional information in terms of the schema. In order to elicit public support for the proper side in the conflict, the United States can be presented as supporting democracy or opposing communism, U.S. allies can be presented as democratic, or enemies can be presented as communist or supported by the Soviet Union. One effect of such motivated elite use of elements of the cold war schema is that the schema can come to dominate conceptions of international conflicts and determine side-taking in support of U.S. policy.

Not every international conflict has been readily interpretable in terms of the cold war schema. The cold war schema is but one example of an extension of the American patriotic schema that has helped Americans distinguish the "good guys" from the "bad guys."

During World War II, for instance, the Nazi enemy schema helped to guide American side-taking. More recently, the Gulf War was clearly framed in terms of the American patriotic schema: the United States, in standing up for Kuwait's right to self-determination, was seen as defending freedom and democracy against an oppressive military dictatorship. Thus, Americans knew that they were the virtuous saviors and that Iraq (and particularly Saddam Hussein) was the terrible villain. In the short run, the use of the American patriotic schema in framing the Gulf War ensured popular support and enthusiasm for the Bush regime and its war effort. In the long run, the war was an exercise in patriotism, a positive demonstration of the truths held in the patriotic schema, and a forum for the repeated recital of those truths.

Like elections, wars have their ritual functions: they allow for the expression and acting out of patriotic sentiments and beliefs in a highly charged context that reifies beliefs and magnifies sentiments. Schematic side-taking does not just allow citizens to make simple sense of complex conflicts: schematic side-taking allows international conflicts to function as demonstrations of the veracity of the American patriotic schema.

11

Recalling Information Consistent
with the Cold War Schema

Lippmann (1922) suggested long ago that stereotypes are self-confirming and resistant to refutation because they are used in processing the very information that is used to evaluate and validate them. More recently, a number of studies (Snyder & Uranowitz, 1978; Rothbart, Evans, & Fulero, 1979; Snyder, 1981) have shown that subjects tend to remember stereotype-consistent information more than stereotype-inconsistent information. These findings have been interpreted as support for Lippmann's claim, since information that reinforces the stereotype is retained while potentially refuting information is lost. The experiment discussed in this chapter tests whether the cold war schema, through its effect on recall of relevant information, serves to confirm itself and resist potential refutation.

Events do not always fit preconceptions, and events have not always fit neatly into the cold war schema. For example, U.S. intervention in pre-Pinochet Chile, while perhaps anticommunist, encouraged the undermining and overthrow of Chilean democracy. U.S. behavior was inconsistent with the schema-based notion that the United States supports democracy. Has information about events that have been inconsistent with the cold war schema been paid attention to, remembered, and taken seriously in the same way that consistent information has? If not, then the cold war schema may have served to maintain its cultural predominance by filtering out information that has not fit it, making it difficult for schema users to test the validity of their preconceptions.

The experiment presented in this chapter tests recall of information that is consistent or inconsistent with the cold war schema. Findings demonstrate tendencies to ignore, distort, or discount information inconsistent with the cold war schema. For example, U.S. opposition to democracy was correctly recalled far less than U.S. support for democracy or U.S. opposition to communism. Because the cold war schema structured memory and recall processes, information consistent with it was more likely to be correctly recalled and incorporated into knowledge. For years, news and rhetoric have been biased in favor of the cold war schema, but these findings show that biased information is only one piece of the picture. Even when information may not have been biased, information processing was.

THE EXPERIMENT

Effects of consistency with the cold war schema on recall were tested in the same experiment that was introduced in the last chapter (see the methods section of Chapter 10). Subjects read news articles that portrayed a superpower intervention on behalf of a government besieged by rebels. In various conditions of the experiment, the superpower was either the United States, the Soviet Union, or "UVW," and the government or rebels were sometimes described as democratic or communist. The fifteen conditions of the experiment are listed in Table 10.1.

In the eight conditions used in this portion of the experiment, two elements of the cold war schema—a superpower and an ideology—were present in the text. The superpower was either the United States or the Soviet Union, and either the government or the rebels were labeled as either democratic or communist. The cold war schema specifies a set of balanced relationships among these four elements, as shown in Figure 11. 1. For each of the four superpower–ideology matchings (U.S.–democratic, Soviet–democratic, U.S.–communist, and Soviet–communist), there is one condition of the experiment that is consistent with the cold war schema and one inconsistent condition:

1. *Conditions Containing the United States and Democrats*
    Consistent: The United States supports a democratic government.
    Inconsistent: The United States opposes democratic rebels.

2. *Conditions Containing the Soviet Union and Democrats*
    Consistent: The Soviet Union opposes democratic rebels.
    Inconsistent: The Soviet Union supports a democratic government.

3. *Conditions Containing the United States and Communists*
    Consistent: The United States opposes communist rebels.
    Inconsistent: The United States supports a communist government.

4. *Conditions Containing the Soviet Union and Communists*
    Consistent: The Soviet Union supports a communist government.
    Inconsistent: The Soviet Union opposes communist rebels.

FIGURE 11.1
Balanced Relationships among the Superpowers and Ideological Actors, According to the Cold War Schema

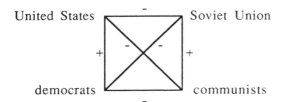

After reading the stimulus article, subjects spent four minutes involved in an interference task, reading a short, irrelevant article. This was intended both to simulate a normal news-consumption situation and to increase schematic effects on recall. The second article was expected to interfere with the subject's immediate, veridical memory of the stimulus text, in the same way that accompanying articles and the passage of time interfere with the memories of normal news consumers for the news reports they read. This was expected to increase subject dependence on schema-based memory in their recall, since schema-based memory has been found to be particularly enduring (Bower et al., 1977; Fass & Schumacher, 1981; Baillet & Keenan, 1986).

Immediately after reading the second article, subjects were presented with a questionnaire and given ten minutes to complete it. They were first asked to summarize the article. Summary recall was used rather than serial recall because it is closer to how people behave in their everyday lives when recalling news reports. People do not attempt to recall news reports word for word, but they often remember and sometimes discuss elements of reports that are salient, meaningful, interesting, or important to them. The summaries provided a measure of what subjects remembered and considered important enough to mention. It was also assumed that summaries would tend to be structured around salient schemata, and would provide clear evidence of schematic effects where they existed (Rumelhart, 1977). Data on recall of the relationships between the superpower (either the United States or the Soviet Union) and the ideological actor (either democrats or communists) were extracted from these summaries.

To test the effects of consistency with the cold war schema on recall, summary recall responses to the inconsistent condition were compared with responses to the consistent condition for each of the four superpower–ideology matchings. All summary recall responses were coded independently by two coders (intercoder consistency was 97%). Cases were coded in random order, and without knowledge of which article the subject had read. Coders recorded (1) any superpower recalled in the summary, (2) any ideology or ideological entity recalled, and (3) whether a supporting or opposing relationship between the superpower and the ideology or ideological entity was stated in the summary.

Ninety-seven percent of the 227 subjects recalled the United States or the Soviet Union in their summaries. Seventy-two percent of those who read of communists mentioned them, while 53% of those who read of democrats recalled them. Forty-three percent of the subjects did not state any superpower–ideology relationship in their summaries. In 90% of those cases this was due, at least in part, to the fact that the ideology was not mentioned in the summary.

Subjects were also asked to describe whatever they found confusing about the article (other questions were also asked, but they are not relevant here). Responses to this question were also coded; if the response included mention of the superpower–ideology relationship as a cause of confusion, this was noted.

Subjects were expected to vary with regard to whether and when they used the cold war schema, how attentive they were to the text, how complete a summary they chose to supply on the questionnaire, and so forth. In addition, interpersonal differences in cognitive style and relevant knowledge lead to variations in the effects of schemata on learning and recall. Findings (Press et al., 1969; Delia & Crockett, 1973) suggest that cognitively simple subjects are more prone than cognitively complex ones to using balance schemata. Fiske et al. (1983) gave subjects descriptions of a fictional country and varied whether the country was identified as communist, democratic, or neither. Subjects who were relatively low in political knowledge tended to recall information that was consistent with the stereotype of the sort of state (communist or democratic) they were told they were reading about, and to exclude from recall information inconsistent with that stereotype. More knowledgeable subjects did not tend to exhibit such consistency-bias.

While interpersonal variations are found in this experiment, this chapter concentrates on how textual variations among the conditions of the experiment lead to different response tendencies. Although there is substantial variation within each condition, this does not detract from the important finding that texts consistent with the cold war schema show a greater tendency to be recalled with detail, clarity, and accuracy than texts inconsistent with the schema. This is not to downgrade the importance of interpersonal differences; a good deal of variation in responses is clearly due to subject variations such as those suggested above.

Four types of responses were distinguished (see Figure 11.2). First, some subjects did not recall the superpower–ideology relationship at all. Second, some of those who did recall the relationship did so incorrectly, recalling support as opposition or vice versa. Third, some of those who correctly recalled the relationship reported that they found it confusing. Fourth, some subjects correctly recalled the superpower–ideology relationship they had read about in the text and did not claim to have been confused by it.

The first type of response ignores the relationship, the second distorts it, and the third finds it confusing. Do subjects tend to respond to relationships that are inconsistent with the cold war schema in these three ways? The fourth type of response processes the relationship without difficulty. Do subjects respond in this fourth way, correctly recalling the relationship without confusion, significantly

FIGURE 11.2
Four Types of Summary Recall Responses

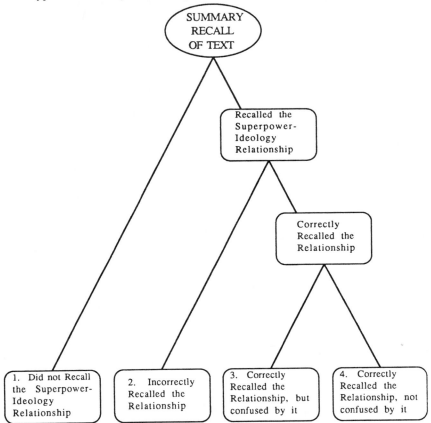

more in consistent conditions? If so, it is reasonable to conclude that the cold war schema serves to bias information processing such that consistent information is more easily processed and learned than inconsistent information. To answer these questions, the percentage of subjects in each consistent condition who gave each sort of response is compared to the percentage who gave that response in the inconsistent condition containing the same superpower and ideology.

EFFECTS OF INCONSISTENCY ON RECALL

Hypotheses concerning the effects of consistency or inconsistency with the cold war schema on summary recall are based on theories and findings in the psychological literature. Heider (1958) predicted that balanced structures would be better recalled than unbalanced structures. Findings have yielded qualified support for this prediction. For instance, DeSoto et al. (1968) found that balanced structures were learned and correctly recalled more than unbalanced structures. Cottrell et al. (1971) found not that balanced relationships are learned more than unbalanced ones, but that they are less likely to be forgotten once they are learned. Balanced and unbalanced structures were correctly recalled with equal frequency one minute after learning, but unbalanced structures were forgotten 24 hours later significantly more than were balanced structures.

In addition, schemata strongly determine what is recalled from a text (Rumelhart, 1977). A large body of experimental literature demonstrates and articulates a variety of schematic effects on memory (Hastie, 1981). Schemata guide perception and storage of stimuli, as well as subsequent retrieval and communication of what is recalled (Brewer & Treyens, 1981). Schema theory suggests tendencies to distort, reject, ignore, forget, or be confused by inconsistent relationships more than consistent ones (Alba & Hasher, 1983). Thus, information consistent with the schema is more likely to be accepted as clear and comprehensible reality than inconsistent information.

This tendency is expected to be manifested in the subjects' summary recall of the text in three alternative ways. First, information that is inconsistent with the schema may be ignored, forgotten, or not considered significant and thus left out of summary recall (Heider, 1958; Sentis & Burnstein, 1979; Cantor & Mischel, 1979; Hastie, 1981). Since the schema provides a framework for selective storing, recalling, and summarizing (Bransford & Johnson, 1972; Zadney & Gerard, 1974; Anderson et al., 1978; Rothbart et al., 1979), inconsistencies may be selected out of the picture.

Second, salient relationships inconsistent with the schema may stand out against schematic expectations as disturbing, confusing anomalies. When both the schematic elements and their relationships are relatively salient, inconsistency elicits a sense that things are out of order, not as they should be. These anomalies may actually stand out and be remembered (a schema-based "von Restorf" effect) more than consistent information (Graesser, Gordon, & Sawyer, 1979; Bower et al., 1979; Hastie & Kumar, 1979; Graesser, Woll, Kowalski, & Smith, 1980), and this may counteract the effects of schema-consistent selection discussed above. The confusing anomaly, however, is not easily incorporated into one's knowledge structure, and there is a tendency to discount it as odd, unrealistic, not to be accepted without explanation (George, 1980).

Third, subjects may ignore the fact that the relationship in the text is different from that in the schema. Subjects may actually read, comprehend, and store inconsistent text as if it were consistent with the schema. Alternatively, they may fill in gaps in stored text with schema-consistent "default" elements while reconstructing the text at time of recall (Minsky, 1975; Bower et al., 1977). Because the cold war schema serves to structure comprehension, storage, and recall, subjects may recall inconsistent information in a way consistent with the schema but not the actual text (Spiro, 1977, 1980a, 1980b). This schema-consistent distortion creates error in recall.

Thus three sorts of schematic effects have been identified:

1. *Schema-Consistent Selection*   Information inconsistent with the schema tends to be recalled less than information consistent with it.

2. *Anomaly Identification*   Information inconsistent with the schema tends to be recalled more than consistent information, and to be considered confusing.

3. *Schema-Consistent Distortion*   Information inconsistent with the schema tends to be recalled as if it were consistent with the schema.

While all three sorts of effects were expected to some degree in all inconsistent conditions, conditions involving communists were expected to elicit somewhat different patterns of responses than conditions involving democrats. As we saw in the word-association study described in Chapter 7, communism brought the Soviet Union to mind and democracy brought the United States to mind for two-thirds of the subjects in that study. While the Soviet Union also brought communism to mind for two-thirds of the subjects, however, only 38% of the subjects mentioned democracy in response to the United States (freedom, not democracy, was the most common response to the United States). In addition, we saw in Chapter 9 that subjects' tendencies to assume the goal of U.S. foreign policy to be opposing communism, and to apply that general goal to U.S. involvement in Nicaragua, was stronger than the tendency to do so for the goal of promoting democracy. These findings suggest that communism is a more salient element of the cold war schema than democracy.

While "communist" is a clear, highly charged, powerful label of a dangerous outgroup, "democratic" is a more ambiguous label, one that has been diluted through use in public discourse to describe political actors from Ferdinand Marcos to Jose Napoleon Duarte to Michael Dukakis and even to Mikhail Gorbachev. "Communist," as a more striking and salient symbol than "democratic," is not as easily ignored or left out of summary recall. Thus an inconsistent relationship involving communists is more likely either to stand out against schematic expectations as a confusing anomaly or to be incorrectly recalled in a manner consistent with the schema. In conditions containing the less salient democratic actors, the democratic nature of those actors is more likely to be ignored in recall. Overall findings fit this general picture.

FINDINGS

Overall findings are presented in Table 11.1. For conditions involving democrats, both superpower–ideology relationships were recalled less when the text was inconsistent with the cold war schema. Of those reading of U.S. support for democrats, 50% recalled a U.S.–democratic relationship, while 32% of those who read of U.S. opposition to democrats did so. Sixty-nine percent of the subjects who read of Soviet opposition to democrats recalled a Soviet–democratic

TABLE 11.1
Recall of Superpower–Ideology Relationship by Consistent and Inconsistent Conditions

	Type of Recall*			
Condition	①	②	③	④
United States and Democrats:				
Consistent Condition (n=26)	50%	0%	0%	**5 0%**
Inconsistent Condition (n=28)	6 8	7	0	**2 5**
Soviet Union and Democrats:				
Consistent Condition (n=29)	3 1	0	0	**6 9**
Inconsistent Condition (n=29)	4 8	1 0	1 0	**3 1**
United States and Communists:				
Consistent Condition (n=29)	3 4	0	0	**6 6**
Inconsistent Condition (n=29)	1 7	3 1	2 4	**2 8**
Soviet Union and Communists:				
Consistent Condition (n=29)	4 8	0	0	**5 2**
Inconsistent Condition (n=28)	4 3	2 1	2 9	**7**

*

① Did not recall the superpower–ideology relationship

② Incorrectly recalled the relationship

③ Correctly recalled the relationship, but confused by it

④ *Correctly recalled the relationship, not confused by it*

relationship, while 52% of those who read of Soviet support of democrats did so. Although neither difference is significant at the .05 level, they are both of reasonable magnitude and in the expected direction. Thus, while findings are not conclusive, they do suggest some schema-consistent selection. In inconsistent conditions there was less of a tendency to store and recall democrats within the framework of the cold war schema, and so there was more of a tendency to leave democrats out of the summaries.

For conditions involving communists, however, no such tendency was found. In fact, both superpower–ideology relationships were recalled more when the text was inconsistent with the cold war schema. Of those who read of U.S. opposition to communists, 66% mentioned a U.S.–communist relationship in their summary recall, while 83% did so in response to U.S. support for communists. Fifty-two percent of subjects who read of Soviet support for communists recalled a Soviet–communist relationship, while 57% of those who read of Soviet opposition to communists mentioned such a relationship. Because of the salience of communists, they did not tend to be left out of the summaries. Since subjects did pay attention to communists, they tended to process inconsistency either by identifying it as a confusing anomaly or by transforming it into consistency through distortion.

Reports by subjects concerning what they found to be confusing in the text support the notion that, especially for conditions involving communists, inconsistency elicits the identification of anomalies which cause confusion. For both inconsistent conditions involving communists, about a quarter of the subjects (29% when the Soviet Union opposed communist rebels, 24% when the United States supported a communist government) mentioned the superpower–ideology relationship as something they found confusing. As expected, inconsistency involving communists stood out as confusing anomalies for many subjects. In addition, 10% of the subjects who read about the Soviet Union supporting democrats claimed to be confused, but nobody in the condition involving U.S. opposition to democrats did. No subject in any of the consistent conditions mentioned the superpower–ideology relationship as a source of confusion.

There is also evidence of schema-consistent distortion. In all of the inconsistent conditions, a portion of those who recalled the superpower–ideology relationships did so in a manner consistent with the cold war schema, not the text they had read. When the United States supported communists, 31% of the subjects incorrectly recalled that the United States opposed the communists. When the Soviet Union opposed communists, 21% incorrectly recalled Soviet support for the communists. In both inconsistent conditions involving communists, of those subjects who recalled the superpower–ideology relationship, close to 40% recalled the schematic relationship rather than the textual one.

When the Soviet Union supported democrats, 10% of the subjects incorrectly recalled that the Soviet Union opposed the democrats. When the United States opposed the democrats, 7% of the subjects incorrectly recalled U.S. support for the democrats. In both inconsistent conditions involving democrats, of those subjects who recalled the superpower–ideology relationship, around 22% recalled the schematic relationship rather than the textual one. No subject in any of the consistent conditions incorrectly recalled a superpower–ideology relationship.

A couple of examples of typical relationship reversals will provide a taste of the phenomenon. Notice that in the first case the subject changed the identity of the communists, while in the second case the subject changed the superpower–rebel relationship.

Text The United States supported a communist government against rebels.

Response "The article was about a guerrilla movement in 'XYZ' that the U.S. was involved in fighting against them. The guerrillas, were, of course, the communist party. The U.S. were the good guys."

Text The Soviet Union supported a government against communist rebels.

Response "Country XYZ was in a state of revolution and the communist rebels need/ wanted the help of the USSR to suppress the opposing force."

Incorrect recall is clearly a result of inconsistency between textual relationships and schematic relationships. These schematic effects were stronger where communists were involved. This lends support to the notion that the salience of communists did not allow subjects to ignore them in inconsistent conditions (in fact they stood out), and forced them to resolve the inconsistency in other ways.

The combined findings are summarized in Table 11.1. Where democrats were involved, inconsistency decreased the percentage of subjects who recalled a superpower–ideology relationship. Inconsistent conditions containing democrats elic-ited a tendency toward schema-consistent selection, which resulted in fewer subjects recalling the superpower–ideology relationship. This was also accompanied by relatively mild tendencies toward anomaly identification and schema-consistent distortion: democratic inconsistency elicited some incorrect recall of the relationships, and very few claims of confusion based on inconsistency.

Where communists were involved, inconsistency increased the recall rate, but substantial percentages of the subjects in these inconsistent conditions recalled the relationship incorrectly, and equally large numbers claimed to be confused by the inconsistent relationship. Thus inconsistent conditions containing communists did not show any tendency toward schema-consistent selection, and most subjects recalled the superpower–ideology relationship. Here, however, there were strong tendencies toward anomaly identification and schema-consistent distortion; many subjects either incorrectly recalled or were confused by the superpower–ideology relationship. Overall, regardless of whether democratic or communist actors were involved, significantly more subjects correctly recalled the superpower–ideology relationship without confusion in the consistent conditions than in the inconsistent conditions.

In all cases, the combined effect of inconsistency with the schema was a clear decrease in the percentage of subjects who correctly recalled the superpower–ideology relationship without claiming to be confused by it. While 50% of the subjects correctly recalled U.S. support for democrats, only 25% correctly re-called U.S. opposition to democrats (chi square = 3.6, df = 1, p = .06). Sixty-nine percent of those who read of Soviet opposition to democrats recalled it without confusion, while just 31% did so in response to Soviet support for democrats (chi square = 8.3, df = 1, p < .005). Sixty-six percent correctly recalled U.S. opposition to communists without confusion, while 28% responded this way to U.S. support for communists (chi square = 8.4, df = 1, p <.005). Correct recall without confusion was the response of 52% of those who read of Soviet support for communists, but of only 7% of those responding to Soviet opposition to communists (chi square = 13.5, $df = 1$, $p < .0005$).

DISCUSSION

These findings have important implications with respect to popular use of relevant news information to test and evaluate the cold war schema. Evidence has been presented of response patterns that reduced the cognitive impact of schema-inconsistent information. Information that is not recalled or considered worthy of mention in a summary, information that is incorrectly recalled, and information that is viewed as strange and confusing is less likely to be learned and incorporated into one's knowledge structure than information that is clearly and correctly recalled. Thus the cold war schema, when used, searched out its own confirmation and guarded against its own refutation.

This means that American news consumers were more likely to pay attention to democratic characterizations of those supported by the United States or opposed by the Soviet Union than to democratic characterizations of those opposed by the United States or supported by the Soviet Union. There appears also to have been a tendency to recall inconsistent information as if it were consistent. Such errors in recall of inconsistent information maintain perceptions of a schema-consistent reality in the face of schema-inconsistent information. The recognition of confusing anomalies (which occurred predominantly in conditions of inconsistency involving communists) creates the opportunity for critical evaluation of the schema, but it also creates the desire to discount or explain away the anomaly, or to force it into fitting the schema after all. Together, these effects constitute a cognitive-cultural bias toward confirmation of the cold war schema and away from its refutation.

Consistent information is not just more likely to be learned and remembered, it is more likely to be communicated to others. Schema-consistent selection and distortion affect what news people hear from friends and acquaintances. Summary recall findings show a tendency to transmit information consistent with the schema, not to transmit information inconsistent with the schema, and to replace inconsistent information with consistent information. The result is a public discourse into which, all else being equal, schema-consistent information is more likely to enter.

All else has not been equal. As was argued in the first section of this book and demonstrated in Chapter 5 (with respect to elections in Central America), there has been a tendency for American politicians, officials, and journalists to present many foreign and international events in ways consistent with the cold war schema. The findings of this experiment imply, however, that even had American news consisted equally of information consistent and inconsistent with the cold war schema, Americans would, at least in the short term, have tended to find confirmation of the schema in the news. The cold war schema interfered with information otherwise capable of cuing alternative perspectives. This increased popular support for U.S. foreign policies that were or could be viewed from the cold war perspective, and allowed politicians and officials to elicit such support by promoting the application of the cold war schema to specific conflicts.

Some critics of U.S. foreign policy have interpreted U.S. interventions in such places as Guatemala, Chile, and Vietnam as antidemocratic. Supporters of these sorts of interventions have countered by depicting them as efforts to preserve democracy in the face of a communist threat. Findings suggest a tendency to attend to and recall information framed in this second manner. Sixty-six percent of the subjects who read of U.S. opposition to communists recalled it in their summaries. Fifty percent of those who read of U.S. support for democrats did so. In contrast, only 25% of those who read of U.S. opposition to democrats recalled it that way, and 7% mistakenly thought they had read of U.S. support for democrats.

Thus, even if public discourse had consisted evenly of arguments by critics and supporters, the prominence of the cold war schema would have created a tendency to find confirmation for supporting arguments and to ignore the critics. One result, as the side-taking findings from Chapter 10 indicate, is a strong tendency to support the United States and its allies. In the case of Vietnam, for instance, effects of the cold war schema may have interfered with the abilities of policymakers and the public to interpret evidence of a flawed and failing policy, made them resistant to critical arguments, and delayed shifts in public opinion and policy. Given the tragedies of Vietnam and other U.S. involvement, such effects should not be taken lightly.

More important still, the ongoing predominance of the American patriotic schema is perpetuated through the schema-guided memory processes it produces. Because the cold war schema and other extensions of the patriotic schema frame American perceptions of the many wars and interventions the nation has engaged in, those events tend to be remembered (or forgotten) and interpreted in ways that reinforce, rather than refute, the American patriotic schema. Regardless of the complex realities of international events, then, the pictures that stick in American minds contain positive proof that the United States fights for freedom and democracy in the world.

12

Conclusion

I'm no linguist, but I have been told that in the Russian language there isn't even a word for freedom.

—Ronald Reagan (Mintz, 1986, p. 26)

Freedom should be the right to be stupid if you want to be.

—Ronald Reagan (Reagan, 1989, p. 426)

Is the "land of the free" the home of the stupid? The answer is no. The sorts of cognitive biases that have been demonstrated in the last six chapters are basic to the way human beings think. Americans have no monopoly on cultural schemata, ingroup favoring, attribution and memory biases, or pressures toward cognitive balance. Nor are these sorts of things an indication of mental inadequacy. Differences in cognitive styles affect how and when these sorts of cognitive effects happen, but even powerful minds are susceptible to the sorts of schema-based information-processing biases shown in this book.

The main point is that biased perceptions of international relations are anchored in a nation's collectively held patriotic self-image, and that these biased international perceptions serve to bolster and perpetuate the patriotic beliefs upon which they are based. This book was written in an effort to explore the cognitive structures and processes through which this occurs.

These dynamics have been demonstrated in terms of American beliefs and perceptions in the post–World War II era. The American patriotic schema has been a long-standing, stable, and pervasive fundamental belief system in American culture, and the cold war schema extended the patriotic schema into world affairs in the cold war era. The biased picture that resulted from viewing world affairs in terms of the cold war schema created the image of a world into which the patriotic schema could comfortably fit. This reinforced and reified the patriotic schema. Thus the American patriotic schema is tied in an interactive fashion with ongoing perceptions of international relations. Ultimately, stable, patriotic public perceptions of national greatness and governmental legitimacy function to ensure a supportive and acquiescent public. This helps secure America's impressive level of political stability. Structures and processes of international perception, then, serve a system maintenance function at the domestic political level.

A variety of methods have been used here to demonstrate this thesis. In Chapter 3, national survey data were used to demonstrate the general pervasiveness of the cold war schema throughout the post–World War II period. Some examples of the use of the cold war schema in American culture (on television, in the cinema, and in academia) were presented in Chapter 4. The case studies presented in Chapter 5 showed how the cold war schema framed television news presentations of Central American elections, and how this framing bolstered the patriotic schema and encouraged public support for U.S. policies toward Central America.

In the second section of the book (Chapters 6 through 11), findings from a series of studies conducted on American university students were used to demonstrate cognitive effects of the cold war schema. The studies presented in Chapters 6 and 7 demonstrated that the cognitive links that comprise the cold war schema could be found in American minds. Chapter 7 went on to demonstrate that the American patriotic schema was strongly and stably held, but that the improving Soviet image was weakening the Soviet component of the cold war schema. The role of pressures toward structural balance in the process of belief system change was also examined. Chapter 9 presented a study that showed how elements of the cold war schema were manifested in perceived U.S. foreign policy goals, and how the general schema was applied to a specific case.

Experimental studies of the effects of the cold war schema were presented in Chapters 8, 10, and 11. In each study, subjects were given news reports concerning superpower involvement in a smaller country. The identities of actors and their acts were varied among experimental conditions, and the resulting variations in responses were measured and compared with hypotheses. The experiment presented in Chapter 8 demonstrated clear and pervasive pro-American attribution biases, as well as some anti-Soviet biases among more conservative subjects. The study presented in Chapter 10 showed a tendency for subjects to favor international actors described as U.S.-supported or democratic, and to oppose actors described as Soviet-supported or communist. The experiment presented in Chapter 11 found a tendency for subjects to ignore, forget, or be confused by information inconsistent with the cold war schema, or to recall it incorrectly as if it were consistent with the schema.

All the cognitive biases demonstrated in these three chapters were guided by elements of the cold war schema. In turn, biased attribution, side-taking, and recall contributed to the construction of an image of international relations that made those elements of the schema seem real. The cognitive processes demonstrated in these experiments were quite different, yet their political consequences were the same. Within the American context, the political consequences of these cognitive effects are two-fold. First, U.S. military interventions get interpreted in a positive light and thus tend to receive popular support, at least initially. This enables American rulers, if they wish, to stage antidemocratic or otherwise destructive interventions with relative freedom. Second, these biased interpretations bolster pro-American stereotypes, which generally serve to elicit supportive popular responses to other American policies and actions. Thus biased perceptions of one U.S. involvement reinforce stereotypes that lead to similarly biased perceptions of others. In the end, citizens' abilities to critically monitor and evaluate U.S. foreign policy is impaired, and the ability of government to pursue unsavory policies with impunity is enhanced.

These phenomena transcend the American context. The United States is not the only nation that sometimes fails to live up to its patriotic self-image. Reality often falls short of idealized stereotypes, and that is when sociocultural and cognitive processes must serve to cushion the clash between the complex world and the simple schema. These processes are structured by the schema and serve to preserve and promote it. When the schema is a patriotic national self-image, processes of self-perpetuation contribute to the maintenance of political order, public acquiescence, and policy support. Thus schema-based cognitive biases function to help foster national unity and stability. Unfortunately, such biases also harden the lines of international intolerance and misunderstanding.

References

Abelson, R. (1973). The Structure of Belief Systems. In R. Schank & K. Colby (Eds.), *Computer Models of Thought and Language*. San Francisco, CA: W. H. Freeman.

Abelson, R. (1981). Psychological Status of the Script Concept. *American Psychologist*, 36, 715–729.

Abelson, R., & Rosenberg, M. (1958). Symbolic Psychologic. *Behavioral Science*, 4, 1–13.

Alba, J., & Hasher, L. (1983). Is Memory Schematic? *Psychological Bulletin*, 93, 203–231.

Allison, G. (1970). Cool It: The Foreign Policy of Young America. *Foreign Policy*, 1, 144–160.

Almond, G. (1960). *The American People and Foreign Policy*. New York: Praeger.

Anderson, R. (1989). Let's Practice-up on Our Quayle-isms Before His Next Visit. *A Slice of the Times*, Dec. 11, 2.

Anderson, R., Spiro, R., & Anderson, M. (1978). Schemata as Scaffolding for the Representation of Information in Connected Discourse. *American Educational Research Journal*, 15, 433–440.

Arno, A. (1984). Communication, Conflict and Storylines: The News Media as Actors in a Cultural Context. In A. Arno & W. Dissanayoke (Eds.), *The News Media in National and International Conflict*. Boulder, CO: Westview Press.

Ashmore, R., & Del Boca, F. (1981). Conceptual Approaches to Stereotypes and Stereotyping. In D. Hamilton (Ed.), *Cognitive Processes in Stereotyping and Intergroup Behavior*. Hillsdale, NJ: Lawrence Erlbaum.

Axelrod, R. (1973). Schema Theory. *American Political Science Review*, 67, 1248–1266.

Bailey, T. (1948). *The Man in the Street*. New York: Macmillan.

Baillet, S., & Keenan, J. (1986). The Role of Encoding and Retrieval Processes in the Recall of Text. *Discourse Processes*, 9, 247–268.

Bartlett, F. (1932). *Remembering*. Cambridge: Cambridge University Press.

Beals, R., & Hoijer, H. (1959). *An Introduction to Anthropology*. New York: MacMillan.

Bennett, W. (1983). *News: The Politics of Illusion*. New York: Longman.

Belsky, L., & Doble, J. (1984). *Technical Appendix to Voter Options on Nuclear Arms Policy*. New York: Public Agenda Foundation.

Bobrow, D., & Norman, D. (1975). Some Principles of Memory Schemata. In D. Bobrow & A. Collins (Eds.), *Representation and Understanding*. New York: Academic Press.

Bower, G, Black, J., & Turner, T. (1979). Scripts in Memory for Text. *Cognitive Psychology*, 11, 177–220.

Bransford, J., & Johnson, M. (1972). Contextual Prerequisites for Understanding: Some Investigations of Comprehension and Recall. *Journal of Verbal Learning and Verbal Behavior*, 11, 717–726.

Brewer, W., & Treyens, J. (1981). Role of Schemata in Memory for Places. *Cognitive Psychology*, 13, 207–230.

Bruner, J., Goodnow, J., & Austin, G. (1956). *A Study of Thinking*. New York: Wiley.

Cantor, N., & Mischel, W. (1979). Prototypicality and Personality: Effects on Free Recall and Personality Impressions. *Journal of Research in Personality*, 13, 187–205.

Carbonell, J. (1978). POLITICS: Automated Ideological Reasoning. *Cognitive Science*, 2, 27–51.

Casson, R. (1981). *Language, Culture and Cognition*. New York: Macmillan.

Cohen, B. (1973). *The Public's Impact on Foreign Policy*. Boston, MA: Little, Brown.

Conover, P., & Feldman, S. (1984). How People Organize the Political World. *American Journal of Political Science*, 28, 95–126.

Cornelius, W., et al. (1985). *Report of the Latin American Studies Association Delegation to Observe the Nicaraguan General Election of November 4, 1984*. Austin, TX: Latin American Studies Association.

Coser, L. (1956). *The Functions of Social Conflict*. New York: Free Press.

Cottam, M. (1986). *Foreign Policy Decision Making*. Boulder, CO: Westview Press.

Cottrell, N., Ingraham, L., & Monfort, F. (1971). The Retention of Balanced and Unbalanced Cognitive Structures. *Journal of Research in Personality*, 13, 187–205.

Dallek, R. (1983). *The American Style of Foreign Policy*. New York: Alfred A. Knopf.

D'Andrade, R. (1981). The Cultural Part of Cognition. *Cognitive Science*, 5, 179–195.

D'Andrade, R. (1984). Cultural Meaning Systems. In R. Shweder & R. LeVine (Eds.), *Culture Theory*. New York: Cambridge University Press.

Deaux, K., & Emswiller, T. (1974). Explanations of Sex-linked Tasks: What Is Skill for the Male Is Luck for the Female. *Journal of Personality and Social Psychology*, 29, 80–85.

Delia, J., & Crocket, W. (1973). Social Schemas, Cognitive Complexity, and the Learning of Social Structures. *Journal of Personality*, 41, 413–429.

DeSoto, C., Henley, N., & London, M. (1968). Balance and the Grouping Schema. *Journal of Personality and Social Psychology*, 8, 1–7.

Destler, I., Gelb, L., & Lake, A. (1984). *The Unmaking of American Foreign Policy.* New York: Simon & Shuster.

Duncan, B. (1976). Differential Social Perception and Attribution of Intergroup Violence: Testing the Lower Limits of Stereotyping of Blacks. *Journal of Personality and Social Psychology*, 34, 590–598.

Edelman, M. (1974). The Political Language of the Helping Professions. *Politics and Society*, 4, 295–310.

Ehrlich, H. (1973). *The Social Psychology of Prejudice.* New York: Wiley.

Ellul, J. (1965). *Propaganda.* New York: Alfred A. Knopf.

Epstein, E. (1973). *News from Nowhere.* New York: Vantage.

Everett, A., Johnson, K., & Rosenthal, H. (1971). *Calley.* New York: Dell.

Fass, W., & Schumacher, G. (1981). Schema Theory and Prose Retention: Boundary Conditions for Encoding and Retrieval Efforts. *Discourse Processes*, 4, 17–26.

Ferguson, T. (1986). The Right Consensus? Holsti and Rosenau's New Foreign Policy Belief Survey. *International Studies Quarterly*, 30, 411–423.

Festinger, L. (1957). *A Theory of Cognitive Dissonance.* Stanford, CA: Stanford University Press.

Finlay, D., Holsti, O., & Fagen, R. (1967). *Enemies in Politics.* Chicago: Rand McNally.

Fishman, M. (1980). *Manufacturing the News.* Austin, TX: University of Texas Press.

Fiske, S., Kinder D., & Larter, W. (1983). The Novice and the Expert: Conditions for Encoding and Retrieval Effects. *Journal of Experimental Social Psychology*, 19, 381–400.

Freud, S. (1961). *Civilization and its Discontents* (trans. J. Strachey). New York: W. W. Norton.

Fulbright, J. (1964). *Old Myths and New Realities.* New York: Random House.

Gallup Poll, The (1972). *Public Opinion, 1935–1971.* New York: Random House.

Gallup Poll, The (1978). *Public Opinion, 1972–1977.* Wilmington, DE: Scholarly Resources.

Gallup Poll, The (1981). *Public Opinion, 1980.* Wilmington, DE: Scholarly Resources.

Gallup Poll, The (1984). *Public Opinion, 1983.* Wilmington, DE: Scholarly Resources.

Gallup Poll, The (1985). *Public Opinion, 1984.* Wilmington, DE: Scholarly Resources.

Gallup Poll, The (1986). *Public Opinion, 1985.* Wilmington, DE: Scholarly Resources.

Gallup Poll, The (1987). *Public Opinion, 1986.* Wilmington, DE: Scholarly Resources.

Gallup Poll, The (1988). *Public Opinion, 1987.* Wilmington, DE: Scholarly Resources.

Gallup Poll, The (1989). *Public Opinion, 1988.* Wilmington, DE: Scholarly Resources.

Gallup Poll, The (1990). *Public Opinion, 1989.* Wilmington, DE: Scholarly Resources.

Gallup Poll, The (1991). *Public Opinion, 1990.* Wilmington, DE: Scholarly Resources.

Gallup Poll Monthly, The (1991). Princeton, NJ: The Gallop Poll, February.

Gamson, W. (1988). A Constructionist Approach to Mass Media and Public Opinion. *Symbolic Interaction*, 11, 161–174.

Gans, H. (1979). *Deciding What's News: A Study of CBS Evening News, NBC Nightly News.* New York: Pantheon Books.

Gati, R. (1974). *Caging the Bear: Containment and the Cold War.* Indianapolis, IN: Bobbs-Merrill.

Geertz, C. (1973). *The Interpretation of Culture.* New York: Basic Books.

George, A. (1980). *Presidential Decisionmaking in Foreign Policy*. Boulder, CO: Westview.

Goodenough, W. (1957). Cultural Anthropology and Linguistics. In P. Garvin (Ed.), *Report of the Seventh Annual Round Table Meeting on Linguistics and Language Study*. Washington, DC: Georgetown University.

Goodenough, W. (1971). *Culture, Language, and Society*. Reading, MA: Addison-Wesley.

Graber, D. (1968). *Public Opinion, The President, and Foreign Policy*. New York: Holt, Rinehart & Winston.

Graber, D. (1980). *Mass Media and American Politics*. Washington, DC: Congressional Quarterly Press.

Graesser, A., Gordon, S., & Sawyer, J. (1979). Recognition Memory for Typical and Atypical Actions in Scripted Activities: Tests of a Script Pointer + Tag Hypothesis. *Journal of Verbal Learning and Verbal Behavior*, 18, 319–332.

Graesser, A., Woll, S., Kowalski, D., & Smith, D. (1980). Memory for Typical and Atypical Actions in Scripted Activities. *Journal of Experimental Psychology: Human Learning and Memory*, 6, 503–515.

Greenberg, J., & Rosenfield, D. (1979). Whites' Ethnocentrism and Their Attributions for the Behaviour of Blacks: A Motivational Bias. *Journal of Personality*, 47, 643–657.

Greenstein, F. (1969). *Children and Politics*. New Haven, CT: Yale University Press.

Hallin, D. (1983). The Media Goes to War: From Vietnam to Central America. *NACLA Report on the Americas*, 17, 4, 2–34.

Harary, F. (1961). A Structural Analysis of the Situation in the Middle East in 1956. *Journal of Conflict Resolution*, 5, 167–178.

Hartz, L. (1955). *The Liberal Tradition in America*. New York: Harcourt Brace Jovanovich.

Harvey, J., & Weary, G. (1981). *Perspectives on Attribution Processes*. Dubuque, IA: Wm. C. Brown.

Hastie, R. (1981). Schematic Principles in Human Memory. In E. Higgins, C. Herman, & M. Zanna, *Social Cognition*. Hillsdale, NJ: Lawrence Erlbaum.

Hastie, R., & Kumar, P. (1979). Person Memory: Personality Traits as Organizing Principles in Memory for Behaviors. *Journal of Personality and Social Psychology*, 37, 25–38.

Head, H. (1920). *Studies in Neurology*. New York: Oxford University Press.

Heider, F. (1958). *The Psychology of Interpersonal Relations*. New York: Wiley.

Heradstveit, D. (1979). *The Arab–Israeli Conflict: Psychological Obstacles to Peace*. Norway: Universitetsforlaget.

Herman, E. (1984). "Objective" News as Systematic Propaganda: The New York Times on the 1984 Salvadoran and Nicaraguan Elections. *Covert Action*, 21, 7–13.

Hesse, P., & Stimpson, T. (1983). *Images of the Enemy on Children's Television*. Presented at a conference on "War Film: Contexts and Images," University of Massachusets, Boston.

Hewstone, M. (Ed.) (1983). *Attribution Theory: Social and Functional Extensions*. Oxford: Basil Blackwell.

Hirshberg, M. (1992). *Consistency and Change in American Perceptions of China*. Presented at the annual meeting of the International Society of Political Psychology, San Francisco.

Holsti, O. (1976). Cognitive Process Approaches to Decision-Making. *American Behavioral Scientist*, 20, 11–32.

Holsti, O. (1987). Public Opinion and Containment. In T. Deibel & J. Gaddis (Eds.), *Containing the Soviet Union*. McLean, VA: Pergamon–Brassey's International Defense Publishers.

Holsti, O. (1989). *U.S. Leadership Attitudes toward the Soviet Union: 1976–1988*. Presented at the annual conference of the Society for Historians of American Foreign Relations, College of William and Mary, Williamsburg, VA.

Holsti, O., & Rosenau, J. (1984). *American Leadership in World Affairs*. Boston, MA: Allen & Unwin.

Holsti, O., & Rosenau, J. (1986). Consensus Lost. Consensus Regained?: Foreign Policy Beliefs of American Leaders, 1976–1980. *International Studies Quarterly*, 30, 375–409.

Holsti, O., & Rosenau, J. (1990a). The Emerging U.S. Consensus on Foreign Policy. *Orbis*, 34, 579–595.

Holsti, O., & Rosenau, J. (1990b). The Structure of Foreign Policy Attitudes Among American Leaders. *Journal of Politics*, 52, 94–125.

Holt, R. (1989). College Students' Definitions and Images of Enemies. *Journal of Social Issues*, 45 (2), 33–50.

Hunt, M. (1987). *Ideology and U.S. Foreign Policy*. New Haven, CT: Yale University Press.

Huntington, S. (1982). American Ideals versus American Institutions. *Political Science Quarterly*, 97, 1–38.

Hurwitz, J., & Peffley, M. (1987). How Are Foreign Policy Attitudes Structured? *American Political Science Review*, 81, 1099–1120.

Hurwitz, J., & Peffley, M. (1990). Public Images of the Soviet Union: The Impact on Foreign Policy Attitudes. *Journal of Politics*, 52, 3–28.

Jaspars, J., Fincham, F., & Hewstone, M. (Ed.) (1983). *Attribution Theory and Research: Conceptual, Developmental and Social Dimensions*. New York: Academic Press.

Jervis, R. (1976). *Perception and Misperception in International Politics*. Princeton, NJ: Princeton University Press.

Jones, E., & Nisbett, R. (1971). *The Actor and the Observer: Divergent Perceptions of the Causes of Behavior*. Morristown, NJ: General Learning Press.

Kalb, M., Koppel, T., & Scali, J. (1982). The networks and foreign news coverage. *The Washington Quarterly*, Spring.

Keen, S. (1986) *Faces of the Enemy: Reflections of the Hostile Imagination*. San Francisco: Harper & Row.

Keesing, R. (1981). Theories of Culture. In R. Casson, *Language, Culture and Cognition*. New York: Macmillan.

Kegley, C. (1986). Assumptions and Dilemmas in the Study of Americans' Foreign Policy Beliefs. *International Studies Quarterly*, 30, 447–471.

Kegley, C., & Wittkopf, E. (1982). *American Foreign Policy*. New York: St. Martin's Press.

Kennan, G. (1947). The Sources of Soviet Conduct. *Foreign Affairs*, 25, 566–582.

Kohut, A. (1988). What Americans Want. *Foreign Policy*, 70, 150–165.

Kroeber, A. (1948). *Anthropology*. New York: Harcourt, Brace & Company.

Kroeber, A., & Kluckhohn, C. (1952). *Culture: A Critical Review of Concepts and Definitions.* New York: Random House.

Larson, D. (1985). *Origins of Containment.* Princeton, NJ: Princeton University Press.

Lau, R., & Sears, D. (1986). *Political Cognition.* Hillsdale, NJ: Lawrence Erlbaum.

Lerner, M. (1957). *America as a Civilization.* New York: Simon & Schuster.

Levering, R. (1978). *The Public and American Foreign Policy, 1918–1978.* New York: William Morrow.

Levering, R. (1988). *The Cold War, 1945–1987.* Arlington Heights, IL: H. Davidson.

Levine, R., & Campbell, D. (1972). *Ethnocentrism.* New York: Wiley.

Lippman, W. (1922). *Public Opinion.* London: Allen & Unwin.

Lodge, M., & Wahlke, J. (1982). Politicos, Apoliticals, and the Processing of Political Information. *International Political Science Review,* 3, 131–150.

Maggiotto, M., & Wittkopf, E. (1981). American Public Attitudes Toward Foreign Policy. *International Studies Quarterly,* 25, 601–631

Mandelbaum, M., & Schneider, W. (1979). The New Internationalisms. In K. Oye, D. Rothchild, & R. Lieber (Eds.), *Eagle Entangled.* New York: Longman.

Mann, J., & Taylor, D. (1974). Attribution of Causality: Role of Ethnicity and Social Class. *The Journal of Social Psychology,* 94, 3–13.

Markel, L. (Ed.) (1949). *Public Opinion and Foreign Policy.* New York: Harper.

Markus, H., & Zajonc, R. (1985). The Cognitive Perspective in Social Psychology. In G. Lindzey & E. Aronson (Eds.), *The Handbook of Social Psychology* (3d ed.). New York: Random House.

Mead, M. (1940). Warfare Is Only an Invention—Not a Biological Necessity. *Asia,* 40, 402–405.

Minsky, M. (1975). A Framework for Representing Knowledge. In P. Winston (Ed.), *The Psychology of Computer Vision.* New York: McGraw-Hill.

Mintz, M. (1986). *Quotations from President Ron.* New York: St. Martin's Press.

Montagu, A. (1964). *The Science of Man.* New York: Odyssey Press.

Montagu, A. (1978). *Learning Non-Aggression.* New York: Oxford University Press.

Nathan, J., & Oliver, J. (1985). *United States Foreign Policy and World Order.* Boston: Little, Brown.

Neisser, U. (1976). *Cognition and Reality.* San Francisco: Freeman.

Niemi, R., Mueller, J., & Smith, T. (1989). *Trends in Public Opinion.* Westport, CT: Greenwood Press.

Nincic, M. (1985). The American Public and the Soviet Union: The Domestic Context of Discontent. *Journal of Peace Research,* 22, 345–357.

Nincic, M. (1988). The United States, the Soviet Union, and the Politics of Opposites. *World Politics,* 40 (4), 452–475.

Nye, J. (1984). *The Making of America's Soviet Policy.* New Haven, CT: Yale University Press.

Orwell, G. (1949). *Nineteen Eighty-Four.* New York: Harcourt, Brace and World.

Parenti, M. (1969). *The Anti-Communist Impulse.* New York: Random House.

Perle, R. (1989). Helping Gorbachev Discard a Broken Idea. *U.S. News and World Report,* Nov. 20, 40.

Pettigrew, T. (1981). Extending the Stereotype Concept. In D. Hamilton (Ed.), *Cognitive Processes in Stereotyping and Intergroup Behavior.* Hillsdale, NJ: Lawrence Erlbaum

Picek, J., Sherman, S, & Shiffrin, R. (1975). Cognitive Organization and Coding of Social Structures. *Journal of Personality and Social Psychology*, 31, 758–768.

Press, A., Crockett, W., & Rosenkrantz, P. (1969). Cognitive Complexity and Learning Balanced and Unbalanced Social Structures. *Journal of Personality*, 37, 541–553.

Price, V. (1988). *On the Public Aspects of Opinion*. Presented at the annual conference of the International Communication Association, New Orleans.

Reagan, R. (1989). *Speaking My Mind*. New York: Simon and Schuster.

Redfield, R. (1941). *The Folk Culture of Yucatan*. Chicago, IL: University of Chicago Press.

Regan, D., Straus, E., & Fazio, R. (1974). Liking and the Attribution Process. *Journal of Experimental Social Psychology*, 10, 385–397.

Rielly, J. (1987). *American Public Opinion and U.S. Foreign Policy 1987*. Chicago, IL: Chicago Council on Foreign Relations.

Rogin, M. (1987). *Ronald Reagan, the Movie*. Berkeley, CA: University of California Press.

Rosenberg, S., & Wolfsfeld, G. (1977). International Conflict and the Problem of Attribution. *Journal of Conflict Resolution*, 21, 75–103.

Rossi, I. (1980). *People in Culture*. New York: Praeger.

Rostow, E. (1990). The impact of Gorbachevshchina on United States Foreign Policy. In U. Ra'anan & I. Lukes (Eds.), *Gorbachev's USSR: A System in Crisis*. London: Macmillan.

Rothbart, M., Evans, M., & Fulero, S. (1979). Recall for Confirming Events: Memory Processes and the Maintenance of Social Stereotypes. *Journal of Experimental Social Psychology*, 15, 343–355.

Rumelhart, D. (1977). Understanding and Summarizing Brief Stories. In D. Laberge & S. Samuels (Eds.), *Basic Processes in Reading*. Hillsdale, NJ: Lawrence Erlbaum.

Sande, G., Goethals, G., Ferrari, L., & Worth, L. (1989). Value-Guided Attributions. *Journal of Social Issues*, 45 (2), 91–118.

Schank, R. (1975). The Structure of Episodes in Memory. In D. Bobrow & A. Collins (Eds.), *Representation and Understanding*. New York: Academic Press.

Schank, R., & Abelson, R. (1977). *Scripts, Plans, Goals and Understanding*. Hillsdale, NJ: Lawrence Erlbaum.

Schlesinger, A. (1967). Origins of the Cold War. *Foreign Affairs*, 46, 22–52.

Schneider, W. (1984). Public Opinion. In J. Nye (Ed.), *The Making of America's Soviet Policy*. New Haven, CT: Yale University Press.

Scott, W. (1965). Psychological and Social Correlates of International Images. In H. Kelman (Ed.), *International Behavior*. New York: Holt, Rinehart & Winston.

Seckler-Hudson, C. (1973). *Our Constitution and Government*. Washington, DC: United States Government Printing Office.

Sentis, K., & Burnstein, E. (1979). Remembering Schema-Consistent Information. *Journal of Personality and Social Psychology*, 37, 2200–2211.

Shapiro, R., & Page, B. (1988). Foreign Policy and the Rational Public. *Journal of Conflict Resolution*, 32, 211–247.

Shultz, G. (1985). The United States and Central America. Washington, DC: United States Department of State.

Sigal, L. (1973). Reporters and Officials: The Organization of Newsmaking and Politics. Lexington, MA: D. C. Heath.

Simmel, G. (1955). Conflict (trans. K. Wolff). Glencoe, IL: Free Press.

Smith, T. (1983). The Polls: American Attitudes Toward the Soviet Union and Communism. Public Opinion Quarterly, 47, 277–292.

Snyder, M. (1981). On the Self-Perpetuating Nature of Social Stereotypes. In D. Hamilton (Ed.), Cognitive Processes in Stereotyping and Intergroup Behavior. Hillsdale, NJ: Lawrence Erlbaum.

Snyder, M., & Uranowitz, S. (1978). Reconstructing the Past: Some Cognitive Consequences of Person Perception. Journal of Personality and Social Psychology, 36, 941–950.

Spanier, J. (1985). American Foreign Policy Since World War II (10th ed.). New York: Holt, Rinehart & Winston.

Spanier, J., & Uslaner, E. (1982). Foreign Policy and the Democratic Dilemmas. New York: Holt, Rinehart & Winston.

Spence, J. (1983). The Great Salvador Election Blitz. NACLA Report on the Americas, 17 (4), 11–15.

Spence, J. (1984). Second Time Around: How to Cover an Election. Columbia Journalism Review, March/April.

Spence, J. (1985). Color it Undemocratic: Nicaraguan Election Coverage. NACLA Report on the Americas, 19 (1), 10–12.

Spiro, R. (1977). Remembering Information from Text: The "State of Schema" Approach. In R. Anderson, R. Spiro, & W. Montague (Eds.), Schooling and the Acquisition of Knowledge. Hillsdale, NJ: Lawrence Erlbaum.

Spiro, R. (1980a). Accommodative Reconstruction in Prose Recall. Journal of Verbal learning and Verbal Behavior, 19, 84–95.

Spiro, R. (1980b). Prior Knowledge and Story Processing: Integration, Selection and Variation. Poetics, 9, 313–327.

Stein, A. (1976). Conflict and Cohesion: A Review of the Literature. Journal of Conflict Resolution, 20 (1), 143–172.

Stephan, W. (1977). Stereotyping: The Role of Ingroup–Outgroup Differences in Causal Attribution for Behavior. The Journal of Social Psychology, 101, 255–266.

Stoesinger, J. (1985). Crusaders and Pragmatists. New York: W. W. Norton.

Sumner, W. (1906). Folkways. Boston, MA: Ginn.

Tajfel, H. (1970). Experiments in Intergroup Discrimination. Scientific American, 223, 96–102.

Tajfel, H. (1981) Human Groups and Social Categories. Cambridge: Cambridge University Press.

Tajfel, H., Billig, M., Bundy, R., & Flament, C. (1971). Social Categorization and Intergroup Behavior. European Journal of Social Psychology, 1, 149–178.

Taylor, D. M., & Jaggi, V. (1974). Ethnocentrism and Causal Attributions in a South Indian Context. Journal of Cross-cultural Psychology, 5, 162–171.

Taylor, S., & Crocker, J. (1981). Schematic Bases of Social Information Processing. In E. Higgins, C. Herman, & M. Zanna (Eds.), Social Cognition. Hillsdale, NJ: Lawrence Erlbaum.

Tesser, A. (1978). Self-Generated Attitude Change. In L. Berkowitz (Ed.), *Advances in Experimental Social Psychology*, Vol. 11. New York: Academic Press.

Thorndike, P., & Hays-Roth, B. (1979). The Use of Schemata in the Acquisition and Transfer of Knowledge. *Cognitive Psychology*, 11, 82–106.

Trout, B. (1975). Rhetoric Revisited: Political Legitimation and the Cold War. *International Studies Quarterly*, 19, 251–284.

Tyler, E. (1871). *Primitive Culture*. London: John Murray.

Walsh, W. (1947). American Attitudes Toward Russia. *Antioch Review*, 7, 183–190.

Weisman, J. (1982). TV and the Presidency. *TV Guide*, March 20.

Whitfield, S. (1991). *The Culture of the Cold War*. Baltimore, MD: Johns Hopkins University Press.

Wilder, D. (1981). Perceiving Persons as a Group. In D. Hamilton (Ed.), *Cognitive Processes in Stereotyping and Intergroup Behavior*. Hillsdale, NJ: Lawrence Erlbaum.

Wittkopf, E. (1986). On the Foreign Policy Beliefs of the American People. *International Studies Quarterly*, 30, 425–445.

Wittkopf, E. (1988). *Americans' Foreign Policy Beliefs, Preferences, and Performance Evaluations*. Presented at the workshop on public opinion and foreign policy at the Annual Meeting of the International Society of Political Psychology, New York.

Wittkopf, E. (1990). *Faces of Internationalism*. Durham, NC: Duke University Press.

Wittkopf, E., & Maggiotto, M. (1983). The Two Faces of Internationalism: Public Attitudes toward American Foreign Policy in the 1970s—and Beyond. *Social Science Quarterly*, 64, 288–304.

Wittkopf, E., & McCormick, J. (1990). The Cold War Consensus: Did It Exist? *Polity*, 22 (4), 627–653.

Wyer, R. (1974). *Cognitive Organization and Change*. Potomac, MD: Lawrence Earlbaum.

Yankelovich, D., & Doble, J. (1984). The Public Mood: Nuclear Weapons and the U.S.S.R. *Foreign Affairs*, 63, 33–46.

Yankelovich, D., & Smoke, R. (1988). America's "New Thinking." *Foreign Affairs*, 67, 1–17.

Yatani, C., & Bramel, D. (1989). Trends and Patterns in Americans' Attitudes Toward the Soviet Union. *Journal of Social Issues*, 45 (2), 13–32.

Zadney, J., & Gerard, H. (1974). Attributed Intentions and Information Selectivity. *Journal of Experimental Social Psychology*, 10, 34–52.

Index

Abelson, R., 18, 27, 181
Alba, J., 202
Allison, G., 71–72
Almond, G., 23, 40, 42, 69
American Civil War Schema, 40
American foreign policy, 51–62;
    American perceptions of, 183–184,
    186, 189, 195, 210–211 (*see also*
    public opinion, American); goals, 60–
    62, 181–187; and ideology, 37, 43,
    58
American Patriotic Schema, 4–6, 18, 37–
    41, 44, 46, 95, 105–6, 161–162, 208–
    210; and conflict, 39–40, 196; and
    culture, 38; and democracy, 38;
    elements of, 38–39; and freedom, 38;
    and free enterprise, 39; and interna-
    tional relations, 39, 209–210; and
    scripts, 39; and subject responses,
    148, 151–152 (*see also* cold war
    schema)
American public opinion (*see* public
    opinion)
American Revolution Schema, 40
Amerika, 99–100

anomaly identification, 203, 205, 206–
    207
Arno, A., 112
Ashmore, R., 26
attribution bias, 163–164; and external
    attribution, 166; and internal attribu-
    tion, 166; and international relations,
    163–164, and the Soviet Union, 167–
    168, 176–180; and the United States,
    164–165, 167–168, 173–175, 178–
    179, 180
attributional consistency model, 166

Bailey, T., 21, 43
balance principle, 35–36; and interna-
    tional relations, 36 (*see also* balance
    schema, balance theory)
balance schema, 35–37
balance theory, 36, 156–157, 166; and
    cold war schema, 188 (*see also*
    balance principle)
Bartlett, F., 26
Beals, R., 32
behavioral tradition, 19–20
Belsky, L., 84

Bennett, W., 115
Bower, G., 28, 199, 202
Bramel, D., 84, 150
Bruner, J., 25
Bush, G., 2, 58–59

Calley, W., 17
Campbell, D., 36
capitalism: and the United States, 136; and freedom, 136
Carbonell, J., 28
Carter, J., 57–58
Casson, R., 28
categorization process, 25–26
China: American attitudes toward, 160, 161
cinema, 101–105
citizen cognition, 18, 21, 25 (see also public opinion)
cognitive dissonance, 159 (see also balance theory)
cognitive preconceptions 19, 20, 128
Cohen, B., 21–22
cold war, 1–3; American goals during, 60–61, consensus, 70, 72; perceptions of, 2; victory, 1–3
cold war culture, 30, 97–106; and academia, 105–106; and cinema, 101–105; and television, 153–159 (see also American Patriotic Schema)
cold war schema, 4–6, 11, 18, 41–46, 48–49, 51–53, 71, 75–76, 80–81, 87, 94–95, 107–108, 129, 144–145, 147, 150, 165, 168, 181–182, 188–189, 190, 195–196, 197, 207–208, 210–211; and accommodation, 52–53, 56–57; and American culture, 97–98 (see also cold war culture); and American foreign policy, 6, 51–52, 141–142 (see also American foreign policy); and American ideology, 43; and balance, 153–156, 161; and children, 101; and conflict management, 52; and detente, 84–87; elements of, 129, 131–142; and El Salvador, 113–120; end of, 59, 94–95; and foreign affairs, 5–6; and foreign news, 107–109, 111, 122; and free association, 128–129;

function of, 44; and intervention, 54, 56, 57; and journalists, 109–110; and Nicaragua, 121–123, 185–186; perpetuation of, 44–45; and recall, 198–201, 202–208; and side taking, 193–196; and subject response, 149–150; and television news, 108–109; and the Vietnam War, 45, 208 (see also American patriotic schema)
cold war script, 28
Communism, 43–44, 203; and oppression, 138; and recall, 203–205, 207; and the Soviet Union, 209–210, 212 (see also Soviet Union)
communist schema, 27
conservatives: attitudes toward the Soviet Union, 151–153, 170; attitudes toward the United States, 151–153, 170
constructionism, 18, 24–25,
containment, 55–56, 61–62; two-track policy, 46–47
Cornelius W., 112–113, 121
Coser, L., 47
Cottam, M., 76
Cottrell, N., 202
Crocker, J., 26
Crocket, W., 200
cultural categories, 26
culture, 28–32; and behavior, 30; and foreign policy, 28–29; and learning, 32; and meaning, 30; and socialization, 32; and symbols, 30

Dallek, R., 48
D'Andrade, R., 26, 28–31
Del Broca, F., 26
Delia, J., 200
democracy, 203; and communism, 42; and freedom, 134–135, 140–141; and the United States, 134–135
democratic myth, 21–22
democratic process script, 39, 119; and the Salvadoran election, 117
DeSoto, C., 201–202
Destler, L., 72
dictatorship, 138–139
Doble, J., 84–87

Dunsmore, B., 120

Edelman, M., 180
Eisenhower, D., 50, 56, 68
Ellul, J., 97
El Salvador: election, 107–108, 112–
    120, 122 (and foreign news, 107–
    108, 112–120); and the United States,
    112–116, 122
Epstein, E., 111, 112

Federal Textbook on Citizenship, 131
Fiske. S., 200
foreign news: and conceptual categories,
    110; and cultural schemata, 108–109,
    110–111; and the Nicaraguan
    election, 108, 112–113, 120–123;
    and the Salvadoran election, 107–
    108, 112–120, 122–123; and schema
    setting, 110; and schematic framing,
    109–110
foreign policy (*see* American foreign
    policy)
freedom: and democracy, 134–135, 140–
    141; and oppression, 42; and totali-
    tarianism, 47–48; and the United
    States, 133–134, 140
free enterprise script, 39
Freud, S., 47
Fulbright, J., 1

Gallup Poll, 62–70, 80, 83–84, 86, 89,
    90–91, 94, 151
Gamson, W., 24
Geertz, C., 29–30
George, A., 32, 37, 202
Goodenough, W., 29, 32
Gorbechev, M., 59; and American public
    opinion, 89, 93
Graber, D., 21–22, 111

Haig, A., 107, 120
Harary, F., 36–37
Hartz, L., 43 , 63
Hasher, L., 202
Heider, F., 35, 144, 201
Heradstveit, D., 166–167
Herman, E., 113, 120

Hesse, P., 101
Hoijer, H., 32
Holsti, O., 19–20, 61, 74, 82
Holt, R., 42
Hunt, M., 37, 58
Huntington, S., 105–106
Hurwitz, J., 23, 44

ideology: American, 43, 58, 63; and
    American foreign policy, 37, 43, 58
ingroup favoring, 33; and differentiation,
    33–34; and loyalty, 33; and self-
    esteem, 33
ingroup–outgroup schema, 33–34; and
    conflict, 47–48; and international
    relations, 34; and stereotyping, 36;
    and the United states, 34–35 (*see also*
    United States, as an in-nation)
in-nations, and out-nations, 169
internationalism: cold war, 74–78;
    cooperative, 78–80; conservative, 76–
    78; liberal, 76–78; militant, 78–80;
    noninternationalism, 76–78; post–
    cold war, 74–75

Jervis, R., 19, 36–37
Johnson, L., 57; and the Vietnam War,
    57

Kalb, M., 111
Keen, S., 47, 78
Kegley, C., 22–23, 42
Kennan, G., 55
Kennedy, J., 50, 56–57; and cold war
    policies, 56–57
Kissinger, H., 57; policies of, 57
Kohut, A., 86, 88
Krause, C., 118
Kroeber, A., 29, 32

legitimation, 55
Lerner, M., 132
Levering, R., 54, 57–58, 72
Levine, R., 36
liberals: and attitudes toward the Soviet
    Union, 151–153, 170–171; and
    attitudes toward the United States,
    151–153, 170

Lippmann, W., 197

Maggiotto, E., 71, 78–80
Maggiotto, M., 71, 78–80
Mandelbaum, M., 71, 76–78, 79
Markel, L., 21
May, E., 59–60
McCormick, J., 69, 73
Montagu, A., 18, 31
Moscow on the Hudson, 101–104
Mundt–Nixon Bill, 65

Nathan, J., 53–54
National Opinion Research Center, 68, 81–82
Nazi enemy schema, 41
news, *see* foreign news
Nicaragua: American perceptions of, 184–187; election, 108, 112–113, 120–123 (and foreign news, 108, 112–113, 120–123); and the United States, 112–113, 120–121
Niemi, R., 64, 81, 150
Nincic, M., 60, 92–93
Nixon, R., 50, 57; policies of, 57
Nye, J., 59–60

Oliver, J., 53–54
Orwell, G, 159
outgroup, *see* ingroup

Page, B., 23
Parenti, M., 17
patriotism, American, 2–3 (*see also* American patriotic schema)
Peffley, M., 23, 44
Pettigrew, T., 34
Press, A., 200
Price, V., 24–25
public opinion: American (and communism, 63–65, 81–82; and containment, 67–70, 83; and cultural exchanges, 68–69; and diplomatic initiatives, 68–70, 85–88; and the end of the cold war, 93–94; and force, 85–88; and foreign policy decision-making, 21–24; and freedom, 84; and

Gorbachev, 89, 93; and Soviet leaders, 89; and the Soviet people, 89–90; and the Soviet Union, 65–67, 83–84, 85–87, 88–94 [*see also* Soviet Union, American conceptions of]; and the United States, 84–85); and cultural schemata, 24–25

Quayle, J., 1

Rather, D., 107
Reagan, R., 16, 50, 58, 116, 209; and Latin America, 58; policies of, 58
recall: and balance structure, 202; and communism, 203–205, 206; schema-consistent distortion, 203, 205; schema-consistent selection, 203; and the Soviet Union, 200, 203–207; and the United States, 200, 203–208
Redfield, R., 29
Red Scare, 56, 81, 83; and ideology, 63
Regan, D., 165–166
Reynolds, F., 117
Rielly, J., 83
Rocky IV, 104–105
Rosenau, J., 61–62, 71–72, 74–76, 79
Rosenberg, M., 35
Rosenberg, S., 166
Rossi, I., 29, 31

Sande, G., 167–168
Schank, R., 27, 181
schema, 4, 25–28, 31–32; and conflict, 112; cultural, 3–4, 18, 28, 30–31, 32; for international relations, 33; and recall, 202–203; stereotypes, 111
Schlesinger, A., 164
Schneider, W., 71, 76–78, 79
Schultz, G., 122, 188
Scott, W., 36
scripts, 27–28, 181–182 (*see also* schema)
Seamans, I., 115
semi-isolationism, 74–75
Shapiro, R., 23
Shepard, G., 107
Simmel, G., 47

Smith J., 119–120
Smoke, R., 83–85, 87–88, 93
Stimpson, T., 101
social cognition, 12–13
sociocultural system, 31
Soviet Union: American attitudes toward, 140–141, 169–171 (changes in, 144–145, 147–154, 159–160, 180); American conceptions of, 41–44, 46, 48, 52–53, 61, 76–77 (see also public opinion, and the Soviet Union); American policies toward, 59–60; and communism, 136, 140; fall of, 48, 59; and the invasion of Afghanistan, 83, 85; and Korean Airlines 007, 83; and oppression, 137; schema, 42, 44 (see also attribution bias, and the Soviet Union and recall, and the Soviet Union)
Spanier, J., 22–23, 164
Spence, J., 112–113, 116, 118–120
Spiro, R., 202
Stein, A., 47
stereotypes, 128, 197; and recall, 197; schematic, 111
structural balance, 144 (see also balance theory)
Sumner, W., 47

Taft–Hartley Law, 65
Tajfel, H., 33–34, 166
Taylor, S., 26

television: cartoons, 101; network news, 108–123; women's wrestling, 98–99

Tesser, A., 26
Threlkeld, R, 117–118
Trout, B., 55
Trudeau, G., 1
Truman Doctrine, 22, 42, 51, 54–65
Truman, H., 50, 54–66
Tyler, E., 29

United States: American attitudes toward, 166, 170, 179–180, 211 (see also public opinion, American); and freedom, 131–133, 140–141; as an in-nation, 38, 48; and the Soviet Union, 139–140 (relations between, 91–92) (see also attribution bias, and the United States and recall, and the United States)
Uslaner, E., 22–13

Vietnam War, 51, 87; conceptions of, 142; effects of, 116; results of, 71–75, 80–81

war, 17–19
Wittkopf, E., 23, 42, 80, 85
Wolfsfeld, G., 166

Yankelovich, D., 83–88, 93
Yatani, C., 84, 150

ABOUT THE AUTHOR

MATTHEW S. HIRSHBERG is a lecturer at the University of Canterbury in Christchurch, New Zealand.